PATHFINDER

SKILLS IN LANGUAGE AND LITERATURE

MICHAEL SMITH

THE EDUCATIONAL COMPANY
Approved Quality System

INTRODUCTION

Pathfinder is the only complete and systematic language textbook written especially for the Junior Certificate English course but it can be used also in the following years. Containing all the necessary language and literary skills required for the Junior Certificate, it uses practical, class-tested methods which are clearly developed for the student using an easy-to-follow step-by-step approach.

Pathfinder is designed as an English Language programme catering for both Ordinary and Higher levels. It can be used for one or two class periods each week and will successfully accompany any reader which the teacher may choose.

Unlike many textbooks, **Pathfinder** is not a collection of bits and pieces. Each module is carefully structured to provide a full and coherent treatment of the topic. By virtue of its detailed treatment, each module constitutes a mini-textbook. The book adheres closely to the format of the Junior Certificate English course. Thus, both teachers and students can be confident that they are covering all the required elements of the course.

CONTENTS

GRAMMAR

A QUICK LOOK AT PARTS OF SPEECH

THE NOUN GROUP

noun: a word that names a person, place, thing or quality

> John, Ireland, radio, beauty

pronoun: a word that is used instead of a noun

> I, you, he, it

adjective: a word that gives more information about a noun

> the *big* man, the *slow* horse, *my* house

THE VERB GROUP

verb: a word that describes an action or a state

> The dog *barks.*
> The soldier *fights.*
> The woman *is* brave.

adverb: a word that gives more information about a verb, an adjective or another adverb

- The dog barks *loudly.*
  (*loudly* tells more about the verb 'barks')
- The man was *amazingly* thin.
  (*amazingly* tells more about the adjective 'thin')
- The boy walked *very* slowly.
  (*very* tells more about the adverb 'slowly')

SOME LINKING WORDS

preposition: a word that links nouns and pronouns with other words

> The newspaper is *on* the table.

conjunction: a word that links sentences and words

> John sat down *and* ate his supper.
> Do you want the book *or* will I leave it in the bag?
> James came *but* William refused to come.

interjection: a word that expresses a feeling or emotion but which has no grammatical connection with the rest of the sentence

> *Oh!*
> *Hello!*

negative participle: *not*

THE NOUN GROUP

NOUNS

A **noun** is a word that names a person, place, thing or quality.

> John, Ireland, radio, beauty

It's your turn!

1. Write ten simple sentences. Underline the noun in each sentence.

2. Write down the nouns in each of these sentences.

(a) The dog bit the postman.
(b) My father bought a new car.
(c) Mary is my friend.
(d) Tim was at my party last week.
(e) I gave the book to my brother.
(f) The helicopter circled the house.
(g) The boat is in the harbour now.
(h) Bad weather held up our departure.
(i) The farmer sold all his cows at the market.
(j) Mrs Jones was very angry with her neighbour.

There's more!

Common nouns and proper nouns – page 25.

PRONOUNS

A **pronoun** is a word that is used instead of a noun.

> I, you, he, me, it, they, who, which, him, them

List of Pronouns

Nominative Case	Objective Case	Possessive Case
I / who	me / whom	mine / whose
you	you	yours
he/she/it	him/her/it	his/hers/its
we	us	ours
you	you	yours
they	them	theirs

Rules for using pronouns

• When the pronoun is the **subject** of the sentence, use the **nominative** case.
> *He* and *I* saw the film.
> *They* have the books.

• When the pronoun is the **object** of the sentence, use the **objective** case.
> John saw *him* and *her* yesterday.

• When the pronoun is used **after a preposition** (a word like *to, for, with, from, by*), use the **objective** case.
> Jane went with *us* to the disco.
> John bought the CD for *us*.
> Mary took the ticket from *him*.
> To *whom* did you give the CD?

• Use a pronoun in the **nominative** case before and after any form of the verb **to be**.
> *I* am the person you want.
> It is *I* who called.
> It was *he* who did it.
> It appears to be *they*.

• Use a pronoun in the **objective** case after **let** and **between**.
> John divided the money between *him* and *me*.
> Let *him* cut the grass.

It's your turn!

1. Write out the pronouns in each of these sentences.

(a) I saw him at school yesterday.
(b) We gave them the money when they came.
(c) I know the person who called to our house.
(d) The book which you left on the desk is missing.
(e) We gave it to the girl who came first in the class.
(f) We saw them leave it on the table.
(g) They could not identify the woman who collected it.
(h) Did you see who took the coat?
(i) We were annoyed with them because they were late.
(j) I met him before but I don't know his name.

2. Choose the correct pronoun and underline it.
(a) The secret was between (she, her) and (I, me).
(b) Paula gave the money to (we, us).
(c) From (who, whom) did he buy the ticket?
(d) I was sure it was (she, her).
(e) Is that (he, him) in the black coat?
(f) Mother sent Mary and (I, me) to the supermarket.
(g) Do you think it was (I, me) who took the book?
(h) She is as tall as (me, I).
(i) It seemed to be (them, they).
(j) I bought the book for (her, she).

ADJECTIVES

An **adjective** is a word that gives more information about a noun.

> the *big* man
> the *slow* horse
> *my* house
> *their* car
> *his* book

It's your turn!

1. Write down all the adjectives in each of these sentences.
(a) My neighbour has a vicious dog.
(b) They live in a large, gloomy house.
(c) Rough seas delayed their ship's departure.
(d) My best friend's favourite food is Chinese.
(e) Frank has a fabulous collection of the latest hits.
(f) Most people prefer to wear bright clothes in summer.
(g) I left my books in your house.
(h) The narrow, winding roads slowed them down.
(i) A strange visitor called at our house last night.
(j) My friend is kind and generous.

THE VERB GROUP

A **verb** is a word that describes an action or a state.

> The dog *barks*.
> The soldier *fights*.
> The detective *is* brave.

It's your turn!

1. Write down the verbs in each of these sentences.
(a) Paul played a good match.
(b) We saw that film before.
(c) Helen is a hard-working girl.
(d) Her father drives too fast.
(e) They volunteered for the job.
(f) They ate their meal with relish.
(g) We worked hard all day.
(h) All my friends were at their party.
(i) He has no money now.
(j) Give her the book immediately!

ADVERBS

An **adverb** is a word that gives more information about a verb, an adjective or another adverb. Adverbs usually tell **where**, **when** or **how**.

- The dog barks *loudly*.
  (*loudly* tells us more about the verb 'barks')
- The man was *amazingly* thin.
  (*amazingly* tells us more about the adjective 'thin')
- The boy walked *very* slowly.
  (*very* tells us more about the adverb 'slowly')

Note: Adverbs often end in **-ly**.

Examples of adverbs

Remember – adverbs usually tell when, where or how.

Time (when)

early
late
today
yesterday
tomorrow
ago
already
immediately
now
seldom
soon
never
shortly
previously
before
after
when

Place (where)

near
far
over there
beside
below
under
further
in
out
everywhere

Amount or Degree (how)

partly
about
exactly
quite
very
almost
completely
fully
scarcely

It's your turn!

1. Write down the adverbs in each of these sentences.
(a) The choir sang badly.
(b) They ate their meal greedily.
(c) He can write well when he takes his time.
(d) They waited very patiently for us all day.
(e) Mary is extremely tall.
(f) She does her work slowly but carefully.
(g) He felt better after the rest.
(h) Our opponents played viciously.
(i) I was extremely relieved when I heard the news.
(j) They moved stealthily and cautiously in the dark.

LINKING WORDS

• •

PREPOSITIONS

A **preposition** is a word that links nouns and pronouns with other words.
• The house is *near* the railway station.
 (The noun *house* is linked to the noun *station*.)
• The newspaper is *on* the table.
 (The noun *newspaper* is linked to the noun *table*.)
• The boat is *in* the harbour.
 (The noun *boat* is linked to the noun *harbour*.)

It's your turn!

1.   Write down the prepositions in each of these sentences.

(a)   Andrew gave the book to his friend.

(b)   Kate bought a present for her father.

(c)   David took the money from his sister.

(d)   The needle is in the drawer.

(e)   They bought a record with the money.

(f)   The book was written by F. Jones.

(g)   Joan sat on the seat beside her friend.

(h)   They knocked at the door.

(i)   They stared through the window.

(j)   The cat jumped over the chair.

Watch out!

These prepositions are often misused, so study them carefully.

abandoned **by**

abide **by** (a judgment)

abide **in** (a place)

absolve **from**

abstain **from**

accompanied **by**

accused **of**

accustomed **to**

acquit **of**

afflict **with**

agree **with** (a person)

agree **on** (some point)

aim **at**

amenable **to**

angry **about/at** (a situation)

angry **at/with** (a person)

ashamed **of**

astonished **at**

blamed **for**

capable **of**

centred **on**

comment **on**

compatible **with**

complain **of**

comply **with**

confer **with**

confide **in**

conform **to**

connive **at**

conscious **of**

convenient **to** (a person)

convenient **for** (a purpose)

correspond **with** (a person)

correspond **to** (something)

defiance **of**

deficient **in**

die **of**

different **from**

disagree **with**

disappointed **with** (a person)

disappointed **in** (something)

disgusted **with** (a person)

disgusted **at** (something)

dislike **for**

divide **among** (more than two)

divide **between** (two)

filled **with**

forgetful **of**

glimpse **of**

good **for**

guilty **of**

impatient **with** (a person)

impatient **of** (something)

independent **of**

indifferent **to**

indignant **at** (something)

indignant **with** (a person)

inflict **upon**

inspired **by** (a person)

inspired **with** (something)

involve **in**
irrespective **of**
interfere **with**

meddle **with**

oblivious **of**
opposite **to**

preferable **to**
prevail **on** (a person)
profuse **in**
protest **against**
pursuit **of**

rely **on**
repent **of**
resort **to**
responsible **for** (something)
responsible **to** (a person)
result **in**

satisfied **with**
similar **to**
suffer **from**

taste **of** (food)
taste **for** (art etc.)
tired **of** (something)

vexed **with** (a person)
vexed **at** (something)
victim **of**

wait **for**
wait **on** (attend to)
write **to**

CONJUNCTIONS

A **conjunction** is a word that links sentences and words.

> I invited him to the party *although* I knew he wouldn't come.
> *Neither* Peter *nor* Patricia liked the holiday.

It's your turn!

1. Identify the conjunctions in these sentences.
(a) Despite my instructions, they were unable to find the hotel.
(b) Mary said that she would not come to the party.
(c) John sat down and ate his dinner.
(d) Do you want the book or will I leave it in the bag?
(e) James came but Mary refused to come with us.
(f) John and James went to the match together.
(g) The teacher was sick and tired of the noise.
(h) They promised to come with us but they let us down.
(i) He was happy although he was tired.
(j) She was miserable despite being rich.

ARTICLES AND INTERJECTIONS

definite article: the word *the*

indefinite article: *a* or *an* (if the word following begins with a vowel)

> *a* dog, *an* apple

interjection: a word that expresses a feeling or emotion but which has no grammatical connection with the rest of the sentence

> *Oh!*
> *Hello!*

PREPOSITIONS AND ADVERBS

· ·

It is easy to confuse prepositions with adverbs because the same words can be used as either part of speech. So remember these two important points.

• A **preposition** always goes with and governs a noun or pronoun.
• An **adverb** usually goes with a verb or an adverb. It usually tells when, where or how.

ADVERBS

1. The man passed *by*.
2. He took *off* his coat.
3. Come *along,* boys.
4. Come *on* or we'll be late.

These examples show us a number of things.
• The adverb *by* modifies the verb *passed*.
• The adverb *off* modifies the verb *took*.
• The adverb *along* modifies the verb *Come*.
• The adverb *on* modifies the verb *Come*.

PREPOSITIONS

1. The book was written *by* F. Jones.
2. He took the book *off* the table.
3. He ran *along* the track.
4. Put the book *on* the table.

Here is what these examples show us.
• The preposition *by* governs the noun *F. Jones*.
• The preposition *off* governs the noun *table*.
• The preposition *along* governs the noun *track*.
• The preposition *on* governs the noun *table*.

It's your turn!

Say whether the underlined words are prepositions or adverbs. Then explain your choices.

(a) He put the money <u>in</u> his wallet.
(b) He sat <u>down</u> when I told him.
(c) She put the parcel <u>down</u> on the floor.
(d) They came <u>late for</u> the party.
(e) They broke <u>open</u> the box.
(f) 'Come <u>in</u>,' I said.
(g) The teacher looked <u>over</u> my work.
(h) Your books are <u>everywhere</u> in the house.
(i) Mary and John came <u>later</u>.
(j) They <u>seldom</u> visit us now.

Some compound prepositions

in spite of
for the sake of
on behalf of
because of
in order to
by way of
in front of

CONJUNCTIONS

· ·

And, **but**, **or** and **that** are the most commonly used conjunctions. A conjunction can be distinguished from a preposition by remembering:

• A conjunction *joins*.
• A preposition *both joins and governs* (or controls) a noun or a pronoun.

Conjunction	**Preposition**
He came *after* I left.	He came *after* me.
She will stay *until* I come.	She will stay *until* Monday.

NAMING PARTS OF SPEECH

• •

The part of speech of every word in these sentences has been named. Can you explain each choice?

The teacher said that my work was well done.

The: definite article
teacher: noun
said: verb
that: conjunction
my: adjective
work: noun
was: verb
well: adverb
done: verb

When the spectators heard the final whistle, they invaded the pitch.

When: adverb
the: definite article
spectators: noun
heard: verb
the: definite article
final: adjective
whistle: noun
they: pronoun
invaded: verb
the: definite article
pitch: noun

It's your turn!

Name the part of speech of every word in these sentences. Then explain your choices.

(a) The water in the lake is deep and blue.
(b) The farmer roared loudly when the dogs entered his field.
(c) Karen often goes to the local library.
(d) The ship's captain quickly gave the order.
(e) The express train arrived early at the station.
(f) The snow settled gently on the rooftops and the trees.
(g) It rained heavily during the night.
(h) The postman left the parcel with my neighbour.
(i) They stopped talking immediately.
(j) The pilot landed the aircraft with great difficulty.

Challenge time

The next group of sentences will give you a challenge! Name the part of speech of every word in these sentences. Then explain your choices.

(a) The police found no useful clues because the crime had been carefully carried out.
(b) The bus stopped for the passengers who were waiting in the rain.
(c) The angry man claimed that he had been robbed on the previous day.
(d) The pudding had been completely burned when the cook took it from the oven.
(e) The shopkeeper complained angrily that her store had been broken into almost every night.
(f) The victorious team returned home late because the train was delayed.
(g) The women do not know the names of the actors.
(h) The children who broke the window ran away quickly.
(i) Tom and Una came to the party although they were not invited.

• • • • • • • •

A BIT OF ORDER, PLEASE

SYNTAX: PUTTING WORDS IN ORDER

• • • • • • • •

Syntax means the **arrangement** or **order** of words in a sentence.

Let's take a look at how words are put together to make a sentence – and to make sense! To understand how a **simple sentence** works, just imagine an archer shooting at a target. This diagram will help.

subject   predicate (verb)   direct object

Archer   Flight of Arrow   Target

SUBJECT

• •

The **archer** = the person or thing the sentence is about = the **subject**

- The **subject** of a sentence **tells who or what** the sentence is about.
- The **subject** of a sentence will always be a **noun** or a **pronoun**.
- It's easy to find the subject – just put **who** or **what** in front of the verb or predicate ('predicate' is just another word that is used for the verb when dealing with syntax). The **who** or the **what** is the **subject**.

The dog bit the man.

the **action** = *bit*

who or **what** bit?

the dog bit

the **subject** = *the dog*

VERB

• •

the **flight** of the arrow = **the action** = the **verb** (the predicate)

The dog bit the man.
the **action** = **bit**
the **verb** (predicate) = **bit**

A **predicate** must be a **finite verb**.

Here's a simple test for knowing whether a verb can be a predicate – just find out if it has a subject. If it has, then it is a finite verb and it can be a predicate.

To find the subject, simply put **who** or **what** before the verb. Look at this example.

The dog bites the man.
who or **what** bites the man?
Answer = *The dog* = subject

9

So the verb *bites* has a subject. It is a finite verb and can be a predicate. Here is another example.

> The man is tired.
> **who** or **what** is tired?
> Answer = *The man* = subject

So the verb *is* has a subject. It is a finite verb and can be a predicate.

DIRECT OBJECT

target = **the aim** of the action = the **direct object**

It is easy to find the **direct object**. Just put **whom** or **what** after the verb (the predicate). The **whom** or **what** is the **direct object**.

> The dog bit the man.

> verb (predicate) = bit
> bit **whom** or **what**?
> bit *the man*
> the **direct object** = *the man*

WRITING A SIMPLE SENTENCE

A **simple sentence** is just what it says – simple!
• A **simple sentence** has **one subject**.
• A **simple sentence** has **one verb** (predicate).
• A **simple sentence** has **one direct object**.

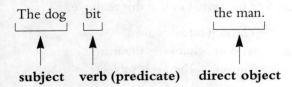

The dog	bit	the man.
↑	↑	↑
subject	**verb (predicate)**	**direct object**

It's your turn!

1. Name the subject, the verb (predicate) and the direct object in each of these simple sentences.

   Then draw a circle around the subject. Underline the verb (predicate). Make a box around the direct object.
   (a) The ball struck the goalpost.
   (b) Jane's father fixed the car.
   (c) The postman delivered the parcel.
   (d) We all enjoyed the disco.
   (e) Mary wrote the letter.
   (f) Peter did his homework.
   (g) My neighbour witnessed the robbery.
   (h) Patrick sent the flowers.
   (i) John bought new shoes.
   (j) My father liked his presents.

2. Write five simple sentences of your own. Then circle the subject, underline the verb and put a box around the direct object.

WRITING A COMPLEX SENTENCE

We can make a simple sentence more interesting – or more **complex** – if we add more information.

• **simple sentence**
  The dog bit the man.

• **complex sentence**
  The dog *that lives next door* bit the man.
  (This tells us more about *the dog*.)

  The dog bit the man *who threw the stick*.
  (This tells us more about *the man*.)

We've added a **clause** to each sentence.
> that lives next door
> who threw the stick

A clause is a group of words containing a subject and a predicate.

THE PRINCIPAL CLAUSE

The **principal clause** expresses the most important part – the principal part – of the whole sentence. Other clauses add further information about some word or phrase. Look at this example.

> Mary wrote the letter which she had promised to her friend.

The principal clause is *Mary wrote the letter*. It is the main part of the sentence.

THE SUBORDINATE CLAUSE

Other groups of words in a sentence are called **subordinate clauses**. A **complex sentence** will have **one principal clause** but may have **many subordinate clauses**.

> The dog bit the man who threw the stick.

principal clause = The dog bit the man
subordinate clause = who threw the stick

The man who drove the truck had a puncture.

principal clause = The man had a puncture
subordinate clause = who drove the truck

Mrs Flynn read the book which she got from the library.

principal clause = Mrs Flynn read the book
subordinate clause = which she got from the library

What's the difference between principal and subordinate clauses?

The **principal clause**
• expresses the *key part* of the sentence
• gives the sentence its *overall meaning*
• can stand *on its own*

The **subordinate clause**
• *depends on the principal clause* to give it sense
• just gives *a bit more information*
• *cannot stand* on its own

Study the following sentence.

> My father, who had his birthday last week, liked his presents.

principal clause = My father liked his presents
• the key part
• the overall meaning
• stands on its own

subordinate clause = who had his birthday last week
• depends on the principal clause
• gives a bit more information
• cannot stand on its own

Try these!
Write out the principal clause and the subordinate clause in each of these sentences.
1. He only visits when he has a little time to spare.
2. Jane sent me flowers because it was my birthday.
3. We all enjoyed the disco which was held in our school.
4. We usually go to the beach when the weather is fine.
5. Peter refused to go to the party which his friends threw for him.

6. My mother lost the scarf which I had bought for her birthday.
7. Jane returned the CD which I lent her last week.
8. We didn't go swimming because the weather was bad.
9. My parents will not allow me to go to a disco until I am sixteen.
10. Unless the weather improves, there will be no match tomorrow.

THE WORK OF SUBORDINATE CLAUSES

There are three types of subordinate clauses:
- **adjectival clauses**
- **adverbial clauses**
- **noun clauses**

ADJECTIVAL CLAUSES

. . . .

An **adjectival clause** does **the work of an adjective**. It gives more information about a noun or a pronoun in some other clause.

> The girl *who was standing at the bus-stop* wore a blue coat.

- The clause *who was standing at the bus-stop* tells us more about *the girl.*
- *The girl* is a **noun**.

Adjectives tell more about nouns or pronouns.

- An **adjectival clause** is a group of words which qualifies (tells more about) a noun.
- An **adjectival clause** is joined or related to the rest of the sentence by words such as the following. (They are called relative pronouns or relative adverbs.) **who, which, that, what, as, where, when, why, whom, whose**

Note: Sometimes a relative pronoun is left out, as in the following sentences.

- The money he wanted could not be found.
(The money *which* he wanted or *that* he wanted...)
- The girl they saw was a stranger.
(The girl *whom* the saw...)

It's your turn!

Identify the adjectival clause in each of these sentences. Point out the noun or pronoun which it qualifies. If a relative pronoun has been left out, put it where it belongs and underline it.

1. The librarian, who was very absent-minded, could not find the book I had returned.
2. The restaurant where we normally eat was closed that day.
3. It wasn't the kind of present I would give my best friend.
4. They never mentioned the time at which I had to come home.
5. The plan you put forward was very interesting.
6. I saw the garden where they planted the tree.
7. The magazine I bought only last week was thrown out with the rubbish.
8. It was the best film I ever saw.
9. The girls who stole my pencil case have been punished.
10. The members of the team who were left behind finally got home.

ADVERBIAL CLAUSES

● ●

An **adverbial clause** does the work of an **adverb**. Adverbs tell more about verbs.

> The children clapped when they saw the clown.

- The clause *when they saw the clown* tells more about when they *clapped*.
- *Clapped* is a verb.

An **adverbial clause**
- gives *more information* about a verb
- *modifies* the verb

KINDS OF ADVERBIAL CLAUSES

- **Time** – tells us **when** something was done.
  I went to the cinema *when I was on holiday*.

- **Place –** tells us **where** something was done.
  She went *where she was told*.

- **Cause** – tells us **why** something was done.
  They came *because they were hungry*.

- **Purpose** – tells us the **reason** why something was done.
  He worked hard *so that he could go to the World Cup*.

- **Result** – tells us the **result** of an action.
  The ship sank quickly, *so no one was saved*.

- **Condition** – tells us the **condition** of an action (the words *if* and *unless* are the signals).
  If I had the money I would go to the cinema.
  I cannot go to the cinema *unless I have the money*.

- **Concession** – tells that there is some **difficulty** about an action.
  Although I have been told that story, I still do not believe it.

Try these!

Identify the adverbial clause in each of the following sentences. Point out the word or phrase it modifies or gives further information about.

1. He will get that job because he wants it so much.
2. We reached home just before it started to rain.
3. I am not allowed to go to the disco unless I get my parents' permission.
4. If I have time I'll go to the match with you.
5. He worked so hard it is a pity he failed.
6. They spent their money so fast they had to come home before they intended.
7. I was really surprised when I opened the door.
8. Two of our friends were left behind because there was no room on the bus.
9. You should be prepared if you want to come with us.
10. The summer camp was closed when we arrived.

Challenge time

Identify the adverbial clause in each of these sentences. Point out the word or phrase which it modifies. Say what kind of adverbial clause each one is.

1. The train had already left when we arrived at the station.
2. He was angry because no one had sent him an invitation.
3. She won't be able to go on holidays unless she starts saving now.
4. They worked so hard that they had to succeed.
5. They always go where they are not supposed to go.
6. We could not visit our friends because the weather was bad all day.

7. I used to go on holidays with my parents when I was younger.
8. The house went up in flames so quickly that the firemen could not save it.
9. We left the party when it became too rowdy.
10. They can come with us if they have the money for their own tickets.

NOUN CLAUSES

• •

A **noun clause** does the work of a noun. The noun which it replaces can be the subject or direct object of the verb in the principal clause.

Many people think that pop music is too loud.

subject = Many people
verb (predicate) = think
what they think = that pop music is too loud

that pop music is too loud = the **direct object** of *think*

A direct object is a noun.
SO *that pop music is too loud* = a **noun clause**

Noun clauses are often introduced by **verbs of perceiving** and **stating**

They saw that _____ (perceiving)
They heard that _____ (perceiving)
They said that _____ (stating)
They declared that _____ (stating)

It's your turn!
Complete these sentences by adding an idea or some information.
1. He knows that _____.
2. She believes that _____.

3. He thinks that _____.
4. He says that _____.
5. She hopes that _____.
6. They declared that _____.
7. She reported that _____.
8. She stated that _____.
9. We wished that _____.
10. They heard that _____.
11. It is true that _____.
12. She understood that _____.
13. He denied that _____.

WRITING OUT THE CLAUSES IN A COMPLEX SENTENCE

Step 1
Identify the **finite verbs**.
Step 2
Find the **subject** of each verb.
Step 3
Find the **principal clause**.

Example
I think that all sports are good for you because they keep you fit.

Step 1
finite verbs = *think, are, keep*

Step 2
who or what *thinks?* = *I* = **subject**
who or what *are?* = *all sports* = **subject**
who or what *keeps?* = *they* = **subject**

Step 3
principal clause = I think

Challenge time

Study these sentences.
- Identify the finite verbs.
- Find the subject of each verb.
- Find the principal clause.

The steps above will help you.

1. The teacher said that my work was well done.
2. When the spectators heard the final whistle, they invaded the pitch.
3. The police found no useful clues because the crime had been carried out so carefully.
4. The bus stopped for the passengers who were waiting in the rain.
5. The angry man claimed that he had been robbed on the previous day.
6. The pudding had been completely burned when the cook took it from the oven.
7. The shopkeeper complained angrily that her store had been broken into almost every week.
8. The victorious team returned home late because the train was delayed.
9. They will begin the match when it stops raining.
10. I know why they refused to come with us.

Examples and Answer Lay-Out

Example 1

I think that all sports are good for you because they keep you fit.

- **clauses**

I think

that all sports are good for you

because they keep you fit

principal clause = I think

subject = I

predicate = think

- **subordinate clause**

that all sports are good for you

subject = all sports

predicate = are

function = noun clause, direct object of *think*

- **subordinate clause**

because they keep you fit

subject = they

predicate = keep

function = adverbial clause of cause, modifying *think*

Example 2

The house which we hoped to buy looked very grand when we saw it that day.

- **clauses**

The house looked very grand

which we hoped to buy

when we saw it that day

- **principal clause** = The house looked very grand

subject = the house

predicate = looked

- **subordinate clause**

which we hoped to buy

subject = we

predicate = hoped

function = adjectival clause qualifying *the house*

- **subordinate clause**

when we saw it that day

subject = we

predicate = saw

function = adverbial clause of time modifying *looked*

Example 3

The general denied that the troops, whom he himself commanded, had shown cowardice.

• clauses

The general denied
that the troops had shown cowardice
whom he himself commanded

principal clause = The general denied
subject = The general
predicate = denied

• subordinate clause

that the troops had shown cowardice
subject = the troops
predicate = had shown
function = noun clause, direct object of *denied*

• subordinate clause

whom he himself commanded
subject = he
predicate = commanded
function = adjectival clause qualifying *the troops*

Try these!

Study these sentences. Then do the following. Refer to the examples when you need help.

- Write out each clause separately and identify the principal clause.
- Identify the kind of subordinate clause and give its function.
- Write out the subject and predicate of the principal clause separately.
- Write out the subject and object of the subordinate clauses separately.

1. There was a lot of noise while the party was going on.
2. The man denied that he was anywhere near the scene of the crime.
3. No one knows where the money is buried.
4. The fighting broke out when their team lost the game.
5. The fire wouldn't light because the logs were damp.
6. The man who was hit by the car made a full recovery.
7. I was very pleased when the teacher praised my work.
8. She was very annoyed when I told her the bad news.
9. He never knows when he should stop.
10. They claimed that I was responsible for breaking the window.

Challenge time!

Follow the instructions above to analyse these sentences.

1. The witness, when he was called to give evidence, stated that he had never seen the defendant before.
2. She said that the person who wrote the letter was quite serious.
3. After the shower had stopped, the group went for a brisk walk to Strawberry Hill from which there is a wonderful view of the beach.
4. I could not forgive her because I knew that she really meant to be difficult.
5. Many who saw the game said later that the result was a big surprise.
6. John went to the station early because he did not know when the train was due.
7. When she heard that her visitors were being neglected she could not hide her rage.
8. He indicated that he was ready to take action if the situation got any worse.
9. When they offered her the award, she refused to accept it because she knew she did not deserve it.
10. No one knows where the pirates buried the treasure because no one lived to tell the tale.

11. He said that he refused to answer their questions because he knew that he was innocent.

12. After they broke down the front door, great sheets of flame could be seen inside the house.

13. You cannot be admitted if you have no ticket because admission is by ticket only.

14. When she was informed of the accident, she broke into tears because she was deeply shocked.

15. When he arrived at the house, they refused to admit him because he was not properly dressed for the occasion.

16. I stopped believing in Santa Claus when I was six because my brother told me the facts then.

17. While the builders were repairing the house, we went on a holiday so that we could avoid the inconvenience.

18. I remember that I did not visit the zoo until I was about seven years old.

19. I hope you will invite me to your party if you are going to have one.

20. I told her that she should stop talking while I was watching the film on the television.

SOME SPELLING TIPS

Our alphabet is made up of vowels and consonants.

Vowels = a, e, i, o, u
Consonants = all the other letters of the alphabet

FORMING PLURALS OF NOUNS

Singular = only one person, place or thing
Plural = more than one person, place or thing

Most nouns form plurals by adding **s** to the end of the word.

one car	two cars
a girl	some girls

It's your turn!
Write the plurals of these nouns.
1. dog
2. cat
3. bag
4. house
5. window
6. desk
7. school
8. pupil
9. teacher
10. chair

Some singular nouns need **es** to make the plural. These nouns end in

s x z sh ch as

one box	two boxes
one church	two churches
one bus	two buses
one class	two classes
one brush	two brushes

It's your turn!
Write the plurals of these nouns.
1. tax
2. bunch
3. loss
4. pass
5. ash
6. buzz
7. fox
8. eyelash
9. stitch
10. address

NOUNS THAT END IN –Y
• When a noun ends in **–y**, look at the letter *before* the **–y.**
If that letter is a vowel (**a, e, i, o, u**) we add **–s.**

toy – toys
bay – bays
key – keys

• When a noun ends in **-y** and the letter *before* it is *not a vowel*, change the **-y** to **-i** and add **-es**.

 party - parties

It's your turn!

Write the plural of these nouns.

 1. donkey
 2. army
 3. day
 4. country
 5. buoy
 6. century
 7. county
 8. boy
 9. ray
10. fly
11. turkey
12. mystery
13. joy
14. jay
15. monkey

SOME IRREGULAR PLURALS

There are no rules for these - you just have to learn them!

 child – children
 tooth – teeth
 goose – geese
 foot – feet
 man – men
 woman – women
 mouse – mice
 louse – lice

Adding -full

When you add **-full** to a word, use only one **-l**.

 wonder – wonderful

Try these!

Add **-full** to the following

 1. use
 2. help
 3. truth
 4. thought
 5. power
 6. watch
 7. waste
 8. hate
 9. peace
10. hope

• When a word ends in **-ll**, drop one **-l** before adding **-ful**.

 skill + ful = skilful
 will + ful = wilful

• When adding **-full** to a word ending in –y, change the **-y** to **-i** if there is a consonant before the **-y**.

 beauty + ful = beautiful
 plenty + ful = plentiful

• If there is a vowel (**a, e, i, o, u**) before the -y, *do not* change the **-y**.

 joy + ful = joyful
 play + ful = playful

PREFIXES AND SUFFIXES

A **prefix** goes **before** the root word.

 think (*root word*)
 rethink (*with the prefix re-*)

A **suffix** goes **after** the root word.

 think (*root word*)
 thinking (*with the suffix -ing*)

RULES FOR PREFIXES

- If the last letter of the prefix is the same as the first letter of the root word, there will be a double letter.

    un (*prefix*) + needed (*root word*) = unneeded

    mis (*prefix*) + spelt (*root word*) = misspelt

- Otherwise, just add the prefix to the beginning of the root word.

    un (*prefix*) + tie (*root word*) = untie

    mis (*prefix*) + print (*root word*) = misprint

RULES FOR SUFFIXES

- Suffixes beginning with a consonant do not change the root word.

    permanent (*root word*) + ly (*suffix*)

    = permanently

    use (*root word*) + less (*suffix*) = useless

- If the root word ends in -y, change -y to -i and add the suffix.

    homely (*root word*) + ness (*suffix*)

    = homeliness

    lonely (*root word*) + ness (*suffix*) = loneliness

A few more important rules

- When a word ends in a silent **-e,** drop the **-e** before the vowel.

    score (*silent e*) + ed (*suffix*) = scored

    love (*silent e*) + ing (*suffix*) = loving

- The **exceptions** to this rule are words that end in **-ce** and **-ge**. These keep the -e before the suffixes **-ous** and **-able.**

    outrage (*root word*) + ous (*suffix*)

    = outrageous

    notice (*root word*) + able (*suffix*) = noticeable

- One-syllable words ending in a vowel + a consonant must double the final consonant adding the suffix.

    drum (*root word*) + er (*suffix*) = drummer

    drum (*root word*) + ed (*suffix*) = drummed

So we get:

    clap – clapping – clapped

    swim – swimming – swimmer

    slim – slimmer – slimming – slimmed

    hop – hopping – hopped

    (If you make a mistake with *hop*, you could get *hoping* or *hoped*!)

- Words of more than one syllable which end in **-l** and a vowel, double the **-l** before a vowel suffix (except with **-ity** and **-ise**).

    compel – compelled – compelling

    enrol – enrolled – enrolling

    appal – appalled – appalling

    control – controlled -controlling

But!

    legal – legality – legalise

    real – reality – realise

It's your turn!

Add a prefix to each of these words to make a new word. If you can think of more than one prefix for a word, try it!

1. run
2. happy
3. do
4. work
5. cover
6. make
7. view
8. take
9. satisfied
10. play

Now try these!

Add a suffix to each of the following to make a new word. Try to form more than one new word if you can.

1. sap
2. rot
3. rat
4. run
5. pat
6. travel
7. equal
8. parcel
9. cancel
10. quarrel
11. neutral
12. capital

Challenge time!

Add as many of these prefixes or suffixes as you can to the following words.

un- im- mis- ir-

-ing -ed -ful -ly

The first one will give you the idea.

1. necessary – unnecessary – necessarily – unnecessarily
2. draw
3. bake
4. love
5. regular
6. print
7. able
8. go
9. reverent
10. spelt
11. beauty
12. lovely
13. empty
14. plenty
15. possible

Is it **ie** or **ei**?

The Rule

i before **e**,
except after c,
or when sounding like **a**
as in 'neighbour' and 'weigh'

You can remember a few exceptions to this rule with this sentence.

The **weird foreigner seizes neither leisure** nor **pleasure**.

WORDS THAT ARE OFTEN MISSPELLED

- If you can think of a rule when writing these words, use it!
- Otherwise, use your memory!
- Look up the meanings of any words which you don't understand.

absence
abundance
accept
accidentally
accommodate
accurate
achieved
acknowledgement
acquaintance
across
addresses
advice
advise
aerial
aisle
aggravate
agreeable
all right
almost
amateur
among
analyse
annual
anonymous
anxiety
apologise
apparent
appearance
appetite
appreciates
appropriate
approval
Arctic
argument
arrange

ascend
assistant
association
athletics
attach
attacked
attention
awful

bachelor
bargain
basketball
beginning
beautiful
believe
benefited
bicycle
biscuit
bookkeeper
brake
breathe
break
breed
Britain
bruise
bulletin
bureau
buried
business

cafeteria
calendar
campaign
candidate
captain

caricature
catastrophe
cemetery
certain
choice
character
choice
clothes
college
column
coming
commission
committee
competent
completely
complexion
conquer
conscience
conscious
consistent
convenience
copies
corps
correspondence
courageous
course
coarse
criticism
cylinder

defense (American)
defence
definitely
deceive
decision
descent
description
desirable
despair
desperate
develop
dictionary

dining
disappear
disastrous
discipline
disease
dissatisfied
doesn't
dutiful

earnest
economical
ecstasy
effect
efficient
eight
eighth
eliminated
embarrass
emphasise –ize
endeavour
enthusiasm
equipment
equipped
especially
essential
etiquette
exaggerate
excellent
exhausted
existence
explanation
expenses
experience
extension
extraordinary

familiar
financial
fascinating
fatigue
February
fierce

fiery
finally
foreign
forfeit
formerly
forty
fragile

gasoline
gauge
genius
government
grammar
grievance
guard
guarantee
gymnasium

handkerchief
happened
haven't
height
heroes
honorary
hoping
hospital
humorous
hungry
hypocrisy

imagination
immigrate
indispensable
incidentally
independent
influence
initial
intelligent
irresistible

knowledge

laid
licence
lighting
likelihood
literature
livelihood
loneliness
losing
lying

maintenance
manoeuvre
marriage
martyr
matinee
meant
medicine
medieval
mentioned
microphone
miniature
minimum
minutes
mischievous
missile
misspelled
monotonous
mortgage
movable
municipal

necessary
niece
ninety
ninth
noticeable
nuisance

occasionally
occurred
omitted
opinion

opportunity
optimistic
orchestra
origin
original

paid
parachute
parallel
parliament
particularly
pastime
perhaps
permanent
permissible
perseverance
personally
perspiration
physical
picnic
planning
pleasant
pneumonia
possess
possibility
practice
precede
preference
prejudice
prisoners
privilege
probably
procedure
professor
pronunciation
propeller
psychology
purpose
pursue

quiet
quite

realise –ize
really
receive
recognise –ize
recommend
referred
rehearse
reign
relief
representative
restaurant
rhythm

sandwich
satisfactory
scarcity
schedule
scissors
secretary
seize
separate
sergeant
severely
shining
siege
similar
sincerely
souvenir
specimen
speech
strategy
strength
stretch
subtle
success
sufficient
superintendent
superior
surprised
syllable
sympathy
symphony

tariff	truly	unnecessary	view
television	twelfth	until	villain
tendency	tying	using	
temperament	tyranny	usually	waist
thoroughly			waste
tomorrow			Wednesday
tournament	umbrella	vacuum	weird
traffic	unconscious	valuable	writing
tragedy	undoubtedly	vengeance	
transferred	unknown	vicinity	

. . . .

GET TO THE POINT

LOOKING AT PUNCTUATION

. . . .

- We must know about **punctuation** and **capital letters** in order to make sense of what we read.

- **Punctuation marks** or **signs** tell us when to begin, when to end and when to pause in our writing.

- When writing **direct speech**, we indicate who is speaking by using punctuation marks.

CAPITAL LETTERS

. . . .

Capital letters are used at the **beginning of every sentence** and for all **proper nouns**.

A **proper noun** is the name of a **particular** person, place or thing.

> Mrs Jones (a particular person)
> Mr Smith (a particular person)
> County Cork (a particular place)
> Mount Everest (a particular place)
> Catholicism (a particular thing)
> Nissan (a particular thing)

It's your turn!
Give *six* proper nouns for *each* of these general terms.
Example: car – Ford

1. cars
2. countries
3. religions
4. mountains
5. names of people
6. rivers

A **common noun** is the name of **any** person, place or thing.

> the girl
> the boy
> the trumpet
> the dog
> the cat
> the religion

It's your turn!
Give *six* common nouns for *each* of these general terms.
Example: cutlery – fork

1. cutlery
2. toys
3. sports
4. games
5. jobs
6. fruits

PUNCTUATION MARKS

• •

FULL STOPS (.)

Use a **full stop** at the end of every **complete statement.**

A **statement** is a sentence which gives **information** or states a particular **fact.**

It's your turn!

Write these sentences correctly by using capital letters and full stops.

1. alice is in sixth year at st mary's school
2. the boy lost his sports bag he was very upset the bag was very big
3. my sister's name is betty she is very tall
4. the boy plays football for his school team he practises every day
5. my family is going to america on holiday we are going in september
6. st patrick's day is on the 17th of march
7. john smith is a very good swimmer he swims with the irish team
8. mrs murray goes to work at 8 o'clock every morning she works in the bank of ireland
9. my father bought a new car last week it is very nice
10. barbara and pat play together after school they are best friends

Abbreviations

A **full stop** is *sometimes* used after **abbreviations**.

Abbreviations *can* be written either *with* or *without* a full stop. Your teachers will tell you which they prefer.

Try these!

Write the abbreviations for these words.

1. road
2. street
3. south
4. father
5. sister
6. avenue
7. doctor
8. mister
9. saint
10. medical doctor

QUESTION MARK (?)

Use a **question mark** at the end of a **direct question.**

> Where did you put the book?
> Is this the correct page?

Watch out!

Watch out for **indirect questions**. These are **statements** which need a full stop.

> **direct question**
> Where did you put the book?
> **indirect question**
> I wonder where you put the book.

It's your turn!

Put a question mark after each direct question.
Put a full stop after each indirect question.

1. What did he see in the room
2. I asked him what he had seen
3. When is Tracy coming home
4. I have no idea when Joan is coming
5. How much money did he give you
6. She doesn't know how much money he gave you
7. When did the film start
8. I wonder when the film will start
9. Did he give you the correct change
10. I don't know how much it should be
11. I'd love to know how they did that
12. I wonder if you'd mind being a bit more quiet

EXCLAMATION MARKS (!)

Use an **exclamation mark** to express **surprise** or **astonishment**. An exclamation mark is also used for **commands**.

> What a lovely day!
> Stop that immediately!

Try this!

Write ten sentences which express surprise or astonishment, or which give commands.

THE COMMA (,)

- A **comma** marks a **pause** in a sentence. The pause is less pronounced than the pause marked by a full stop
- Use a **comma** to separate nouns in a **list**.

> Jack, Maura, Tim and Tina got top marks.
> They bought apples, oranges, bananas and pears.
> (Do not use a comma before *and*).

- Use a **comma** to separate two or more words which are the **same part of speech**.

The verbs in this example are separated by commas. There is no comma before *and*.

> She stumbled, stopped, stared and walked on.

Try these!

Insert commas where they are needed in these sentences. It might help if you say the sentence aloud to show where the natural pauses come.

1. John picked up the book opened it and then flung it away.
2. They saw tigers lions bears and elephants.
3. John Mary Patrick and Billy went to the concert.
4. The vegetables meat diary produce and bread are on the left of the entrance.
5. The child opened the door looked in quickly and then slammed it shut.

- Use a comma between **nouns in apposition**. These are words that are in the same grammatical position.

> Mr Jones, the postman, is late this morning.

- *Mr Jones* and *the postman* are both nouns.

- *Mr Jones* is the subject and *the postman* is the noun in apposition.

> We saw our neighbour, Miss Field.

Try these!

Insert commas where they are needed in these sentences.

1. Madrid the capital of Spain is a beautiful city.
2. Williams the goalkeeper put in a poor show.
3. He went to the local shop O'Brien's around the corner.
4. Miss Moore the principal is very fair.
5. I have to visit the dentist Mr Murphy.
6. My best friend Terry Walsh is an excellent musician.
7. Miss Stone my mother's boss is coming for dinner.
8. Our neighbour Mr Flynn has just left hospital.
9. Jane's class went to the concert with their teacher Mr Ford
10. We saw the sailing ship 'The Asgard'.

- Use a **comma** after an **adverbial clause** at the beginning of a sentence.

> When he came home that evening, they discussed the problem.

Try these!

Insert commas where they are needed in these sentences.

1. After he saved enough money he went on a holiday.
2. Before she passed away she had a few last words to say.
3. When they had eaten they went out to play.
4. After he had painted the room he tidied up the mess.
5. When the team is prepared then we'll play.
6. Because it was Sunday they went to church.
7. Ever since he broke his leg he has been afraid to play tennis.

• Use a **comma** to separate **direct speech** from the rest of the sentence.

> 'I come here quite often,' he said.

QUOTATION MARKS (" ") OR (' ')

• Use **quotation marks** to indicate **direct speech**, **quotations** and **titles** of book, poems, plays or films.

> You can use either double quotes " " or single quotes ' '.

> "We won't stay any longer," he said.

> Ann said, 'That was a terrific film.'

> Everyone in the class has read "The Little House on the Prairie".

> Did he see 'Jurassic Park'?

Quotation marks are usually placed **after** full stops, commas and question marks in direct speech.

Watch out!

Look at the book title and film title in the last example. The quotes come *before* the punctuation.

When introducing a quotation, use a comma *before* the quotation marks.

> They called, "Don't come in yet."
> The garda shouted, 'Put that dog on a lead!'

It's your turn!

Insert *double quotation marks* in each of these sentences.

1. It's a boring film, John said. I'm leaving.
2. Where did you put my book? Mary asked her mother.
3. I saw Star Wars five times.
4. Let's go home, Pat said. It's getting late.
5. He never does what he's told, his father complained.
6. Who reads books like Treasure Island now?
7. Who starred in The Mission?
8. I hate exams, Pat said. I never do well in them.
9. I don't know where he lives, Maura said. Is it far from here?
10. Have you read The Diary of Adrian Mole?

THE COLON (:)

Use a **colon** to introduce a **list**.

> Write a note on each of the following men: Napoleon, Julius Caesar and Alexander the Great.

> Here's what you'll need: pencils, pens, paper and crayons.

Try these!

Insert a colon in the appropriate place in each sentence.

1. There are three vegetables I hate parsnips, cabbage and sprouts.
2. Four countries competed Ireland, France, Wales and Scotland.
3. Which of the following rivers is in England the Seine, the Thames, the Liffey or the Tiber?
4. In what countries are the following cities Madrid, Naples, Rouen, Oporto?
5. My favourites fruits are peaches, pears, bananas and oranges.

THE APOSTROPHE (')

• The **apostrophe** is used for **contractions** and **to show possession**.

Contractions

Sometimes when speaking or writing, we shorten words.

I am becomes *I'm.*

These are called **contractions**.

An apostrophe is used to show where the letter has been left out.

Try these!

Change these words to contractions. Don't forget to put the apostrophe where a letter has been left out.

1. he is
2. did not
3. could not
4. she is
5. what is
6. I have
7. here is
8. there is
9. is not
10. it is

• Sometimes an apostrophe replaces *two letters* to form a contraction.

I will becomes *I'll.*

Try these!

Change these words to contractions. Put in the apostrophe to replace the two letters.

1. can not
2. we will
3. we have
4. he will
5. they will
6. I have
7. we have
8. it will
9. she will
10. would have

Apostrophe of possession

• An **apostrophe of possession** uses **'s** to show that something belongs to someone.

Tom's car
Mary's coat

This is more convenient than writing or saying:

the car of Tom
the coat of Mary

Try these!

Put in an apostrophe to show possession.

1. Tonys car is very big.
2. Bettys dress is pretty.
3. The ships deck is extremely wet.
4. The students bag is quite heavy.
5. The cats paw is sore.
6. The mans hat is big.
7. The babys skin is soft.

8. The girls hair is shiny.
9. Terrys job is satisfying.
10. Janes hat is blue.

• When a noun is *already plural* and ends in **–s**, we put an apostrophe *after* the **–s**.

> the schoolbags of the girls
> = the girls' schoolbags
> the caps of the boys = the boys' caps

It's your turn!
Put in the apostrophe to show possession.
1. the ladies hats
2. the parties leaders
3. the cats paws
4. the boys coats
5. the countries politicians

Challenge time
Change each phrase to the possessive form.
Watch out for nouns which are already plural.
1. the dog of Jack
2. the dresses of the girls
3. the leg of Mary
4. the feathers of the birds
5. the feather of the bird
6. the books of the library
7. the cars of the salesman
8. the cameras of the photographers
9. the toys of the kittens
10. the menus of the restaurant

• If a person's name ends in **–s** and has **only one syllable**, we add **'s.**
> Yeats's poems

• If a person's name ends in **–s** and has **more than one syllable**, we add only the apostrophe.
> Elvis' guitar
> Lewis' video

DIRECT SPEECH
Study these before testing yourself!

Note: When a different person is speaking, you must start a new paragraph. It may help if you say the conversation aloud first.

Example 1
Without punctuation
Im ready when you are he said standing up to go where did you put the tickets I asked I gave them to you he replied

With punctuation
> "I'm ready when you are," he said, standing up to go.
> "Where did you put the tickets?" I asked.
> "I gave them to you," he replied.

Example 2
Without punctuation
where do you think youre going the porter asked inside I replied showing him my ticket Im afraid that ticket was for last weeks performance he growled

With punctuation
> "Where do you think you're going?" the porter asked.
> "Inside," I replied, showing him my ticket.
> "I'm afraid that ticket was for last week's performance," he growled.

Test yourself

Write the following passages correctly. Use capital letters, full stops, commas, apostrophes, question marks and quotation marks where they are needed. Remember to start a new line when a different person starts to speak.

1. i saw him last sunday i said was he in good humour john asked yes i answered and he wants go to the match with us

2. you cant come in mary said this is a private party but we were invited we protested wheres your invitation then mark asked im afraid i left it behind

3. how much money have you got i asked not enough im afraid mary said thats too bad i sighed we dont have enough to get in

4. how much does this cost i asked the shop assistant ten pounds she replied thats more than i can afford

5. did your mother give you permission i asked of course she did maura replied what time should you be home before eleven i answered

6. what time do you go to school at i asked half eight john answered thats too early for me im afraid i said

7. are you coming to my party next tuesday asked mark id love to said ann do you want me to bring some of my new tapes

8. what are you doing henry asked john im waiting for paul he answered

9. mrs jones the grocers wife isnt in the shop at the moment said john

10. you can come if you like said john i do not want to replied the boy im happier at home

WORDS CAN TRIP YOU UP!

LET'S TRY TO AGREE!

When writing a sentence, we must know the **rules of agreement.**

Rule 1

When the **subject** is **singular**, the **verb (predicate)** must be **singular.**

> The *man goes* to work.
> The *girl runs* to school.

Rule 2

When the **subject** is **plural**, the **verb (predicate)** must be **plural.**

> The *men go* to work.
> The *girls run* to school.

It's your turn!

1. Each of these sentences has a single subject and a single predicate.
   Underline the subject. Draw a circle around the predicate. Then change each subject and predicate to plural.
   (a) The coat is black.
   (b) The boy kicks the ball.
   (c) The girl likes to read.
   (d) The child fell on the floor.
   (e) The woman has black hair.
   (f) The table is big.
   (g) The man opened the gate.
   (h) The dog likes meat.
   (i) The woman waves good-bye.
   (j) The boy jumps over the wall.

2. Write a predicate which will agree with the subject. See how many correct predicates your class thought of.
   (a) The houses _____ big.
   (b) The boy _____ the ball.
   (c) The girls _____ to read.
   (d) The ball _____ the goal post.
   (e) The wind _____ the tree down.
   (f) The ferry _____ late.
   (g) My father _____ a new car.
   (h) The shop _____ before six.
   (i) Her friend _____ her books.
   (j) We _____ house three times already.

Rule 3

All of these words are **singular**. When they are used as **subjects**, they must have **singular predicates**, or verbs.

each	anyone
every	anybody
neither	everyone
either	nobody
none	

The next example is easy because *-one* is part of each word.

> Everyone *is* present.
> Anyone *is* allowed to visit the park.
> Everyone *is* welcome in our home.
> No one *is* coming with us.

These are a bit harder – but it's easy when you know how. Just try putting *one* into the sentence and see if it works.

> Each of the girls *takes* her coat.
> Each (*one*) of the girls takes her coat.
>
> Neither of the men *was* right.
> Neither (*one*) of the men was right.
>
> *Is* either of those books in your bag?
> Is either (*one*) of those books in your bag?

This one is even trickier. Here's how you can tell.

> None of the coats *was* mine.
> (*Not one*) of the coats was mine.

It's your turn

Use *is, are, was* or *were* to complete each sentence. Make sure the word you choose agrees with the subject. (Check the rules!)

1. Each of the apples _____ sweet.
2. Neither of the children _____ here.
3. Neither of the girls _____ happy.
4. None of the jokes _____ funny.
5. Nobody _____ at home.
6. Everyone _____ at the party.
7. Not one of the players _____ successful.
8. Neither of my friends _____ there.
9. Each of us _____ going home.
10. Anyone _____ able to do that.

Rule 4

A singular subject is sometimes followed by a phrase beginning with *like, as well as* or *with*. If the **subject** is **singular**, the **verb** must be **singular**.

> Mary, like all her sisters, *is* very punctual.
> John, with his two friends, *is* coming home today.
> Ann, as well as her brother, *was* at the party.

Rule 5

When **two singular subjects** are joined by *and*, they need a **plural verb**.

> John and Mary *are* friends.

Make it easy for yourself – change *John and Mary* to *they* and see whether your sentence makes sense.

> (*They*) are friends.
> The boy and his father *have left* the house.
> (*They*) have left the house.
> My sister and I want to go.
> (*We*) want to go.

Rule 6

If **two singular subjects** are separated by *either…or* or *neither…nor*, they need a **singular verb**.

> Either John or Mary *knows* the right answer.
> Either (*one*) knows the right answer.
> Neither John nor Mary *told* the truth.
> Neither (*one*) told the truth.

Rule 7

If **two plural subjects** are separated by *either…or* or *neither…nor*, they must have a **plural verb**.

> Either the boys or the girls *are* right.
> Neither the boys nor the girls *know* where the book is.

It's your turn!

Choose the correct word and write each sentence. Check the rules if you need help.

1. Either John or Mary (is, are) to blame.
2. Mary, with her two sisters, (was, were) invited to the party.
3. Both Jim and Michael (is, are) coming to see us.
4. Why (does, do) everyone come whether invited or not?

5. Both the men and women (was, were) invited.
6. Ann, like Patricia, (is, are) prepared to work hard.
7. Neither of the two books (was, were) lost.
8. Everyone of us (was, were) wrong about James.
9. Neither of the two men (were, was) satisfied with the deal.
10. Neither Patricia nor Barbara (was, were) able to finish the race.

USING I AND ME

The **first person pronoun** *I* is used when it is the subject of a verb.

> I went to the cinema last night.
> *Who* went to the cinema?
> Answer = I = subject

> **Note**: Although it is not grammatically correct to say 'It is me', common usage has made it acceptable.

What happens with a plural subject?

> Tim and (I, me) went to the cinema.

Just leave out *Tim and* – does the sentence make sense? Would you say

> *Me* went to the cinema.

or

> *I* went to the cinema.

So the correct usage is

> *Tim and I* went to the cinema.

When the word is not the subject of a verb, the first person form is *me*.

> He gave the book to *me*.
> It works well for *me*.
> He saw *me* coming along the street.
> Between you and *me*, I don't really like sport.
> She says she is just like *me*.

What happens with plurals?

> They went swimming with Martha and (I, me).

Just leave out *Martha and*. Which of these makes sense?

> They went swimming with *I*.

or

> They went swimming with *me*?
> Always use **me** after *to, for, with, by, from, of, between, like*.

Try these!

Choose the correct word and write the sentence.

1. There was always trouble between him and (I, me).
2. Mary, like (me, I), hates violence.
3. Are you coming to the match with (I, me)?
4. They are not like (I, me) in any way.
5. There was a difference of opinion between them and (I, me).
6. He was running like (I, me) when he fell.
7. The money was shared between him and (I, me).
8. Tara and (I, me) stayed to help our teacher.
9. They decided to ask my brother and (I, me)
10. The boys snatched the packages from Sarah and (I, me).

WHAT'S THIS I HEAR?

• •

WORKING WITH HOMONYMS

Homonyms are words that **sound the same** but which are **spelled differently** and have **different meanings**. It's easy to confuse them, so learning them by heart is probably the best thing to do.

allowed (permitted)
aloud (out loud)

altar (a communion table, as in a church)
alter (to change)

bear (an animal)
bare (without a covering; to lay bare)

berth (a ship's station at anchor)
birth (to give birth; a birth)

blue (colour)
blew (the wind blew)

bored (to have made a hole; to be fed–up)
board (a flat piece of wood; the provision of meals, as 'room and board')

brake (of a car)
break (to break open; to cause damage)

buy (purchase)
by (alongside; 'by' someone)

coarse (rough)
course (as a golf course; a subject for study)

four (the number 4)
fore (up front)
for (on behalf of)

heard ('I heard the music.')
herd (a herd of animals, as deer or cattle)

hear (to listen)
here (a place; opposite of 'there')

hoarse (with a throaty voice)
horse (an animal)

knew (they knew)
new (not old)

key (to a door)
quay (in a harbour)

loan (with money)
lone (to be alone, on one's own)

pair (two)
pear (fruit)
pare (to peel)

practice (noun, as in a doctor's practice)
practise (verb, meaning to carry out)

reel (spool)
real (actual)

right (to turn right; to be right; correct)
write (to write a letter)

sail (a sheet of canvas, as in a ship's sail)
sale (the selling of goods at a reduced price)

scene (spectacle)
seen (verb)

scent (smell)
sent (verb)

sea (ocean)
see (verb)

soar (fly high)
sore (to feel pain)

sow (seed)
sew (clothes)

site (a location, as a building site)
sight (eyesight)

sole (the underside of the foot)
soul (a person's spirit)

there (place; opposite of 'here')
their (belonging to them)
they're (contraction of 'they are')

to (part of a verb – to go, to think; towards – to the beach)
too (also)
two (the number 2)

veil (of a bride)
vale (valley)

weak (not strong)
week (seven days)

waist (part of the body)
waste (to misuse; anything left over after use)

who's (contraction of 'who is')
whose (possessive, as 'Whose coat is it?')

What's the difference?

Write each sentence by using the correct word.

1. The landlady provided room and (bored, board).
2. That race (coarse, course) is the finest in the country.
3. I always thought he was a (lone, loan) wolf.
4. We set (sale, sail) as soon as possible.
5. How to dispose of (waist, waste) is now a major problem.
6. (Practice, Practise) makes perfect.
7. There were great bargains at the (sail, sale).
8. I found her an extremely (course, coarse) person.
9. We saw a large (herd, heard) of deer in the park.
10. No matter what I say, he refuses to (altar, alter) his ways.
11. I was not (allowed, aloud) to go to the disco.
12. Last (weak, week) we went to the cinema.
13. There is a pretty (veil, vale) near our house.
14. I like to (by, buy) magazines.
15. I keep the (quay, key) in my pocket.
16. I like the (sent, scent) of the roses.
17. Turn (write, right) when you get to the end of the street.
18. It's a complete (waist, waste) of time.
19. My father is working on a building (sight, site).
20. I was at the (seen, scene) of the accident.

LISTEN AGAIN

their   there   they're

• *their* is a **possessive adjective** and is always followed by a **noun**.

    their coat, *their* garden, *their* latest record

• *there* can be an **adverb,** meaning *in that place*.

    I saw him standing *there*

    He put the book down *there*.

• *there* can be used with a **verb.**

    There is no money in my pocket

    There has been a lot of trouble recently.

• *they're* is a **contraction** of *they are*.

    They're not very friendly.

    They're waiting for us to make up our minds.

What's the difference?

Write the following sentences using *there*, *their* or *they're*. (Watch out for the last few!)

1. Tonight _____ is a party in my house.
2. The children are playing with _____ toys.
3. The bus stops over _____.
4. The girls put on _____ coats.
5. Tomorrow _____ going to the cinema.
6. Mary is over _____.
7. Next week _____ going on holidays.
8. _____ very brave to climb up _____ in _____ bare feet.
9. When they reached _____ destination they camped _____ with _____ friends.
10. In only they had stayed _____ we could have saved _____ lives, but _____ never going to be found now.

Remember!

there = over there, in that place
their = possessive, belonging to them

Challenge time!

Write these sentences correctly, using *their* or *there* .

1. I saw them standing _____ a minute ago with _____ friends.
2. I put _____ money in the drawer over _____.
3. When they reached _____ destination they camped _____ for two days.
4. If they had listened, _____ would have been no trouble about _____ passports.
5. After a few minutes _____ was a great explosion down _____.
6. We stood _____ sadly watching _____ retreating figures.
7. We stayed _____ for lunch last week with _____ family.
8. He sat down _____, and not all _____ pleading could get him to move.

9. If I had _____ money I would not stay _____.
10. _____ is no danger to _____ property now that _____ is a watchdog.

TO AND TOO DON'T MAKE TWO!

• •

• *to* means movements towards.
    We walked *to* the house.
    He gave it *to* her.
• *to* is also used to form the infinitive of a verb.
    He likes *to eat*.
    We are going *to swim*.
• *too* means more than enough.
    He bought *too* many books.
    There is *too* much violence on TV.
• *too* can mean *also* or *as well as*.
    She has a ticket *too*.
    They *too* will probably be late.
• *two* is the word for the number 2.
    He has *two* tickets for the show.
    Two of us won the prize.

What's the difference?

Write these sentences using *to*, *too* or *two*.

1. I gave her the money _____ buy the _____ books.
2. My sister came _____ although she was not invited.
3. He got sick because he ate _____ much.
4. It is _____ late _____ turn back now.
5. They sent me _____ tickets _____ many.
6. It is not good _____ work _____ hard.
7. He is _____ short _____ be a guard.
8. _____ many people nowadays eat _____ much.
9. The _____ boys were _____ late _____ go.
10. He knew _____ much _____ be fooled by those _____ girls.

A few tricky ones

These groups of words are often confused.
Study them!

where (place)
were (verb)
we're (contraction of *we are* or *we were*)

thought (past tense of *think*)
taught (past tense of *teach*)

quiet (peaceful)
quite (rather – as in 'He was feeling quite well.')

does (form of the verb, *to do*)
dose (as medicine)

breath (as in 'a breath of air')
breathe (verb)
breadth (width)

Remember!

where = place
were = verb
we're = contraction of *we are* or *we were*

Try these!

Write these sentences correctly. Use *where*, *were*
or *we're*.

1. That is the town _____ I used to live.
2. Today _____ going to the zoo.
3. _____ are you going on holidays?
4. The boys _____ playing a football match
   yesterday.
5. We _____ very happy when our team won
   the match.
6. Tonight _____ having fish for dinner.
7. _____ very happy to be living _____ we
   are.

8. We _____ very busy doing our exams last
   week.
9. I cannot remember _____ I left my book,
   but _____ still looking.
10. Next year _____ going to Spain _____ we
    have always had fun.

Remember!

who's = contraction for *who is*
whose = possessive, as in 'Whose hat is this?'

It's your turn!

Complete each sentences by using *whose* or
who's.

1. _____ coat is that?
2. The girl _____ bag was stolen was sad.
3. The doorbell rang and my sister asked
   '_____ that?'
4. The girl _____ singing is very nervous.
5. The boy _____ leg is broken is now in
   hospital.
6. The man _____ son won the race is very
   proud of him.
7. The woman _____ over there is very
   talkative.
8. That is the actress _____ mother is also
   famous.
9. That is the actor _____ tipped to win an
   Oscar.
10. The girl _____ sick is absent from school.

What's the difference?

Choose the correct word to complete each
sentence.

1. The teacher who (taught, thought) English
   left the school.
2. I stood (there, their) for a long time.

3. I had to take a large (does, dose) of medicine.
4. The girl is very (quiet, quite) now.
5. The (breath, breadth) of the door is too narrow.
6. There's not a (breath, breathe) of fresh air in here.
7. After a while he (taught, thought) no more about it.
8. No one knows what he (does, dose).
9. The sight of it took my (breath, breadth) away.
10. Homework is usually (quiet, quite) boring.

USING ITS AND IT'S

• *its* is a possessive adjective like his or her.

  I know where *its* entrance is.

  Its controls are behind the panel.

• *it's* is the contraction for *it is*.

  It's in the car.

  It's the best shop in town.

Try this if you're not sure – put *it is* in the blank. Does it make sense?

  The dog is chewing (it's, its) bone.

  The dog is chewing *it is* bone.

No! So the answer must be –

  The dog is chewing its bone.

What's the difference?

Complete each sentence by using *its* or *it's*.

1. (Its, It's) not what I thought it would be.
2. (Its, It's) good to know the difference.
3. I know where (its, it's) hidden.
4. (Its, It's) engine is in the back.
5. She saw where (its, it's) wheel went.
6. (Its, It's) nowhere to be found.
7. (Its, It's) colour is too bright for me.
8. Did you notice (its, it's) size?
9. I don't like (its, it's) shape.
10. (Its, It's) too fast for me.

IS IT OF OR OFF?

• *of* usually shows possession, a sense of belonging to. It can also mean *among*. It can be used with *on account of* or *because of*.

  The roof *of* the house is damaged.

  He gave me two *of* his records.

  One *of* my friends had an accident.

  Because *of* that meeting we are no longer friends.

• *off* indicates direction, as *away from*.

  The boat went *off* course.

  He ran *off* when I shouted at him.

  The plate fell *off* the table.

What's the difference?

Write these sentences, filling in the blanks with *of* or *off*.

1. I picked the book _____ the ground.
2. He ran _____ without saying a word to either _____ us.
3. Two _____ the ships veered _____ course.
4. We switched _____ the television and went for a walk.
5. He took _____ his jacket and gave it to one _____ his friends.
6. We set _____ as soon as one _____ us spotted the distress signal.
7. He was excused because _____ illness.
8. The dish slipped _____ the edge _____ the shelf.
9. The police say that he was pushed _____ the platform at the back _____ the stage.
10. As soon as they saw us they cleared _____ as if they were in a bit _____ a hurry.

DOUBLE NEGATIVES

If a verb is negative, do not use other negative words or phrases in the sentence, like *nothing, no one, never, no*.

Wrong – They do not have no money.
Right – They do not have any money.

Wrong – They never saw no on.
Right – They never saw anyone.

Wrong – They never go out no more
Right – They never go out any more.

COMPARISON OF ADJECTIVES

When using adjectives, there are three degrees of **comparison**.

- **Positive** = used when only **one** person or thing is referred to.
  I like the *big* book.
- **Comparative** = used when **two** persons or things are referred to.
  I prefer the *bigger* book. (bigger of the two)
  The comparative degree is usually formed by adding **-er** to the positive.
- **Superlative** = used when **more than two** persons or things are referred to.
  She wanted the biggest book. (biggest of them all)
  The superlative degree is usually formed by adding **-est** to the positive.

A few exceptions

Of course, there are usually a few exceptions to every rule. The following comparisons do not use *-er* and *-est*.

Positive	Comparative	Superlative
good	better	best
bad	worse	worst
much	more	most
many	more	most
little	less	least

Try these!

Fill in the blanks with a word from the list above. (It is possible for more than one of these words to be correct.)

1. Of the two coats, I like the black one _____.
2. Pat's behaviour in school is _____ than John's.
3. They always have _____ money than their brother.
4. He is _____ in maths than I am.
5. He is the _____ student in the whole class.
6. Things are bad but they can always get _____ .
7. Who got the _____ seat at the cinema?
8. I worked harder than John but he got _____ results.
9. I like salt on my food but I prefer _____ pepper.
10. Teachers always say that a student can do _____.

FORMING IRREGULAR ADJECTIVES

We do not add **-er, -est** to adjectives ending in -al, -ed, -ic, -ile, -ine, -ode, -ous and some others. Instead, we use *more* and *most*. For example, we do not say –

beautiful-er	*but*	more beautiful
comic-er	*but*	more comic
delicious-er	*but*	more delicious
hostil-er	*but*	more hostile

The following adjectives end in -*or*. They are followed by *to* instead of *than*.

superior to	senior to
inferior to	junior to

DOUBLE COMPARISONS

It is a common mistake to use **double comparison of adjectives.**

Wrong: She was the most wisest person I ever met.
Right: She was the wisest person I ever met.

Wrong: It was the most hottest summer in years.
Right: It was the hottest summer in years.

GOOD AND WELL

- *Good* is an adjective, so we say –
  The food was good.
  (*food* is a noun which is qualified by the adjective *good*.)
- *Well* is an adverb, so we say –
  She cooks well.
  (*cooks* is a verb which is modified by the adverb *well*.)

What's the difference?

Chose either *good* or *well* to complete each sentence.

1. She does her job very (good, well).
2. She never eats (good, well) when she is sick.
3. I always try to do my homework (good, well).
4. When you are rushing you never get anything done (good, well).
5. He felt that he did (good, well) in the interview.
6. I never do very (good, well) in exams.
7. I don't know how (well, good) she did in her test.
8. They did (good, well) in getting the results they got.
9. She did (good, well) but it wasn't her best.
10. He played (good, well) in very bad conditions.

ADVERBS

- Adverbs are usually formed by adding -*ly* to the adjective (positive degree).

  He walked *slowly* along the road.
- The comparison of adverbs is formed by using *more* or *most*.

  He walked *more slowly* than I did.
  Of them all, he walked *most slowly*.

Some exceptional adverbs

Positive	Comparative	Superlative
fast	faster	fastest
hard	harder	hardest
soon	sooner	soonest
near	nearer	nearest
long	longer	longest
loud	louder	loudest
late	later	latest
far	farther	farthest
well	better	best
badly	worse	worst
much	more	most
little	less	least

A mixed bag!

There is an error in each of these sentences.
Rewrite each sentence by correcting the error.
Then give a reason for making the correction.
(Don't be afraid to check the rules!)

1. You must promise not to tell no one.
2. There were a great crowd present.
3. His work is superior than yours.
4. It was the best summer sail we ever went to.
5. He built that wall very good.
6. It was to cold to go for a walk.
7. Were do you think you're going?
8. Their was a very big crowd at the match.
9. This writer's mistakes are easy detected.
10. Noreen is the smaller of the five sisters.
11. He always does his work good.
12. They brought the boat alongside the key.
13. Do either of you know were the house is?
14. None of us were at home at the time.
15. Neither of the cars were any good.
16. He asked me for a lone.
17. I had taken the smallest of the two cakes.
18. We never do good in our tests.
19. Their is not in this wide world a valley so sweet.
20. Mary and me are going fishing.
21. Everyone intending to go on the excursion were waiting at the bus stop.
22. I didn't recognise nobody at the party.
23. I near broke my sides laughing at the clown.
24. The invitation to the concert was sent to my parents and I.
25. Where did you get them sweets?
26. I didn't do nothing, but I got the blame.
27. The boy was very quite in the room.
28. I gave the CD too my friend.
29. There never there when you want them.
30. I'm not saying no more.
31. The old lady set down for a rest.
32. He kept the quay in his pocket.
33. John put the violin into it's case.
34. That programme board me completely.
35. Me and Joseph went to school together.
36. He knows where yous are.
37. I got the money off my father to buy the bicycle.
38. Whose coming to the match with me?
39. The prices in that shop is ridiculous.
40. None of the houses were destroyed.

EXPOSITORY OR FACTUAL WRITING

An expository or factual composition has five main functions.
- **To set forth a subject**
- **To explain what it is**
- **To describe and analyse how it works**
- **To trace its history and development**
- **To give your personal judgment of its value**

Exploratory Questions

Before tackling an expository essay, it is a good idea to ask yourself some questions. The following list shows the kind of questions you might ask yourself.

- What is the subject? If necessary, use a dictionary to help you with this, but do not give a dictionary-style definition.
- How does it work? This question may refer to an object, an idea or a system of some kind, such as 'democracy'.
- When and how did it come into existence?
- What is its use?
- What value has it now?
- What value did it have in the past?
- Does it make sense?

GENERAL PLAN FOR EXPOSITORY COMPOSITION

INTRODUCTION
Paragraph 1 = Definition
What is it?
- Examine the *key words* (the main words) in the topic.
- Do not produce a dictionary-style definition of these key words.
- Show that you have a reasonable understanding of what you are asked to write about.

MAIN BODY
Paragraphs 2 and 3 = Descriptive Analysis
- **When** did the object or thing come into existence? (Time)
- **How** did it come into existence? (History)
- **Who** thought of the object or idea in the first place?

Paragraph 4 = Function
What does it do?
- What is the **function or purpose** of the object or idea?
- Of **what use** is it? Of what use was it?

CONCLUSION
Paragraph 5 = Assessment
Its value?
- Explain the **importance or unimportance** of the object or idea.
- What **value** has it?

USING THE PLAN: SKETCHING AN EXPOSITORY ESSAY

• •

TOPIC: TOURISM

Introduction = Definition
What is it?
- Organised travel and visits to other countries
- The package tour
- Travel and accommodation arrangements made by a commercial company

Main Body = Descriptive Analysis (paragraphs 2 and 3)

When did it come into existence?
- Modern tourism began in this century.
- Middle–class and working–class people began to earn more money. They had longer holidays. They wanted to fulfil their dreams of visiting places which they had only heard of or read about.

Main Body = Function (paragraph 4)

Its use?
- Gives many people the chance to experience other cultures, other ways of life.
- Gives many people a break from the monotony of their own everyday working lives.
- 'A change is as good as a rest!'

CONCLUSION: ASSESSMENT
Its value?
- Relaxation
- Cultural experience
- Broadening the mind
- Tolerance of differences among different people

Does it work?
- Has the values listed above
- There is the danger that too much tourism can damage a country's natural beauty and its culture.
- Culture becomes a product to be bought and sold.

EXAMPLE OF USING THE PLAN

• •

TOPIC: TOURISM

Tourism can be described as travel for business or pleasure. A whole industry has developed which arranges holiday destinations and the accommodation and services which people require. This is often called the 'package holiday' business. With this kind of highly organised tourism, everything is laid on by the travel agent. There are also other kinds of tourism, including back-packing and self-catering holidays.

Tourism has only emerged recently as a growing industry. In the early part of this century, a holiday for most people was a day-trip to the seaside. A few hours' play at Bray or Bundoran or Blackpool, and it was home again, back to reality. In the past, it was common for someone to be born in a small village, to grow up and live their entire lives without ever straying very far from home. However, as working conditions improved and pay increased, many people began to save up to take an annual holiday, sometimes to the old seaside resorts or to relations in the country. Then developments in technology (such as aeroplanes) and increased advertising meant that people developed a curiosity about the wider world. This, combined with cheaper travel fares, has produced the mass movement of people around the world every year.

Tourism serves many purposes. It exposes people to other cultures and other ways of life, although the real culture is often hidden from well-off tourists in their four-star hotels. They do not see the ways in which the ordinary people live and work. In some places, they do not see the shanty towns that may be so close to them.

People often take holidays for a change of scenery, to have a change in the pace of life. Tourism also means a great deal to the holiday destinations that are at the heart of the business. There is a flow of money into the local economy and a development in the region's infrastructure of roads, railways, hotels and shops. It provides employment for local people and makes life in many of these places more pleasant.

Of course, tourism has its dangers. The natural environment of many tourist places has been the victim of unregulated tourist exploitation. Beaches and seas have been polluted. Forests have been cut down. Historic old buildings have been knocked down to make way for new multi-storey hotels. And native cultures have been turned into phoney shows for tourists who

think they are seeing the 'real thing'.

In general, though, it seems to me that tourism has produced more good than bad. It has brought enormous pleasure to countless millions of people. By exposing people to different cultures and different lifestyles, tourism has made a contribution to tolerance and understanding among the different peoples of the world.

USING THE PLAN: SKETCHING AN EXPOSITORY ESSAY

TOPIC: SPEED
Introduction
Paragraph 1 = Definition (What is it?)
- What kind of speed do you think you are asked to discuss?
- All kinds of mechanical speed?
- The speed of your own body?
- Mechanical speed seems the most likely answer.
- It offers the best scope for a composition.
- What does mechanical speed involve?
- Cars, trains, aeroplanes, ships, telecommunications, television, satellites etc.
- Speed in farming and factory production

MAIN BODY
Paragraphs 2 and 3 = Descriptive Analysis
- Although simple machines were known in the past, the science of mechanics (of machinery) was only properly developed in the 17th century. At that time, scientists tried to solve the mysteries of the physical universe, of the world we can see, touch, hear, smell and taste.

- Laws that control energy (force) and motion were discovered.
- Speed began to be understood.
- The laws of physics were put to use in designing machines.
- The first great successes: the use of steam energy and the invention of the mechanical loom. Both of these were developed during the Industrial Revolution.
- This took place at the end of the 18th century and the opening years of the 19th century, first in England and then in America.
- Machines became so efficient that they killed off many craft industries which made things by hand.
- Machines were soon able to do things much more quickly than any person could.

Paragraph 4 = Function (What does it do?)

- The purpose of speed is to produce things quickly so that more and more goods and services can be produced, and produced more cheaply.
- Goods, raw materials and finished products can be moved about faster.

CONCLUSION
Paragraph 5 = Assessment (Your personal judgment))

- Human beings have come to depend on machines.
- Computers can make complicated calculations which are impossible for a human being to do as quickly and as accurately.

- As human life becomes more and more controlled by machines, and as machines can operate much faster than people, human beings who work with them often find it hard to cope with them. There is a danger in this.
- Is modern technology using up the earth's resources (coal, gas, oil, timber etc.) at a speed so fast that the earth may soon be unable to support human life?
- Are machines making people redundant as workers because people cannot compete with the speed of machines?
- There are speed limits built into the human body and mind which human beings may be unwise to go beyond.

It's your turn!

1. Write out the first paragraph along the lines sketched out above.
2. Write out paragraphs 2, 3 and 4 as sketched out above. You are free to add or subtract from the suggestions given.
3. Complete the essay.

USING THE PLAN: SKETCHING AN EXPOSITORY ESSAY
• •
TOPIC: THE PROBLEM OF LITTER

Note: This is an expository composition. Pay attention to the *problem* aspect of the topic. It is not just about *litter*, but about *the problem of litter*.

INTRODUCTION

Paragraph 1 = Definition (What is it?) Give a definition of litter.

- Litter usually means odds and ends of paper, beer and soft drink cans, plastic wrappings, bottles etc. which are thrown away on streets, in parks, in places of recreation, in rivers etc.
- Litter is accepted as a problem. It is a bigger problem in some places than in others. Dublin City, for example, has a bad name for litter and is often called 'dirty Dublin'.

MAIN BODY

Paragraphs 2 and 3 = Descriptive analysis The litter problem was not always been with us.

- In the past, people had very little to throw away. They were more careful about waste.
- The problem of litter got worse because of the kind of society we live in now, a society known as the consumer society for which everything is packaged.
- We are also called 'the throw-away society'.
- Work out the connection between the consumer society of mass production (things being made in their thousands and millions) and the litter problem.

Paragraph 4 = Function (What does it do?)

- Litter causes many problems.
- Describe as many of these problems as you can.

CONCLUSION

Paragraph 5 = Assessment (Your personal judgment)

- The importance of solving the litter problem.
- In a world in which there is less and less of everything, people should waste as little as possible.
- Can we avoid litter?
- How can we encourage people to stop littering?
- Could litter be recycled (used again)?

It's your turn!

1. Write the first paragraph along the lines sketched out above.
2. Write paragraphs 2, 3 and 4 as sketched out above. You are free to add or subtract from the suggestions provided.
3. Complete the essay.

USING THE PLAN: SKETCHING AN EXPOSITORY ESSAY

• •

TOPIC: KEEPING A DIARY – ITS PLEASURE AND VALUE

Note: This is an expository type of composition. At the same time, it gives you scope for personal writing and for the expression of your own views and experiences.

INTRODUCTION

Paragraph 1 = Definition (What is it?)

- What is a diary?
- When did people start keeping diaries?
- What kinds of people keep a diary?
- Why do people keep diaries?

MAIN BODY

Paragraphs 2 and 3 = Descriptive Analysis

- Describe the pleasures involved in keeping a diary.
- The pleasure of self-expression.
- The pleasure of making sense of what happens to you every day.
- The pleasure of reliving your experiences by being able to read about them again in your diary.

Paragraph 4 = Function (What does it do?)

- Define the different uses which you think a diary can have.
- Describe the kind of diary you are interested in keeping, and explain why.

CONCLUSION

Paragraph 5 = Assessment (Your personal judgment)

- Analyse and describe the value of keeping your diary.
- Its value in helping you to understand yourself, of finding out your faults and weaknesses.
- The value of understanding other people better by noting down your observations.
- The value of seeing yourself more objectively (as others might see you).
- How it helps you to improve yourself.
- Explain the difference between diaries that have value for the general public (because they may contain eye-witness accounts of important events, such as Anne Frank's diary) and diaries that, though they may have little value for others, have great personal value for the people who keep them.

Try these!

1. **Sport**
   (a) Draw up a list of exploratory questions and answers using the guidelines above.
   (b) Sketch out a plan for the essay.
   (c) Write a full composition on the topic.

2. **The good and bad effects of science**
   Answer (a), (b) and (c) as above.

3. **Exploring a library**
   Answer (a), (b) and (c) as above.

4. **Computers**
   Answer (a), (b) and (c) as above.

5. Consider the question of **food prices** from the point of view of a housekeeper, a farmer and a shopkeeper.
   Answer (a), (b) and (c) as above.

6. **The energy crisis**
   Answer (a), (b) and (c) as above.

Challenge time

Write a composition on one of the following topics.

1. Medicine
2. Travel
3. Employment
4. The year 2000
5. The influence of television
6. The importance of the past
7. Leisure
8. Choosing a career
9. Education
10. Films
11. The motor car
12. Space travel
13. The schoolboy or schoolgirl, in fact and in fiction

REPORTS

A student may be asked to write many kinds of reports.
• Report on **a local even**t – a sale of work, school sports day etc.
• A **book report**
• Report on a **film or television programme**
• Report on the year's **activities** of a club
• Report on a **drama production**

Questions to answer

Think about the following before writing your report.
• Who asked you to write the report – a teacher, a newspaper?
• Where will the report appear – local paper, school paper?
• For whom is the report intended – teacher, students, readers of a particular paper?

WRITING ABOUT AN EVENT

A report about a particular event should contain:
• **information**
• **impressions**
• It may also contain **bias** or **prejudice.**

INFORMATION
• **What** is the nature of occasion – a local sports festival, a school trip?
• **Where** did the event take place – your city, town, area, abroad?
• **When** did the event take place – day, date, time?
• **Who** was present – size of attendance, any important people?
• **Description** of event(s)

IMPRESSIONS

In addition to the facts, the reporter usually gives his or her own personal opinion of the event. This opinion should be both reasonable and fair.

Questions to answer
• Did the event go as the organisers had planned ?
• Did anything unusual happen?
• Was anything special said (quotation) or done?

SAMPLE REPORT

Read this report and talk about whether it tells where, when, who, what. What is your impression of this report?

A school trip to Italy

Arriving exactly on schedule at Milan airport, we went by coach to Milan. Although our stay there was very brief, we managed to visit the beautiful cathedral before leaving for Sirmione. We were soon introduced to a shocking facet of Italian living – the high prices – when we had to buy lunch. With our pockets now emptier, we toured around nearby Lake Garda, Italy's biggest lake as well as one of her most beautiful stretches of water. From there we set off for Venice, passing through Verona on the way, site of one of Italy's largest colosseums.

Upon reaching Venice, we checked into the Hotel Vienna where we had a very pleasant meal – this time it was part of the package! Rising the next morning at the unearthly hour of 7am, we had a continental breakfast of coffee, rolls and peach jam (not appreciated by the bacon and egg fans among us!).

The morning was spent in and around the ancient and magnificent city of Venice, 'Queen of the Adriatic' as she is sometimes called. We went by coach to the Piazza Roma and by waterbus to St Mark's Square before returning to the hotel after another late night.

After strolling around the city the next morning, we reached our meeting point only to discover that one of the buses had broken down. Undeterred, our good-natured driver ferried two separate loads of exhausted students and teachers back to the hotel. Next day, on a new bus, we were off to Florence to see the famous Ponte Vecchio. Our friendly guide told us that this was the only bridge there that had survived the German army's retreat from Italy at the end of World War II.

That night came our first truly Italian meal – there were more choices of pastas and sauces than we had ever heard of! Most of us loved it, but of course Tom Miller wanted a hamburger. Next morning, after an early night, Florence was once more the venue for our sightseeing. We saw the fabulous Golden Doors of the Baptistery which Michelangelo described as being 'fit to be the gate of Paradise'.

After Florence there was Pisa and its famous Leaning Tower, a truly amazing sight. Early to bed again so we could be up at 4am and off to Rome in time for 'Urbi et Orbi', the pope's blessing.

Upon receiving the pope's blessing, we visited many famous places: the Colosseum, the Arch of Constantine and of course the Vatican itself. We seemed to visit every church and cathedral in Rome! But it was well worthwhile. And finally, we all threw a coin into the Trevi Fountain, an old tradition for anyone who wants to return to Rome again – and we all do!

It's your turn!

Write reports on the following.

1. An accident you witnessed
2. The opening of a new local swimming pool
3. Your favourite TV series
4. A school charity walk
5. An art exhibition in your school
6. The launch of a Buy Irish campaign in your school
7. A parent-teacher meeting
8. A career talk you attended
9. A talk to your class by an anti-drugs expert
10. The appointment of a new principal in your school

SAMPLE SPORTS REPORT

Read this report and see whether it gives all the information it should – what, where, when, who. Are there any ways in which you might improve the report?

Under-14 Cup Team

It was Sunday, 20 May, and we arrived on a sultry day at Coolmines School. There was a good-sized crowd. We were feeling in fine form. We'd had friendlies before against other schools, and we'd had ample training. We were playing on an all-weather pitch, much to the disapproval of the team.

Twenty minutes into the first half, we hit the net. We had got the breakthrough we needed. In the second half we scored again, this time through a great run by Brendan Byrne who finished it with a chip over the goalie. They pulled one back but it wasn't enough. We were on our way to the Quarter Finals.

Reports to write

1. Write a report for the school magazine of a fund-raising sponsored walk.
2. Your local newspaper has asked you to write a report on your school awards day. Write a vivid and interesting report on this event.
3. Write a report for the school magazine of a local event (sports day, parade etc.).
4. Write a report for the school magazine of an educational trip, either here or abroad, in which you took part.
5. Write a report for a local newspaper of a film you have seen.
6. The new principal of your school wishes to introduce a few changes. Write a report for him/her, as you have been requested, on school life from the student's point of view.
7. An accident has occurred in your school. Write a report of what happened as if you were an insurance investigator.
8. Write a report for a local newspaper of a fire you witnessed.
9. You have attended a huge open-air pop concert. Write a report of the event.
10. Write a report of your meeting with a sports or entertainment personality.

BIAS IN REPORTS

Bias means giving a report a certain slant. This means that the reporter's own views and opinions come into the report. Even when a reporter's bias is obvious, any criticisms or praises should be reasonable and fair. However, this is not always easy to do if someone is reporting on something in which they believe passionately – or on something which they object to strongly.

Questions to answer

• Is the report impartial? (not taking sides)

• Does the reporter give a particular slant to the information? Does he/she present impressions which they hope will persuade the reader to see things in a certain way? An example of this might be a report of a foxhunt written by someone who is opposed to blood sports.

• A reporter may express his or her bias by distorting the information – by leaving out essential bits of information, for example. He or she may highlight their impressions by using words that have either good or bad associations (connotations) for the reader.

SAMPLES OF BIASED REPORTING

1. Read the following report carefully. Point out any details and aspects of the presentation which may make you think that the report is biased. Why do you think the reporter refers to the firm and the location as 'H_____ Rabbits of X_____'? Why are words such as 'range', 'germ-free', 'business', 'money-making machine' and 'interesting' written with quotation marks?

A Visit to a Rabbit Breeder

An opportunity to attend a guided tour and 'introductory weekend' at a rabbit farm – so naturally I had to go.

H_____ Rabbits of X_____ offer New Zealand White rabbits, Dutch, Half-lop, Californian and black French Simonoire – a recent addition to the 'range'. They also provide 'germ-free' animals.

It is a rather ramshackle place with low-level tatty sheds. This general seediness truly reflects the nature of the 'business'.

The day started with a talk by Mr S, director of the company, who terrorised a tiny rabbit by slapping it onto some scales while describing the animal as a 'money-making machine'. He spoke with a certain amount of pride in his tough 'I'm-not-soft' presentation.

It was explained in great detail how cheap it is to start up a rabbit farm; any old shed will do, and there's little or no control over conditions. There were a few 'interesting' stories of people killing all their rabbits with doses of Jeyes fluid, and the like.

2. Read the following report carefully. Point out any details and aspects of presentation which make you suspect that the report is biased. Write down any words with which you are not familiar. Check their meanings in a dictionary. How is the bias shown in this report different from that in 'A Visit to a Rabbit Breeder'?

As we stood looking at the front elevation of 'The Heath', Company's Homes' latest venture, with its elegant cladding, PVC fixtures for easy maintenance, and the stained glass features on windows and front door, a gaggle of geese flew from the nearby park, just behind the houses, across to the Island, perhaps a quarter of a mile away as a bird flies.

This epitomises the area, one of the most prestigious suburbs of Dublin. It is small, and in this instance, small is beautiful. Unexpected delights bordering the sea, it has an added advantage – everything is within easy reach.

For leisure there is the lovely park with its world-famous rose gardens. A vibrant tennis club, swimming pool, rugby and cricket grounds and plenty of facilities for soccer abound. There are two very good secondary schools and a primary school nearby.

And all this is just ten minutes from the city centre. It is also close to the East Link Bridge for people with connections on the south side of Dublin. And it is near the DART line. No wonder houses here are at a premium.

(from *The Irish Independent*)

Reports to write

Write a biased report on the following.

1. A greyhound coursing event from the viewpoint of: (a) a member of the Irish Council Against Blood Sports; or (b) from the viewpoint of a member of a coursing club.
2. A leak at a nuclear plant, from the viewpoint of an anti-nuclear protester.
3. A seal cull from the viewpoint of: (a) a supporter of the Worldwide Fund for Nature (WWF); or (b) a local fisherman.
4. A visit to an old-fashioned zoo from the viewpoint of a member of Zoo Check.

5. A whale hunt from the viewpoint of a member of Greenpeace.
6. An oil spillage at sea as reported by: (a) a spokesperson of the oil company involved; (b) a spokesperson for the local environment awareness group.
7. A mugging as reported by a policeman.
8. Damage to a battery-hen farm as reported by the owner of the farm.
9. An industrial dispute as reported by: (a) a striker; or (b) the owner of the business.
10. A school expulsion as reported by: (a) the student involved; or (b) the school principal; or (c) the student's parents.

BOOK REPORTS

Students will be asked to write book reports throughout all their years at secondary school. A good book report should answer most of the following questions.

- **Name of the author**
- **Title** of the book
- Information **about the author** – where he or she comes from, the time during which they were writing
- **Other works** by the author
- The **author's reputation** – something about what people think of him or her
- **Anything special** about the writing of this specific book – for example, was it written in special circumstances such as wartime?
- **Type of book –** Books fall into a few very broad categories.
    - ★*Non-fiction* – a book about something which actually happened
    - ★*Fiction* – a true-sounding book about imaginary happenings
    - ★*Fantasy* – a book with magical characters or happenings
    - ★*Autobiography* – a book about a person's life written by that person
    - ★*Biography* – a book about a person's life written by someone else
- **Subject matter** – Working-class life, politics, sport, country life, cookery etc.?
- **Theme** – What idea or ideas does the author have about the subject matter?
- **Techniques** used in the book. How does the author organise the material in the book?
- Has the book a distinctive **tone** and **style** – humorous, serious, scholarly, mysterious?

SAMPLE BOOK REPORT

Roald Dahl is one of the most popular authors of young people's fiction. Some of his work appeals to the very young – like *James and the Giant Peach*. Older readers enjoy books like *Danny, Champion of the World*. This report is about a book called *Boy* – part of Roald Dahl's autobiography. It was written by a Junior Certificate student.

• •

Boy by Roald Dahl

Roald Dahl was born of Norwegian parents in Wales in 1916. He was educated both in day schools in Wales and boarding schools in England. The first volume of his autobiography, 'Boy', gives an account of his early years in Wales, life with his family there and school life.

Dahl has written many books for children and adults. He firmly established his quirky style of writing while writing short stories for magazines. Later, in the 1960s and 1970s, he wrote his novels. His love of children was always in evidence in his children's books, especially in 'The Witches' and 'Charlie and the Chocolate Factory'. His 'Tales of the Unexpected' ran as a top-rated television show which ran for many years. Roald Dahl died in 1990.

'Boy' is a humorous book, focusing on the author's life in early decades of the twentieth century. It is a fascinating portrait of pre-television home life, pre-plastic bag sweetshops, pre-jet travel. Unlike some long-winded autobiographies, this book is as good a read as the author's fiction. Some readers may find it even more interesting because it is true.

'Boy' describes in great detail the author's Norwegian-influenced home life in Wales, his annual trips to Norway on a steamer, his summer holidays in the fjords – all told in a witty and truthful manner. The book moves slowly from the time before he was born and his parents' lives to his early years in kindergarten and primary school. The next section deals with boring school: the regulation uniform, trunks and tuck boxes, washing with cold water, not being allowed out of bed at night no matter how weak your bladder, putting sugar on the dormitory corridors to announce the stealthy approach of the demonic matron, and warming the toilet-seats for the 'boazers' or prefects. Again all of this is told in a humorous and sometimes sinister way. Roald Dahl obviously held strong views on the cruelty he was exposed to as a child.

The book ends with Roald Dahl aged about twenty years, leaving school for good and finding a job with the Shell Oil Company. This story is taken up in his second volume of memoirs, 'Going Solo', in which he tells about his working life and the time he spent in the RAF as a pilot.

'Boy' is distinctive Dahl, written in a simple but never vulgar style. It has colourful characters and a direct manner of presentation. It is compulsive reading.

SAMPLE BOOK REPORT

The Chronicles of Narnia is probably one of the most loved of fantasy adventures. This book report, written by a Junior Certificate student, tells about the author and his work, concentrating on *The Lion, the Witch and the Wardrobe*. Does it make you want to read the book – if you haven't read it already?

The Lion, the Witch and the Wardrobe
by C.S. Lewis

The author of this novel was born in Belfast in 1898 although he spent almost all his life in England, especially in Oxford where he was a professor of literature. He is perhaps best known for his magnificent 'Chronicles of Narnia'.

Lewis wrote several books based on the magical land of Narnia. He began with 'The Magician's Nephew' and ended with 'The Last Battle'. The adventures of Prince Caspian and the 'Voyage of the Dawnreader' have been dramatised for television, as well as the most famous of the Narnia novels, 'The Lion, the Witch and the Wardrobe'.

The story gives an account of the lives of four young children who were sent to a large house in the English countryside during the Second World War. This was a war that Lewis himself experienced and therefore the plight of the children was a subject very close to his heart.

'The Lion, the Witch and the Wardrobe' tells about the journey of the four young children from the harsh realities of war-torn England into a fantastic land of adventure, excitement and, in the end, of happiness and joy.

The novelist shows how the children escape from the harsh discipline of their everyday lives and enter an enchanted land of adventure. The children are transformed from ordinary schoolchildren into royalty as they grow up in the land of Narnia. There they become trusted and respected leaders.

The author contrasts the themes of reality and fantasy. The description of the large, cold, stone country house is contrasted with the vivid and magical imagery of Narnia. An obvious theme explored in the novel is the battle between good and evil. The lion Aslan symbolises strength, hope, power and goodness in contrast with his opponent, the Snow Queen, who is the embodiment of evil, treachery and bitterness.

The novel represents every child's dream, to enter a magical land forgetful of the strains and stresses of the real world, to fulfil his or her fantasy as a prince or princess. The wardrobe symbolises the doorway from reality to fantasy, providing the children with an escape route from their daily lives.

The book is hugely popular among children. It is a journey of fantasy, combining danger and excitement with occasional lapses into humour. The characters return after spending many years in Narnia only to discover that no time has passed in the bleak country house from which they had set out. No one in the household would believe their remarkable account – except the old professor. The children are left with the image of the lion Aslan in their minds and the thought that they have resolved the conflict in Narnia.

The author continues his story in other novels as the children return to their beloved Narnia in times of trouble and embark on other adventures.

Book reports to write

1. Write a book report on any novel (a work of fiction) which you have read.
2. Write a book report on a sports book you have read.
3. Write a report on any non-fiction (true) book you have read.
4. Choose a fantasy novel which you have enjoyed and write a book report which would encourage others to read it.

DESCRIPTIVE WRITING

There are two kinds of descriptive writing
- **Pure description**
- **Suggestive description**

PURE DESCRIPTION

In writing pure description, the writer is an **impartial observer**. The writing should be:

- **specific** (dealing with actual things)
- **factual** (containing hard information)
- **scientific** (not just a matter of opinion)

Pure description should concentrate on the **observable facts** – the things you can hear, see, touch, smell and taste. Pure description is found in science book, dictionaries, encyclopedias and reference books of all kinds.

The following example of pure description is taken from a science book by Maurice Barton entitled *The True Book about the Seas*. It is specific, factual and scientific. (Remember to look up any words which you do not understand.)

A Planet Is Born

More than two-thirds of the surface of the earth is covered by seas and oceans. There are many theories to account for the origin of the earth. These need not concern us here. We need to know only that at some time, variously estimated at three or four and a half thousand million years ago, it came into being as a mass of molten material revolving in space, and from this, today, we have a nearly spherical mass, slightly flattened at the poles, and nearly eight thousand miles in diameter. As the original molten mass cooled, we have to suppose that a hard crust formed over its surface. The intense heat within, together with the shrinking, opened up cracks in this cooling surface through which flowed lava and steam. The lava solidified on the outside of the crust, and, as the eruptions followed each other, the foundations of the land masses grew. At the same time, the steam hung in a mantle of water vapour around the earth. As it cooled, water poured from it in violent rains. This water filled the spaces between the masses of lava flow, and thus were born the oceans. The heavy rains also wore down the surfaces of the lavas and the particles from them were deposited as sediments, which in turn formed some of the layers of rock we see today.

Think about it

1. What features of this extract show that it as pure description? Look for specific, scientific and factual details.
2. What do you think is the function of this piece? How effectively does the passage perform this function?

It's your turn

Write a paragraph of pure description on the following. Remember that you must write as an impartial observer. Use reference books of your choice to find out more. Be sure you use this information by writing in your own words.

1. Railways
2. Beaches
3. Life in the garden
4. House for sale
5. A geography field trip
6. An historical event
7. Farm work
8. From tadpole to frog
9. A landscape
10. The motor car

SUGGESTIVE DESCRIPTION

Suggestive descriptive has a number of functions. It must highlight:

- **qualities**
- **impressions and appearance**
- **mood and atmosphere**

In suggestive description, the writer describes persons, places or events, telling us how he or she feels or wants us to feel about them.

Suggestive description should be:
- **colourful**
- **imaginative**
- **personal**
- **impressionistic**

Suggestive description is usually combined with *narrative writing*. (Look for Narrative Writing in the Table of Contents.)

This example of suggestive description is from C.S. Lewis' novel, *The Voyage of the Dawntreader*. In it, the children are looking at a picture of a ship which becomes more and more real to them.

> The things in the picture were moving. It didn't look at all like a cinema either; the colours were too real and clean and out-of-door for that. Down went the prow of the ship into the wave and up went a shock of spray. And then up went the wave behind her, and her stern and her deck became visible for the first time, and then disappeared as the next wave came to meet her and her bows went up again. At the same moment, an exercise book which had been lying beside Edmund on the bed flapped, rose and sailed through the air to the wall behind him, and Lucy felt all her hair whipping round her face as it does on a windy day.

Think about it

1. What words and phrases in this passage would you not expect to find in pure description?
2. Rewrite the passage in the manner of pure description.

ELEMENTS OF SUGGESTIVE DESCRIPTION
Qualities

In suggestive description, *adjectives* are used to suggest the qualities of things. When the words *day* and *dog* are qualified by adjectives, as in the following examples, we see much more interesting pictures.

The day
The *blustery* day
The *balmy* day

The dog
The *gentle* dog
The *wolf-like* dog

When writing suggestive description:

- **Choose those details or features** that are important and interesting to you.

- **Choose details** that you think will **interest the reader.**

- Keep details to a **minimum.**

- Choose details that fit in with and help to create the **mood** you want to create.

Try this

Comment on the details or qualities underlined in this extract from Stephen Crane's novel, *The Red Badge of Courage*. Say what they contribute to the description.

The cold passed reluctantly from the earth, and the retiring fogs revealed an army stretched out on the hills, resting. As the landscape changed from brown to green, the army awakened, and began to tremble with eagerness at the noise of rumours. It cast its eyes upon the roads, which were growing from long troughs of liquid mud to proper thoroughfares. A river, amber-tinted in the shadow of its banks, purled at the army's feet; and at night, when the stream had become a sorrowful blackness, one could see across it the red, eye-like gleam of hostile camp-fires set in the low brows of the distant hills.

Concrete words and images

Concrete words and images create actual people, places and objects in readers' imaginations. Readers should feel that they could hear, see, touch, smell and taste what is being described. In this extract from D.H. Lawrence's short story, 'Adolf', the narrator's father, a coal miner, has come home with a surprise for the children. Lawrence has used concrete words and images (underlined) to bring the scene to life for us. Comment on the effect which these words and images have on you.

My mother hastily poured out his tea. He went to pour it out into his saucer. But instead of drinking he suddenly put something on the table among the teacups. A tiny brown rabbit! A small rabbit, a mere morsel, sitting against the bread as if it were a made thing.

CREATING MOOD AND ATMOSPHERE

- **Decide** on the *mood or atmosphere* which you want to create. For example, the atmosphere of a thriller should be one of suspense, excitement, curiosity.
- **Choose** words and images that will help to create this mood.

Try this

This sample of suggestive description is from a ghost story. Read it a couple of times. Then describe the mood and atmosphere it creates. Say how this is done.

That was the worst of Ravenal Hall. The passages were long, the rooms were musty and dull, even the pictures were sombre and their subjects dire. On an autumn evening, when the wind soughed through the trees in the park, and the dead leaves whistled and chattered, while the rain clamoured at the windows, small wonder that folk with gentle nerves went astraying in their wits.

(from 'When I was Dead' by Vincent O'Sullivan)

Think about it

This is a description of a hunter's wife in the days of the North American Indian. Alone in her animal-skin lodge in the forest, she is waiting anxiously for her husband's return.

One evening during the winter season, it chanced that he remained out later than usual and his wife sat alone in the lodge, and began to be agitated with fears lest some accident had befallen him. Darkness had already fallen. She listened attentively to hear the sound of coming footsteps; nothing could be heard but the wind mournfully whistling around the sides of the lodge. Time passed away while she remained in this stage of suspense, every moment augmenting her fears and adding to her disappointment.

Suddenly she heard the sound of approaching footsteps upon the frozen surface of the snow. Not doubting that it was her husband, she quickly unfastened the loop which held, by an inner fastening, the skin-door of the lodge, and throwing it open she saw two strange women standing before her.

COMMENTING ON THE PIECE

PURE DESCRIPTION

The writer does not crowd his description with details. Instead, he has carefully selected only those details which emphasise or heighten the wife's isolation and fear.

- evening
- the winter season
- later than usual
- sat lonely
- darkness
- the wind mournfully whistling
- around the sides of the lodge
- the sound of approaching footsteps
- the frozen surface of the snow

CONCRETE WORDS AND IMAGES

As the story is set on a dark winter's night, the writer uses images of sound and touch rather than visual images – the wind mournfully whistling, the frozen surface of the snow, the skin covering of the door, approaching footsteps.

MOOD AND ATMOSPHERE

The mood of this piece is tense and anxious. The author places the hunter's wife in:
- a lonely setting
- at evening time
- during the winter
- when it is dark
- when her husband's return is overdue

It's your turn

Write a paragraph describing one (or more) of the following. Try to create a definite mood.

1. A derelict house
2. Walking down a deserted street at night
3. Your first summer swim in the sea
4. A child lost in a crowd

MORE MOOD AND ATMOSPHERE

The next extract is a powerful example of creating mood and atmosphere. In this scene, the hero of the story, Stephen Dedalus, is a young boy at boarding school. He has a high temperature and is in the school infirmary which is in the charge of Brother Michael. The writer, James Joyce, wants to create a mood of a boy only half-conscious of what is happening around him. Stephen's mind is wandering. Read the passage a couple of times. Then work out how Joyce has created the mood and atmosphere he wanted.

It was queer that they had not given him any medicine. Perhaps Brother Michael would bring it back when he came. They said you got stinking stuff to drink when you were in the infirmary. But he felt better now than before. It would be nice getting better slowly. You could get a book then. There was a book in the library about Holland. There were lovely foreign names in it and pictures of strangelooking cities and ships. It made you feel so happy.

How pale the light was at the window! But that was nice. The fire rose and fell on the wall. It was like waves. Someone had put coal on and he heard voices. They were talking. It was the noise of the waves. Or the waves were talking among themselves as they rose and fell.

He saw the sea of waves, long dark waves rising and falling, dark under the moonless night. A tiny light twinkled at the pierhead where the ship was entering: and he saw a multitude of people gathered by the water's edge to see the ship that was entering their harbour. A tall man stood on the deck, looking out towards the flat dark land: and by the light at the pierhead he saw his face, the sorrowful face of Brother Michael.

(from *Portrait of the Artist as a Young Man* by James Joyce)

Think about it

1. What specific words in the above passage are rich in suggestions?
2. Show how these suggestions contribute to the mood and atmosphere.
3. What effect is Joyce trying achieve by the use of repetitions?

It's your turn

A. Write a paragraph of suggestive description on each of the following. In each case, write your description from the point of view of the person or thing named.

1. A fireman rescues someone from a burning house
2. A dog waiting in the pound for someone to adopt it
3. A kidnap victim
4. A miner trapped in a collapsed pit
5. A person on his/her first flight
6. A patient being prepared to go to the operating theatre
7. A stray cat

B. Write a paragraph describing one of the following. Use concrete words and images. Underline these words and images when you have finished your piece.

1. An airport
2. A seaport
3. A crowd going to a football match
4. Queuing for the cinema
5. A visit to a hospital
6. A visit to the dentist
7. Christmas morning
8. Setting up a tent
9. A road accident
10. A fall of snow
11. A house on fire

AN EXAMPLE OF DESCRIPTIVE WRITING

● ●

This piece was written by a Junior Certificate student. The instructions were: 'Write a descriptive piece on the subject "My First Date".'

My First Date

'If I said you'd a nice body, would you hold it against me?' I remembered his pathetic chat-up line as I packed for the beach. Collapse-proof deck chair: Check! The beach gear: Check! Oversized floppy hat: Check! And, finally, a book, to reflect my intellectual abilities: Check!

It was a dull day but I was confident that the sun would in due course burst through those overhanging grey clouds. I was covered from head to toe with fake tanning-lotion which was very flattering to the hot-pants and floral one-piece I was wearing. Need I say that diamonds and pearls do not mix well with sand and oil. I tried the more bohemian and chintzy look, and went for a collection of exotic coral stones on a piece of string.

His 'beach gear' consisted of ripped shorts and a faded T-shirt. Under his left arm was a towel rolled up, sausage-like, and in his right hand was a package of sandwiches wrapped in tinfoil. We set up camp and I sat on my deck chair reading my book.

The sun was finally blazing nicely, so I suggested we take a plunge. Suddenly, to my amazement, I realised that everyone on the beach was intrigued by me. The lifeguards wanted to know 'Who's the girl on the deck chair?' And the boys strained over their Raybans to get a closer look. My impeccable tropical taste in swimwear and beach accessories fooled them all. It was either this or the fact that an ice-cream van had just pulled up beside us. I'm exaggerating, of course, but only slightly.

He offered to buy me a choc-ice. So much for romance and horseback galloping through the shallow waters and seething foam of the beach. I was hungry, though, and I indignantly accepted the ice cream. 'Wonderboy', on ordering the ice creams, moved awkwardly from one foot to the other while searching frantically in his pockets. They cost me all the spare change I could find at the bottom of my beach bag. My cheeks weren't red with sunburn when I was handing the coins over, but with sheer mortification.

Speaking of sun, it was starting to get a bit chilly, so I sat in my deck chair, wrapped in towels, listening to a football commentary kindly provided by Loverboy himself! It started with a drop you wouldn't even notice, then two, then three and by the fourth I was halfway up the beach, clutching my chair and bags. Heaven's floodgates were opening and as Loverboy ran ahead of me I struggled to maintain my balance. I abandoned the collapse-proof chair and sprinted home in floods of rain and tears.

My bouffant hair lay limp on my blotchy face. My clothes or lack of clothes resulted in weeks of antibiotics and 'flu tablets. My first date was definitely my worst date, and it might well be my last!

It's your turn

1. Write an account of this first date from the boy's point of view.
2. This story is written in the first person – the story-teller is using 'I' and talking about herself. Rewrite the story in the third person – told about the girl by someone else.

Topics for Descriptive Writing

1. Describe a beautiful place you know in a city
2. My favourite singer or actor
3. A view from the top of a hill
4. Getting up in the morning in summer and in winter
5. My hopes and fear
6. Helping around the house
7. Things that make me laugh
8. Pets I have had
9. Buying new clothes
10. A river well known to you
11. My idea of a perfect holiday
12. Your favourite place in the countryside
13. The most fascinating place in my neighbourhood
14. The city or countryside at night
15. Things that depress me
16. My favourite film
17. My family
18. A nightmare
19. Shopping with Mother
20. A holiday that went wrong

NARRATIVE WRITING

A piece of narrative writing should:
- tell **a story**
- present **an action**
- tell **what happened**

Questions to ask

When working on a piece of narrative writing, first ask yourself these questions.
- **Point of view:** *Who* is doing the telling?
- **Plot:** *What* is happening? *Why* is it happening?
- **Theme:** What is the *meaning* of this action?
- **Characters:** *Who* is doing what?
- **Setting/Place:** *Where* did this happen?
- **Setting/Time:** *When* did this happen?

POINT OF VIEW

Decide on the **point of view** from which the narrative or story is to be written.

- **First person narrative**
  Should the action of the story be written in the *first person* — by an 'I'? That 'I' can be real or imaginary.

- **Third person narrative**
  Should the action be described by a *third person*? This is someone who sees and knows everything and presents the story from many points of view.

- **One character focus**
  Should the writer focus attention on *one character* and describe the story's action from that character's point of view?

A FIRST PERSON NARRATIVE

This piece is written by 'I'. It may be a real 'I' or an imaginary 'I'. (Sinbad is the narrator's younger brother.)

I had to go down to my parents. Sinbad kept crying, bawling over and over like a train. He wouldn't stop.
— I'll burst you if you don't.
I didn't know how they hadn't heard it. The hall light was off. They were supposed to leave it on. I got to the bottom of the stairs. The lino at the hall door was freezing. I checked: Sinbad was still whining.
I loved getting him into trouble. This was the best. I could pretend I was helping.
(from *Paddy Clarke Ha Ha Ha* by Roddy Doyle)

A THIRD PERSON NARRATIVE

In this short piece, a third person is telling the story. He or she is an outside observer who appears to know about everything that is going on.

The budgie was nowhere to be seen. It had been in its cage when the three girls had gone upstairs to see Joan's new stereo unit. How long had they been upstairs? Less than half an hour, they all agreed. Was the door of the cage closed? No one could remember. They had no interest in the budgie. It was Joan's father's. He's had it for six years. A friend of his had given it to him.

Mary and Pat felt Joan's mounting panic. She'd be accused of having let it out of its cage. Her brother Joe would insist on that. It must be in the house somewhere. It was a sly old bird and was probably hiding deliberately to cause all this trouble.

A THIRD PERSON NARRATIVE WITH A PARTICULAR FOCUS

This is also a third person narrative. But this time, the focus is on Bruce.

The telephone rang. Bruce felt a sick sense of disappointment. Perhaps it was his father telephoning from Brisbane to say he would be delayed yet another day. It wasn't like his father to disappoint him, and besides, he knew that Bruce had to go back to the school next day, and it would be a week before the long hols began.

Bruce listened as his aunt answered the telephone. Then the sound of a car coming up the winding road cut across her voice.

He heard the change-down into low gear at the steepest part of the winding road leading to his home, 'Karingel', where it was perched on the hillside, high above the Gold Coast town of Southport, Queensland. When he looked to the left he saw, far below, the long dreaming beaches of pale gold and the sapphire seas breaking on them. The car drew up beside him.

(from *Tiger in the Dark* by Mary Elwyn Patchett)

It's your turn

Rex, the family pet, has to be taken to the vet's to be put down. He is very old and sick and his life has become one medical problem after the other.

1. Write a paragraph describing the scene from *your own point of view (first person narrative)*.

2. Write a paragraph describing the scene in *third person narrative form*, taking into account *everyone's point of view*.

3. Write a paragraph describing the scene in third person narrative form. This time, *focus on the point of view* of your younger brother whose favourite pet Rex is.

CREATING CHARACTERS
. . . .
There are five basic ways of creating characters. Sometimes, this creation involves a combination of more than one of the following.

- How they **look**
- What they **do**
- What they **think**
- What they **say**
- What **other characters** think and say about them

A FEW GUIDELINES

- Don't bother to describe 'walk-on' or minor characters.
- Don't try to describe everything about a character.
- Select a few features that will make the character stand out as different from the others.
- Keep direct description to a minimum.
- Let the character's actions show the kind of person he or she is.

A CHARACTER DESCRIPTION

This piece is told in the first person. In it, a very definite character begins to take shape.

And so my apprenticeship began, as a shop-boy in a 'fashionable' show shop in the high street. The owner was a small fattish man with a swarthy, tired face, green teeth and eyes the colour of muddy water. He looked as if he were blind and I made funny faces at him to see if he really was.

'Stop screwing your face up,' he would say in a soft, but menacing, voice.

It was nasty to think that those bleary eyes could actually see me and I just did not believe it. Perhaps he was only *guessing* that I was pulling faces.

'I said stop screwing your face up,' he repeated – this time in an even softer voice. As he spoke his blubbery lips barely parted. Then I heard that rasping, whispering voice again:

'And don't scratch your arms! You're in a high class shop now, in the high street, don't forget!'

(from *My Apprenticeship* by Maxim Gorky)

It's your turn

Write descriptions of each of the following characters. In developing your characters, try to avoid stereotypes or caricatures (characters who are not individual in any way).

1. Describe an eccentric member of your family.
2. Describe a school bully .
3. Describe a pop star you are fond of.
4. Describe your best friend.
5. Describe a tough policeman.
6. Describe an American tourist.
7. Describe a kind and gentle person you know.
8. Describe a teacher you had in Primary School.
9. Describe a neighbour.
10. Describe a sports star you admire.

CREATING THE SETTING

Setting means both **time** and **place**.

- **Time**: *When* did the action take place? Is there anything special about this particular time – an especially hard winter, past, present, future?

- **Place**: Action must take place *somewhere*. The reader should feel as if he or she were really there. If the place is very important, it should be presented at the beginning. Use sensory details – images of sounds, sights, smells – to establish an impression of the place, an atmosphere.

SETTING THE SCENE

A very good example of setting a scene is in the first paragraph of Ambrose Bierce's short story, 'An Occurrence at Owl Creek Bridge'. The scene is that of a military execution during the American Civil War of the 1860s. The main character is Peyton Farquhar, the man to be hanged. The action of the story is the hanging and the events that have led up to it.

A man stood upon a railway bridge in Northern Alabama, looking down into the swift waters twenty feet below. The man's hands were behind his back, the wrists bound with a cord. A rope loosely encircled his neck. It was attached to a stout cross-timber above his head, and the sack fell to the level of his knees. Some loose boards laid upon the sleepers supporting the metal of the railway supplied a footing for him and his executioners – two private soldiers of the Federal Army, directed by a sergeant, who in civil life may have been a deputy Sheriff. At a short remove upon the same temporary platform was an officer in the uniform of his rank, armed. He was a captain. A sentinel at each end of the bridge stood with his rifle in the position known as 'support', that is to say, vertical in front of the left shoulder, the hammer resting on the forearm thrown straight across the chest – a formal and unnatural position, enforcing an erect carriage of the body. It did not appear to be the duty of these men to know what was occurring at the centre of the bridge; they merely blockaded the two ends of the foot plank which traversed it.

It's your turn

Set the scene for each of the following.
1. A wet winter's day in the city
2. A crowded beach in summer
3. Someone trapped in a lift in a high-rise building late at night
4. Being alone at night for the first time
5. A hold-up in a shop
6. In the zoo when a wild animal has escaped
7. Your school's annual sports day
8. An accident
9. A cold damp Monday morning
10. Christmas Eve in a department store

DIALOGUE

Dialogue is another word for direct speech. Dialogue should do the following.
- Tell us something about the character who is speaking.
- Tell us something about the character who is being spoken about.
- Tell us something about the plot.
- Suggest atmosphere.

A FEW GUIDELINES

When using dialogue, remember –
1. Use double (" ") or single (' ') quotation marks.
2. Use a comma before the quotation marks when the dialogue is introduced by *she said* or *they said* etc. For example:
   'Don't go yet,' they answered.
3. The quotation marks are usually placed outside the dialogue at the end.
4. Start a new paragraph to indicate when a different character is speaking. For example:
   'I'm not yet ready,' said John.
   'Hurry up or we'll be late,' Mary shouted.

USING DIALOGUE

Look at how dialogue is used in the following short piece. What does it suggest to you about the two characters? What suggestions is the dialogue giving to us about the plot?

'You're afraid of your own shadow!' John said. 'It's not ghosts you're afraid of. It's your parents!'

'And what about you?' Bill answered back. 'I suppose you don't care what your parents will do if you're not home till after midnight!'

'I'm not worrying about them. I'll tell them that I'm staying overnight in your house. Simple as that!' John grinned smugly.

'But suppose they ring up my house?' Bill worried. 'I'll be in big trouble then as well as you.'

'Chicken! You're afraid of everything and everyone! This is a great chance for us to find out what's going on at that house. Don't tell me you don't want to know.'

Bill felt himself cornered.

It's your turn

1. Write a dialogue between two characters in which each of the characters speaks four times. Convey the impression that one of them is a bully and the other is his or her victim.

2. Write a dialogue among three characters in which each character speaks three times. Two of the characters are trying to persuade the third, who is shy, to go to a disco.

3. Write a dialogue between a girl and her mother in which each of the characters speaks four times. They are arguing about the 'bad' company the daughter is keeping.

4. Write a dialogue between two soldiers in which each of them speaks about four times. They are about to be executed for desertion.

5. Write a dialogue between a child and his or her father in which each of the characters speaks about five times. The father wishes to bring the family's pet dog to the city pound.

6. Write a dialogue between a teacher and a student in which each of them speaks about six times. The student feels that he or she has been wrongly accused of some kind of misbehaviour.

7. Write a dialogue between a son and a daughter in which each of them speaks about seven times. They are arguing about household chores. Reveal sexist attitudes in the dialogue.

8. Write a dialogue between two friends in which each of them speaks about six times. One of them has been very late in keeping an appointment. Make your dialogue convey a distinct impression of the two characters.

9. Write a dialogue between a son or daughter and a parent in which each of the characters speaks about six times. They are arguing about the son or daughter keeping late hours.

10. Write a dialogue between two students in which each of them speaks six times. One of them has done something for which the entire class is going to be punished unless the culprit owns up.

GENERAL PLAN FOR NARRATIVE COMPOSITION

EXPOSITION

Setting/Plot/Character

- An action begins in a given situation.
- Set the scene or develop the setting already given. At the same time, decide about the nature of the action (the plot).
- At the end of the first paragraph or at the beginning of the second, introduce the main character, whether it is yourself as first person narrator, or someone else.
- Think ahead to what the outcome of the action is going to be.

COMPLICATION

- The action should pass through stages of tension and complication.
- Create two or three complications. Involve someone (another character or characters) or something which prevents the action from taking its obvious course.

CLIMAX

- Tension builds up to a breaking-point.
- Build up interest, excitement and suspense. For example, a character is hanging from a cliff ... Will he/she fall? Will the grass clump to which he/she is clinging give way? Will someone come to his/her rescue in time?

DEVELOPING THE PLOT

- The action of the story develops into a new situation.

It's your turn

Using this plan as your model, sketch out a narrative for the following.

1. A holiday romance
2. A holiday misadventure
3. A ghost story
4. A science fiction story
5. A family conflict
6. A school day that went wrong
7. My first disco
8. The day my brother tried to walk my dog
9. Two sisters and one boyfriend
10. When Granny came to live with us

USING THE PLAN

Study the following example of using the plan to create a story.

EXPOSITION

A tramp arrives in a small country town. He is young, handsome and well-spoken. He calls at a large run-down mansion on the outskirts of the town. He thinks there is a good chance that he will get some work at the mansion for which he will be paid – if not in cash, then in food and perhaps lodging. A refined old lady answers his knock at the front door. She is impressed by his handsome appearance and his quiet, educated tone of voice. She offers him a meal in return for chopping some logs.

COMPLICATION

The old lady is so taken by the young tramp that she offers him more work. In return, she gives the tramp board and lodging. Soon the old lady begins to treat the tramp as a son. But the tramp is becoming impatient with the old lady's mothering.

CLIMAX

The relationship between the tramp and the old lady becomes increasingly tense as the old lady's attentions intensify.

DEVELOPMENT OF THE PLOT

Should the tramp go away? But he has no money. One day he accidentally sees the old lady taking some cash out of a suitcase. Later he finds out that the suitcase is full of money. He decides to steal it. As he is stealing the money, the old lady enters the room. There is a struggle and the old lady falls, hitting her head off a corner of the fireplace. Panicking, the tramp tries to escape without making any effort to cover up the accident. He is quickly arrested and confesses his guilt. In prison, he learns that the old lady was enormously rich and that shortly before her death, she had willed him her entire fortune because she liked him and because he reminded her of her long dead son.

USING THE PLAN

● ●

THE SKETCH

• Topic

Write a short story beginning 'The river was reaching danger level.'

• Exposition

The river was reaching danger level in the village where you and your family are spending your holidays. It is raining hard and the river has swollen and is now on the point of breaking its banks. Someone (yourself, your father, or someone else) has decided to get help for the small community of trapped villagers who are gathered together in the church.

• Complication

The village's telephone wires have been knocked down in the storm. All the roads are flooded and the village is cut off from the nearest town down-river where everyone knows help is at hand. Although the current of the river is dangerously fast, the main character decides to launch a small boat.

• Climax

The difficulties and dangers involved in launching the small boat.

• Development of the plot

The main character's life-and-death struggle against the power of the flooded river. Perhaps the engine of the boat cuts out. Finally reaching the town and alerting the rescue services. The difficulties of evacuation.

EXAMPLE OF THE COMPLETED NARRATIVE

Write a short story beginning 'The river was reaching danger level.'

The river was reaching danger level. For weeks there had been perfect summer weather, one cloudless day after another. The crops had been thriving in the sunshine. The villagers seemed always in good humour, the young children playing outside from early morning till dusk, enjoying the fine weather, while the old people sat in the shade, self-satisfied as the heat eased the aches from their tired arthritic joints. Then, with no more warning than a sudden show of clouds followed by a few claps of thunder, it began to rain. And it rained and rained and rained.

For three days it rained down non-stop on this small village of San Martin in the south of Spain, where my family and I were spending our holidays. For three days the heavens seemed intent on drowning us all in an endless downpour. The long dry period before had hardened the earth so that the rainwater poured across the land's surface, washing away some crops and topsoil, filling up every channel, rushing into streams and rivulets and finally roaring in torrents into the river on a bank of which San Martin was situated. By the second day, you could notice that the level of the river had risen. By the third day it was obvious to everyone that the river was reaching danger level.

Until then, no one had panicked. Everyone, including the oldest inhabitants of the village, those with the longest memory, was convinced that the torrential rain would stop. The crops would suffer some damage but other than that, no great harm would be done. So we, as visitors, felt no reason to be alarmed. But everyone was wrong.

By evening on the third day, it was clear to everyone that a state of emergency existed. Flooding was widespread. The river was rapidly swelling above its banks and the telephone and electricity cables were down. And still it was raining heavily. The entire population of the village, including myself and my family, gathered in the church, the sturdiest building about. More importantly, it was located on the highest level, on a small hill that rose some metres above the general level of the village.

As the evening darkened, the village councillors and elders debated what was to be done. All agreed that outside help was necessary. But how was that to be got? The roads could not be used. The nearest place of possible help was a large town, La Huerta, about six kilometres down-river. There was even a military base there and rescue services were sure to be available, despite the possibility that La Huerta itself might be in trouble.

In the end, with time running out, it was my father who came up with a solution. We had brought a small speed-boat with us on our holiday and it might just be possible for my father to launch this boat and reach La Huerta.

He admitted the danger involved, but said that it was better to try anything than just to wait and be drowned.

The first problem was to get the boat from the house where we were staying. This house was beside the church and I had a good view of the efforts of my father and two village men carrying the boat to the river's edge. I could see the speed at which branches and other flood debris were being swept along by the current.

The pouring rain added to their troubles. Finally they reached what was left of a wooden pier. In seconds, the boat, heavy with the weight of its outboard engine, was in the river. My father jumped into the boat. The two villagers blessed themselves and then the boat and my father were swept away by the river. Painfully, some seconds passed before the sound of the outboard engine roared into the night. Everyone in the church sighed with relief. We were thinking of the certain death my father would have met had the engine failed to start.

My father did reach La Huerta. Just barely, to judge by the hair-raising near-mishaps he told us about later. It was almost impossible for him to steer the boat and his safety was constantly threatened by the branches and debris that swept by him. But four kilometres down-river, the force of the current had slackened on account of the gradient of the river bed, and he had managed to berth at La Huerta.

There he immediately alerted the rescue services. They were on the point of launching a full-scale evacuation operation when, as suddenly as it had started, the rain stopped. It was like a miracle, and I have often wondered whether the many prayers said by all of us in that little village church of San Martin had some influence on the sudden ending of that summer storm.

EXERCISES: NARRATIVE TOPICS

1. 'It was almost dark when we were leaving the town.'
   (a) Develop a setting for the story that begins with the above sentence.
   (b) Outline a plot for the story.
   (c) Describe the appearance of one of the characters in the story.
   (d) Sketch out a plan for the story using the formula: Exposition – Complication – Climax – Development of plot.
   (e) Write the full story.
   (f) Use dialogue.

2. 'Broken glass covered the street and already a crowd had gathered.'
   (a) Develop a setting for the story that begins with the above sentence.
   (b) Outline a plot for the story.
   (c) Describe the appearance of one of the characters in the story.
   (d) Sketch out a plan for the story using the formula: Exposition – Complication – Climax – Development of Plot.
   (e) Write the full story.
   (f) Use dialogue.

3. 'It seemed an impossible task but I had to prove I was no coward.'
   (a) Develop a setting for the story that begins with the above sentence.
   (b) Outline a plot for the story.
   (c) Describe the appearance of one of the characters in the story.
   (d) Sketch out a plan for the story using the formula: Exposition – Complication – Climax – Development of plot.
   (e) Write out the full story.
   (f) Use dialogue.

4. 'The day was fine, ideal for a trip to the island.'
   (a) Develop a setting for the story.
   (b) Outline a plot.
   (c) Describe two of the characters who will appear in the story.
   (d) Sketch out a plan for the story.
   (e) Write the full story.
   (f) Use dialogue.

5. 'You're afraid to do it,' my friend said.
   (a) Develop a setting for the story.
   (b) Outline a plot.
   (c) Describe two or three characters who will appear in the story.
   (d) Sketch out a plan for the story.
   (e) Write the full story.
   (f) Use dialogue.

6. 'It was four o'clock in the morning when I heard a loud knock at the front door.'
   (a) Develop a setting for the story.
   (b) Outline a plot for the story.
   (c) Describe the appearance of two or more characters who will appear in the story.
   (d) Sketch out a plan for the story.
   (e) Write out the full story.
   (f) Use dialogue.

EXERCISES: NARRATIVE TOPICS

1. 'School finished at three o'clock and I started for home with a strange feeling that something terrible was going to happen to me.' Continue this story.

2. Write a short story beginning with the words, 'When I woke up there was not a sound to be heard ...'

3. Write a short story beginning, 'Far away the train whistled.'

4. Write a short story beginning, 'It's so hard to be kind to some people.'

5. Write a short story beginning, 'Suddenly we saw a dim light in the distance.'

6. Write a short story beginning, 'Nobody thought it could be done.'

7. Write a short story beginning, 'The darkest hour is just before dawn.'

8. Write a short story beginning, 'You'll never catch me baby-sitting again.'

9. Write a short story beginning, 'In the half-light every object seemed strange, but there was no going back now.'

10. Write a short story beginning, 'When I heard the cry of a child, I decided to investigate.'

11. Write a short story beginning, 'Of course I was criticised afterwards, but I wasn't sorry.'

12. Write a short story beginning, 'I could never resist a challenge.'

13. Write a short story beginning, 'This is your local Garda Station.'

ARGUMENT/DEBATE

Argument/Debate essays are written for a number of reasons:

- **to convince** the reader that a **certain viewpoint** (a certain way of looking at something) is **more right or sensible** than another viewpoint
- **to convince** the reader that a certain viewpoint, judgment or opinion is **wrong or foolish**
- **to convince** the reader that a certain assessment or judgment is **more right or more sensible** than another assessment or judgment

WORKING OUT A PROPOSITION

A proposition is a statement such as
    'People in glass houses shouldn't throw stones.'
You can **believe** it, **refuse to believe** it or simply **doubt** it. A proposition involves a judgment which may be true or false.

TWO KINDS OF PROPOSITIONS

- A proposition involving **facts.** These may be true or false.
    'There is life on Mars.'
Such a statement can be scientifically checked.

- A proposition involving **obligation** – whether something *should* or *should not* be done.
    'People should not be over-ambitious.'

The proposition involved in a topic for argument may be obvious (whether there is life on Mars). It may have to be worked out (whether being over-ambitious is a good or a bad thing).

WORKING OUT A PROPOSITION

Example 1
Topic
    'The things that money can't buy.'

Things to consider
- We are living in a society in which many people believe that money can buy everything.
- But are there things that money can't buy? Love? Happiness? Health? Friends?
- Things such as love, happiness, health and friends are generally seen as the most desirable things in life.
- So, what should we think?
- We should not live as if money were everything. We should realise the importance of other things apart from money.

Proposition

Having listed the things which we should consider, we can now state the proposition:

The search for riches should not be considered the most important thing in life.

Example 2
Topic
'School as we know it is a thing of the past.'

Things to consider

• The type of education which most schools still insist on is outdated.
• Most schools make students study things which are of no use to them today – things like history and geography.
• Today's kind of education does not prepare the student for living in the modern world.

Proposition

'Today's educational system, with its teaching methods, its range of subjects and its class-structured schools, should be changed.'

It's your turn

A. Write out **a list of things to consider** in dealing with each of these topics.

1. 'Children should be seen and not heard.'
2. 'Parents should be seen and not heard.'
3. 'Adults can learn a great deal from teenagers.'
4. 'Young people should do something to earn their pocket money.'
5. 'Everyone should get a day off when Ireland plays an international match.'
6. 'Science and technology should not be allowed to destroy the world.'
7. 'Children under 15 should not be allowed in video shops.'
8. 'Students should not watch TV on school days.'
9. 'School holidays should be abolished.'
10. 'Pubs should be closed all day on Sundays.'
11. 'People should work for the dole.'
12. 'Students should be represented on the Boards of Management of their own schools.'
13. 'People should look at themselves before criticising others.'

B. Work out the following propositions by making a list of things to consider. Then state the proposition.

1. 'Don't be ambitious. It is the road to unhappiness.' Is this good advice?
2. The motion for your next school debate is: 'A woman's place is in the home.' Write out the speech you would write for or against the motion.
3. You are on a committee which was set up to interest pupils in the arts – music, painting, drama. Write out the suggestions that you would put forward to the other members of the committee.
4. 'He who hesitates is lost.'
5. 'Love thy neighbour as thyself.'
6. 'War is unhealthy for children and other living things.'
7. 'Zoos should be abolished.'
8. 'Video games are bad for children.'

WRITING A PARAGRAPH

Let's review how to write a good paragraph. It will help you to organise your thoughts for presenting a good argument for debate.

The paragraph is **a unit of composition**. It usually deals with
• a *single* idea
• a *single* argument or *one stage* of an argument
• a *single piece or facet* of a description

It is also used to indicate a different speaker in a *dialogue*. In *narrative writing*, a paragraph often indicates a stage in the development of the plot.

The simplest kind of paragraph begins with **an opening statement** which indicates what the paragraph will be about.

The **concluding sentence** of the paragraph sums up the content of the paragraph. It prepares the reader for the next stage in the development of the topic.

Example 1

Study this opening paragraph from an article by Robin Buss on 'Animation'

> There have been many false dawns in British cinema over the last decade, but only one certain success: the animation branch of the industry. There are several reasons for this. Animation is television-friendly, and has been well supported by television itself – especially Channel 4 and S4C. And commercials can provide animators and studios with the money they need for other work. The medium is also relatively low-tech and inexpensive – needing to be fed more with brainwaves than with bucks – so it is easily accessible to young people or to college and art students. Anyone with the right ideas and the necessary patience can make animated films on the kitchen table.
>
> (*The Independent on Sunday*,
> 13 November 1993)

Comments

• The opening sentence clearly indicates where the paragraph is taking the reader – towards an explanation of the success of animation, as compared with the failure of other forms of cinema.

• The last sentence prepares the reader for a discussion that will focus on the comparative cheapness of animation.

Example 2

Here is another example which uses the formula for a good paragraph:

- **Opening topic sentence**
- **Development**
- **Concluding summary sentence** – preparing the reader for the paragraph which follows.

(Look up the meanings of the underlined words or phrases to show that you understand them.)

> Machines that perform better than people – whether at digging up a road or calculating income tax – cause us little grief. 'But to be able to *think* – that has been a very human prerogative,' writes Roger Penrose, an Oxford mathematician, in his book *The Emperor's New Mind*. 'If machines can one day excel us in that one important quality in which we have believed ourselves to be superior, shall we not then have surrendered that unique superiority to our creations?' Some scientists – Professor Penrose not included – believe the day of the thinking machines will come. Yet research, for the moment at least, offers little prospect of creating anything other than a pale imitation of that greatest of all human attributes: thought.
>
> One of the most difficult problems in the race to design computers with 'artificial intelligence' is knowing exactly what intelligence is, and how to recognise it ...
>
> (Steve Connor, *The Independent on Sunday*,
> 7 November 1993)

Comments

- The *opening topic sentence* is about competition between machines and people.
- This idea is then *developed* into competition between computers and human beings in the activity of 'thinking'.
- The *concluding summary sentence* focuses on 'thought'. It prepares the reader for the next paragraph which will concentrate on the meaning of 'thinking' or 'intelligence'.
- This will take the essay further in the over-all discussion about the competition between computers and human beings in the areas of thinking and intelligence.

PARAGRAPHING IN NARRATIVE WRITING

Paragraphing in narrative writing is usually a way of unfolding the plot in stages. Each paragraph indicates a step in the development of the action. It is less tightly controlled than a paragraph in argument/debate writing.

Here is a good example of paragraphing in narrative writing.

> All the way from Dublin my travelling companion had not spoken a dozen words. After a casual interest in the countryside as we left Kingsbridge, he had wrapped a rug about his legs, settled into his corner, and dozed.
>
> He was a bull-shouldered man, about sixty, with coarse, sallow skin stippled with pores, furrowed by deep lines on either side of his mouth.
>
> (from *Up the Bare Stairs* by Sean O'Faolain)

Comments

- The opening paragraph provides a setting for the story and introduces the main character.
- The second paragraph logically follows on, giving the reader a detailed description of the character.
- The plot is hinted at by suggesting that some interaction will take place between the narrator and the character he is introducing.

It's your turn

A. Argument/Debate

Write an introductory paragraph on the following topics, using this formula.

- Opening topic sentence
- Development (Why has the topic come up now?)
- Concluding summary sentence

1. Space Travel
2. Pop Music
3. The Drug Culture Today
4. Unemployment
5. The Environment
6. The Generation Gap
7. The Video Library
8. Feminism
9. Reading
10. Religion

B. Narrative/Description

Write well-organised paragraphs that begin with these sentences.

1. A storm was brewing.
2. After an hour or so, it seemed to me that I was being followed.
3. It was a sound I had never heard before.
4. A large crowd had gathered on the bridge and people were jostling each other as they peered over the parapet.
5. The sound of glass crashing in the middle of the night always stirs up fear.

6. We would have to pass the house that we had heard so much about.
7. My younger brother was nowhere to be seen.
8. The old man was obviously in trouble.
9. Why was the policeman calling at our door?
10. An strange, unearthly glow lit up the horizon.

C. Write an introductory and follow-up paragraph on each of the following topics.
1. The Collecting Mania
2. Television Soaps
3. Why visit art galleries?
4. Pop music is the classical music of our time.
5. Boredom is the scourge of our age.
6. We are only as free as the money we have.
7. Humanity will never outgrow the need for war.
8. If there really were ghosts ...
9. Time Travelling
10. Blood Sports

GENERAL PLAN FOR WRITING ARGUMENT/DEBATE

It is easy to develop a good argument if you follow this plan.

INTRODUCTION
1. If a proposition is not obvious, *work it out* first. Then *state the case* to be argued, whether for or against.
2. *Define the terms* of the proposition. Examine the key words.
3. Give a *brief background* history for the topic. For example, why has this topic of debate come up now? This discussion should be kept to a minimum. It should be used to stimulate ideas.
4. What *issues* are involved in the topic?

ARGUMENT
1. *Present the evidence* for or against. Use statistics, facts, authorities on the subject.
2. *Use* the evidence to make your case.
3. *State the conclusion* you have reached. What have you decided?
4. *Argue* against the opposite views.
5. *Anticipate* and deal with (find flaws in) any objections to your point of view.

CONCLUSION
1. *Sum up* the basic points of the argument.
2. *Show how* these tie in with the topic of debate.

USING THE PLAN: SKETCHING THE ESSAY

This example of sketching out the general plan for writing ARGUMENT/DEBATE should be studied and imitated.

TOPIC
'Today's teenagers are selfish.'
What do you think?

INTRODUCTION
The proposition is already given. So decide whether you are going to agree or disagree with it. Let us suppose you are going to argue against the proposition.

The key word is 'selfish'. So this word should be closely examined and defined.
- Selfishness means caring about oneself and having little or no consideration for others.
- Why should teenagers be singled out as selfish?

- Are teenagers more likely to be selfish than adults? If so, why is that so?
- Are teenagers today more selfish than teenagers in the past?

ARGUMENT

- Many adults feel that teenagers today show little respect or gratitude.
- Parents believe that this lack of respect and gratitude shows itself in disobedience and lack of consideration. For example, teenagers often insist on going to places their parents disapprove of. They also stay out later than their parents want them to.
- Many teenagers do not keep to the rules of behaviour laid down by their parents. However, many parents lay down rules which now make little sense because of changes in social habits.
- Parents are adults. They often forget how they saw the world when they were teenagers themselves.
- Adults are used to thinking about others more often than teenagers.
- Adults find it easier to be concerned with things apart from themselves. They have more experience than teenagers. Many adults expect teenagers to behave as if they have had such experience.
- Teenagers today face many difficulties. They are trying to find out who they are. They are trying to discover their own abilities and limitations. As a result, teenagers are bound to be more concerned with themselves than most adults are.

CONCLUSIONS

- Teenagers don't always wish to be selfish. They may seem self-centred, but this is just a part of growing up.
- If you want to discover who you are, you are bound to spend a great deal of time and energy thinking about yourself. You therefore spend less time and energy thinking about how others feel.
- Adults often forget that they, too, were once teenagers.
- Teenage selfishness is not always selfishness, but a way for teenagers of getting to know themselves.

Try this

Using the suggested plan, write your own plan for this motion for your next school debate.

'Young people should be made to spend some of their holidays helping others.'

USING THE PLAN

. . . .

SKETCHING AN ARGUMENT/DEBATE ESSAY

Topic

'There is too much violence on television.'
What do you think?

Note: This is an Argument/Debate composition. You may argue for or against the statement. You may also present the arguments for or against in an impartial way. Remember – it is violence *on television*, not just violence, that is the issue of debate.

Introduction

- State your **viewpoint.**
    - ★There *is* too much violence on television.
    - ★There *is not* too much violence on television.
    - ★Looking at the evidence both for and against, you have not been convinced one way or the other.
- State **what you understand** by violence on television.
- Give **some examples**.
- Give **your views** on the connection between violence on television and violence in real life.

Argument

- Present the **evidence** to support your viewpoint either for or against, or show that the evidence does not prove the case one way or another.
- Consider **views which are opposed** to yours and argue against them.
- **Anticipate** and argue against possible objections to your viewpoint.

Conclusion

- Sum up the basic points of your argument.

EXAMPLE OF ARGUMENT/DEBATE

Topic

'To co-educate or not to co-educate: that is the question.'

Co-education means educating both sexes in the same school. In Ireland, some children spend their entire school lives at single sex school, while others go to co-educational schools. This good example of argument/debate was written by a Junior Certificate student.

As the Junior Certificate approaches and the months rapidly pass, I wonder what things would be like if I were still at a single sex school. I don't know if it is an advantage or disadvantage to have been at both, but in the end what is past is past and it is the present that is important.

I do wonder if having a pack of hormone-crazy teenagers of both sexes in a school from nine o'clock until four isn't a little bit of a danger to their education. Does mingling with the opposite sex suddenly become more important than mingling with a few textbooks, and does a compatible class become the scene of a slagging match for one girl? I think it does.

From the age of four, I attended a co-educational primary school. I now realise that being there helped me later in the disco! It meant that, although afterwards I went to a single sex school, I still knew the boys in my area and could be friends with them without it interfering with my schoolwork. Which, when you become a teenager, is all that really matters.

I spent one year in a rural convent school before I came to Dublin, to a co-ed school. I found that an all-girls' school makes it easier for us shyer teenagers to be ourselves. Not having boys in the classroom and playground allows us to open up, to develop our personalities and opinions without having to impress all the time.

In a co-ed school, competition is based on your popularity rating among your peers. Whereas in an all-girls' school, the competition for popularity isn't so strong. In most cases, that competition is converted into competition to be first, to beat the best and to have A's all over your report. Best friends are easier to come by, too. There are no walls built around individual groups: the 'popular' group who spend their time impressing the boys; the 'less popular' ones; the 'smart' group; the 'less mature'. The list goes on and go.

One advantage of mixed schools is that they help boys and girls develop friendships and therefore help them mature. But single sex schools make it easier to be taught sex education. Those embarrassing questions can be appreciated by girls together but are mocked by a mixed group. And the boy-girl friendships which you would expect in a mixed school, and which are good, never last long. Girls are used to a boy being a close friend one day and an acquaintance the next.

I have been to a co-ed primary, to a convent secondary school for a short time and am now in a co-ed school. If I were a parent, I would send my child to a mixed primary school and then to a single sex school. I think sending my children to these school would be in their interest and would be good for their future.

(Meg Lynch, a Junior Certificate student, *Education Matters*)

Your views

1. How convincing did you find this essay? Give reasons for your answer.
2. What other arguments can you add to those already presented in the essay?
3. Can you spot any flaws in the essay? If so, say what they are.

A FEW PITFALLS

When preparing your case for an argument/debate, it is easy to fall into a few traps along the way. Think about the following pitfalls when organising your case.

GENERALISATIONS

Having made some specific observation, we may make a statement which we see as being *usually* or *always* true.

For example, two of your best friends have let you down in some way (*a specific observation*). You go on to make the *generalisation* that 'Not even one's best friends can be trusted'.

Another example of generalisation might be this. Having read that a group of robbers betrayed one another to the police, you go on to make the generalisation that 'There is no honour among thieves'.

Both of these statements are only generalisations. Just because you have been let down *once* does not mean that this *always* happens.

SWEEPING STATEMENTS

A statement may be based on *inadequate evidence* (too few observations). It is then described as a sweeping statement. Here are a few examples of this.

- 'Women are bad drivers.'
- 'Television has destroyed family life.'
- 'Teenagers today have no respect for anyone.'

Sweeping statements are not effective in argument because they do no stand up to close inspection – for example, mentioning one woman racing driver is enough to show up a statement about women being bad drivers. However, sweeping statements may still be useful if they are qualified by words such as 'some', 'most', 'many', 'often', 'sometimes', 'usually'. For instance, instead of saying 'Women are bad drivers', you could qualify this and say 'Some women are bad drivers'.

BIASED STATISTICS

Statistics are numerical facts which are often used to support a particular point of view. However, the effectiveness of statistics depends on *their source*.

- Who compiled these statistics?
- Is this person/agency reliable?
- Are the statistics based on good, objective research?

For example, you may want to use a few statistics about TV-watching and the ways in which it affects young children. Would you rely on statistics from someone who had never had a TV because they have always been opposed to TV? Since such a person is probably biased, you would have to be careful about any statistics which they present.

CONFUSING FACTS WITH OPINIONS

Fact

When a statement can be backed up with a lot of evidence, it is much more persuasive. It is more likely to be accepted as true.

For example: 'More illnesses are associated with old age than with youth.' While there are many childhood illnesses, old people are more likely to get sick than younger people.

Opinion

When a statement is not supported by evidence, it may not be accepted as true – even though it *may be true*. Without evidence, a statement is simply one person's opinion of something, based only on his or her own experience and nothing more.

Usually, statements of opinion have little value in argument. They should be avoided. An example of an opinion might be 'Sport is a waste of time.' Without any evidence, this is only an opinion.

FALSE PREMISES

Statements are sometimes based on assumptions which may be false. Look at this statement.

'The meal was terrible. There was garlic in it.'

The assumption is that garlic always makes a meal bad, which it doesn't. A person may not like garlic – but this does not make a meal terrible.

Try these . . .
Working in stages

Follow these stages for preparing each of the propositions.

- State the *arguments in favour* of the proposition.
- State the *arguments against* the proposition.
- Sketch out *a plan* of the composition.
- Write the *introductory paragraph*.
- Write a *full composition* on the topic.

1. 'Young people today have too much money.'
2. 'School holidays are too long.'
3. 'Most adults seem to have forgotten what it is like to be young.'
4. 'Advertising is becoming a nuisance.'
5. 'Homework is a waste of time.'
6. 'Smoking should be prohibited in shops, restaurants, cinemas and other public places.'
7. 'Some people are never happy.'
8. Why I would or would not like to have a summer job.

SOME TOPICS FOR DEBATE-TYPE ESSAYS

Here are a few topics on which you can write debate-type essays. Revise what you have already learned about writing paragraphs and organising your thoughts.

1. The reasons why you would or would not like to emigrate.

2. The motion for your next school debate:
   'The spirit of adventure is dead today.'
   Write out the speech you would make for
   or against this motion.

3. 'The world is still deceived by ornament.'

4. Is the motor car the curse or blessing of the
   twentieth century?

5. The motion for your next school debate:
   'Parents don't understand young people
   today.' Write out the speech you would
   make for or against this motion.

6. 'Fools rush in where angels fear to tread.'

7. The things money can't buy.

8. The motion for your next school debate:
   'School does not prepare us for life.' Write
   out the speech you would make for or
   against this motion.

9. Argue the changes you would like to see
   made in your school.

10. 'The school as we know it is a thing of the
    past.'

11. The motion for your next school debate:
    'Reading is a waste of time.' Write out the
    speech you would make for or against this
    motion.

12. 'Full-time, regular employment is a thing of
    the past.'

13. 'There is no need for hunger in the modern
    world.'

14. 'All the signs are that there will be a Third
    World War and that it will come sooner
    than later.'

15. What I like or dislike about teenagers.

ORGANISE YOUR OWN CLASS DEBATE

BASIC FORMAT FOR AN ORAL DEBATE

1. A *motion* or proposition is selected.
2. A *chairperson* is appointed.
3. Two *teams* of four debaters are selected.
4. The two teams are given *time to discuss* the
   subject of debate.
5. One member of each team is appointed the
   proposer of the motion and should be allowed
   8 to 10 minutes to put the motion. The
   other members of the team are allowed 3 or
   4 minutes to speak on the motion.
6. Speakers *from the floor* are allowed about 2
   minutes each to respond to the debate.
7. Finally, each proposer is allowed 3 or 4
   minutes to *reply* to the debate.
8. The chairperson conducts a *vote* and
   announces the result.
9. In *formal debates*, a member of either side of
   the debate proposes a Vote of Thanks to the
   chairperson and the Adjudicating Panel (the
   panel of judges) if there is one.

TOPIC

The motion for your class debate is:
   'Examinations should be abolished.'
Write out the speech that you would make for
or against this motion.

Dividing the class in two, the teacher could
assign each half of the class the task of
preparing, in writing, the arguments for or
against the proposition. Students could
present their arguments orally to the class.
The whole class could write down both
sets of arguments. Two groups of students
may be selected to debate the arguments in
class.

INTRODUCTION

- *Open* with 'Mr Chairman/Ms Chairwoman, Ladies and Gentlemen.'
- *State* your viewpoint. Say whether you are for or against the motion.
- *Define* what you understand by 'examinations'.
- *Explain* whether you mean all kinds of examinations or only some kinds, such as written public examinations like the Junior Certificate Examination.
- *Explain* why you think getting rid of examinations has become a topic of debate now.
- *Outline* the opinions involved.
- *Ask* whether examinations are necessary to traditional education, which is probably the type of education you are receiving.

ARGUMENT

- *Present the evidence* which you think supports your viewpoint. (Make sure you use only evidence that proves your case.)
- *State* your conclusion.
- *Consider* opposing views and state your arguments against them.
- *Anticipate* and *argue against* any objections to your viewpoint.

CONCLUSION

- *Sum up* the basic points of your argument.

LETTER WRITING

LAY-OUT

Every letter you write should have the following plan or lay-out.

your address _____
_____
_____

_____ date

_____
_____ inside address (receiver's address, with functional letters)
_____

_____ greetings

_____
_____
_____
_____
_____
_____ body
_____
_____

closing _____

handwritten signature _____

signature in block letters/typed _____

24 Woodstock
Gorey
Co. Wexford

13 May 19xx

Mr M. Black
The Superstore
Cork

Dear Mr Black,

• This is the usual lay-out for a letter. Personal letters generally leave out the inside address (the receiver's address).
• Leave a margin of about 3cm/1" on all four sides of the page. This will give your letter a tidy appearance.
• Take care to space out your letter as in this example.

Yours sincerely,

John Ryan

PERSONAL LETTERS

This section will help you to write better personal letters. These include letters such as the following.

1. Letter to a pen friend
2. Letter to a friend who has moved away
3. Holiday letter
4. Letter of encouragement
5. Letter of sympathy
6. Thank-you letter
7. Seasonal greeting
8. Letter of apology
9. Letter of invitation
10. Letter of congratulations

LETTER TO A PEN FRIEND

• Millions of people throughout the world find it interesting and great fun to start a pen-friendship – and keep it going. Some of these pen-friendships may last a lifetime.
• Through pen friends, we can learn a great deal about another country, its people and culture.
• Many good things have come from pen-friendships – romances and marriages, knowledge of foreign languages, travel to distant places.
• Starting a pen-friendship can be the beginning of a great adventure.

Finding a pen friend

Many teen magazines have advertisements for pen friends. You could take out such an advertisement yourself, or you could answer the ad from a person who interests you. Some high-tech agencies even have computerised pen friend services.

Guidelines for your first letter

Your first letter to a pen friend should have this information.
- Your age
- The members of your family
- Your school (what it's like, teachers, sports)
- Your house, neighbourhood etc.
- Your hobbies and interests
- Your daily routine

After exchanging a couple of letters, you can begin to share experiences with your pen friend.

SAMPLE LETTER TO A PEN FRIEND

10 Jones Drive
Dublin 5
Ireland

May 12

Dear Pietro,

I'm delighted to write to an Italian boy. I don't study Italian in my school but my sister Lorna knows a little Italian and she can help me make a start.

I'd like to tell you a little about my family. My mother spends most of her time looking after us all. On Saturdays she works in a fashion shop in the city centre. She is very good humoured and a brilliant cook.

My father loves sports and pottering about the garden, especially at weekends. He knows quite a lot about Italian soccer from watching it on TV. We always watch the matches together, and we also go to school matches whenever we can.

Apart from Lorna, that's my sister who knows a little Italian, I have one other sister, Mary, who is 10, and two brothers. John is 17 and in his last year in secondary school. William is 22 and a university student. The 'other' member of our family is Boxer, our bull terrier.

My favourite hobby is playing soccer with our local youth club. During the season we play a game nearly every weekend. My position is centre-forward.

School is not always great fun. It's probably the same for you. But I do my best because I know that education is important to my future. I like history and physical education best of all my subjects.

We live in a semi-detached house about 10 km from the centre of the city. We have brilliant neighbours. In fact, my best friend, Tom, lives just down the street.

I hope you will write to me soon and tell me about your life and your family in Italy.

Your new pen friend,

Michael

Letters to write

1. Introduce yourself to a 13-year-old girl or boy who lives in Hong Kong.
2. You were at a great party recently. Write a letter to your pen friend in New York telling him or her about it.
3. Your pen friend in Japan has asked you to tell him or her about how Irish parents treat their teenage sons and daughters. Write a letter which tells both the good and bad points.
4. Your pen friend in Paris is thinking of visiting Ireland and wants to know what Irish people think about France and the French. Tell your French friend about Irish attitudes towards food, fashions, films, sports, art etc.

LETTER TO A FRIEND WHO HAS MOVED AWAY

Guidelines and Ideas
- A friendly letter
- Thanks for letter received
- Give news about
  - yourself
  - mutual friends
  - school
  - activities such as sports, hobbies, clubs etc.
  - your family
  - special occasions such as birthdays
  - outings
  - pets
  - visitors
  - Ireland
  - weather
  - holidays
  - festivals
- Ask for information about
  - food
  - travel
  - school etc.
- End by saying you: enclose a photograph of some recent happening; send best wishes from all his/her friends; look forward to hearing from him/her again soon.

SAMPLE LETTER TO A FRIEND WHO HAS MOVED AWAY

24 Wexford Street
Newbridge
Co. Kildare

13 May 19xx

Dear Jane,

I was delighted to get your letter. Only a month has gone by since you left but it feels like years!

I'm still at the same old school doing the same old things. Mary Evans has got a new boyfriend who is really gorgeous! Sheila Tyler finally decided to get her hair done like Kylie Minogue. She looked very odd for a while, but we've all got used to it now. Actually, she looks pretty good!

My parents finally let me go to the school disco, and I really enjoyed it. The one condition was that I had to be home before 11.30. I'd have liked to stay longer, but I know how much they worry about me. Anyway, after all that dancing I was pretty whacked by then!

Write to me again soon. I'm looking forward to hearing from you. Say hi to your parents – and pet the cat!

Best wishes,

Tina

Letters to write

1. Your older sister is living in the United States. Bring her up to date on recent happenings in your family.
2. A friend you have known since you were a child has emigrated to Australia with his or her family. Write a letter telling him or her how you and your friends are. Ask for news about life in Australia.
3. Your brother is working and living in Dublin. He has not been home for some time. Write a letter to him about recent happenings in your hometown.
4. Your friend is living in London. Someone you both know has been in an accident. Write and tell your friend what happened.
5. Your friend has written to you asking about your plans for the summer holidays. In answering the letter, ask about your friend's own plans.

A HOLIDAY LETTER

When you are on holidays, away from your family, the letter you send home could express things like this.

A few ideas
- How you are
- That you are safe and comfortable
- That you like your accommodation
- That you are getting on with the people you are with
- That you are enjoying yourself
- Interesting experiences you have had
- The date of your arrival home

Letters to write

1. It's your first holiday outside Ireland. Write a letter to your best friend describing your experiences.
2. You are in France or Spain on a student-exchange holiday. Write a letter to your parents telling them how your visit is going.
3. You are a city person on your first holiday in the countryside. Write a letter to a friend telling him or her about life on the farm at which you are staying.
4. Your grandmother gave you the money to go on a school holiday to Euro-Disney. Write a letter to her telling her how you are getting on.

SAMPLE HOLIDAY LETTER

14 New Street
Donegal

24 July 19xx

Dear Mam and Dad,

I arrived here safe and sound in the Donegal Gaeltacht. The people in the house where I'm staying are really friendly. There are three other girls from Wexford staying in the house. Though we've just met, they seem very nice.

The weather is not so good but there's nothing new about that! The locals say that it will probably get better soon. We go to school every day. I thought it would be boring, but in fact it's good fun. There are lots of indoor activities to keep us amused when the rain is pouring down!

The scenery is fantastic – mountains and beaches and winding country roads. You should come here yourselves for a holiday some year.

I miss you both very much, though that's not stopping me from enjoying myself. See you on 14 August .

With love,

Louise

LETTER OF ENCOURAGEMENT

A friend/relation is trying to achieve something, in sport, exams etc. You want your letter to show that you are interested and that you care.

Some ideas
- Say how you heard about what your friend/relation is trying to achieve.
- Write about your friend/relation, not yourself.
- Make your friend/relation feel that his or her efforts will be worthwhile.

SAMPLE LETTER OF ENCOURAGEMENT

> 19 Wood Street
> Galway

3 September 19xx

Dear Karen,

I met your mother the other day and she told me that, although you got very good results in the Leaving Cert, you still need extra points to study medicine at university.

I know you've always wanted to be a doctor. I remember you talking to me about it years ago. I even remember the time you practised on me as your 'patient', tying bandages round my head!

I know you'll make a great doctor some day. Study hard. You have the ability and I know that you'll achieve your ambition.

> All good wishes,
> Marie

Letters to write
1. Your friend has been chosen for a selection test to represent Ireland in some sport. Write a letter to him or her giving your reaction to this news.
2. Your friend, who always wanted to go into acting, has been chosen for a 'bit part' in a television film. Write a letter giving your response to this news.

LETTER OF SYMPATHY

The purpose of a letter of sympathy or condolence is to express your concern for the friend or acquaintance whose life has been affected by sickness or death.

Guidelines
- Say how you heard the bad news.
- In the case of a death, express your regard and respect for the person who has died.
- Keep your letter short, simple and restrained.

SAMPLE LETTER OF SYMPATHY

15 October 19xx

Dear Mary,

I was so sorry to learn about the death of your Uncle John. I knew he had been ill for some time and how upset everybody was. He was a good and kind person and I know how fond of him you were and how much you respected him.

Although I didn't know your uncle very well, I want to express my sincere sympathy with you and all the members of your family at this sad time.

> Yours sincerely,
> Paula

Letters to write
1. Your friend's mother has had a serious operation. Write a letter asking about how she is and how the operation went.
2. You friend's father has died suddenly. Write a letter expressing the shock you felt on hearing such sad news.

THANK-YOU LETTER

- Thank-you letters are usually written in response to receiving a present or to someone doing you a favour.
- Thank-you letters should be written immediately.
- A short note is quite acceptable.

Guidelines

- Express your thanks for the gift or favour received.
- Say something pleasant about the gift or favour.
- Describe the favourable reaction of friends to the gift.
- Do not end your letter too abruptly.

SAMPLE THANK-YOU LETTER

19 William Street
Cork

17 September 19xx

Dear Pat,

This is just a brief note to thank you and all your family for the wonderful time we had on holidays on your farm. Joseph is still talking about the hens and rabbits and all the other animals on the farm that he made friends with.

We hope that you can visit us in Cork soon. That will give us the chance to return your kindness.

Once again, many thanks for all your hospitality. Regards from all of us here in Cork.

Best wishes,

Tracy

SAMPLE THANK-YOU LETTER

23 Abbey Street
Mullingar

17 September 19xx

Dear Joan,

Many thanks for the concert ticket you sent me for my birthday. You know how much I love that group.

My friends here are green with envy.

I hope you're well and that we can meet soon.

Once again, many thanks for such a thoughtful gift.

Best wishes,

Alice

Letters to write

1. You were sick in hospital and had few visitors because the hospital is so far away from your home. Write a letter to a friend who came to visit you often.
2. You were not prepared for your Maths test. Your friend, who is very good at Maths, spent many hours helping you. Write a thank-you letter to him or her.
3. You were looking for a book about a pop group. You found out it was not available either here or in Britain. At your mother's suggestion, you wrote to your uncle in New York, hoping that he might be able to get the book there. He got the book right away and sent it to you as a present. Write him a thank-you letter.
4. You are in France on a school holiday. You have run out of money and have written to your parents asking them to send you what they can. In response, they sent you extra money and made no complaints that could have ruined your holiday. Write a letter thanking them.

SEASONAL GREETINGS

When to write
- Christmas
- Easter
- St Patrick's Day
- Valentine's Day
- New Year
- Birthdays
- Wedding Anniversaries
- Mother's Day
- Father's Day

Letters to write

1. A school friend is now living in Australia. Write a short note to accompany your Christmas card. Recall the good times you had together in the past.
2. Write a note to accompany a St Patrick's Day card you are sending to an uncle living in the United States.
3. Write a note to accompany a Christmas card you are sending to a pen friend in Japan. As your Japanese friend may not know much about Christmas, write a little about this.
4. Write a note to accompany a Christmas card you are sending to a cousin in London who is ill.

LETTER OF APOLOGY

You should always write a letter of apology when you have let someone down by:
- not keeping an appointment
- not keeping a promise
- some kind of bad behaviour

Guidelines
- State your apology and mention your offence.
- Give details of what went wrong/excuse.
- Ask about the inconvenience caused and offer new arrangements, if appropriate.

Letters to write

1. You were rude to a teacher who criticised your bad behaviour. You now realise you were in the wrong. Write him or her a letter of apology.
2. Your friend invited you to a birthday party, but you were busy that day and forgot all about it. Write a letter of apology to your friend.

SAMPLE LETTER OF APOLOGY

11 Clare Street
Newbridge
Co. Kildare

18 May 19xx

Dear Paul,

I am very sorry I wasn't there on Wednesday as arranged. I arrived at the forest carpark at 12.15 – one hour late. I wasn't surprised that you weren't there but I still waited for another half hour in case you were late too. Finally I gave up and went home.

Here's what happened. My Dad gave me a lift as arranged and we set off in good time. About 20 km from Newbridge, the car began to overheat and we pulled in to a garage. They told us the problem was in the water pump and that it would take two hours to fit a new one. Dad wouldn't let me hitch, as you can imagine, so there was nothing I could do.

I was really disappointed to miss the Fleadh. I can't wait to hear all the details, so get in touch soon. Next year I promise I'll get started a day in advance!

Best wishes,

Barry

LETTER OF INVITATION

When to write

When you are having a party or some other special social event.

Guidelines
• State the occasion and the date and time at which people are invited.
• Give details of the function.
• Say how much you hope they can attend.

SAMPLE LETTER OF INVITATION

Mill House
Abbey Field Road
Dublin 20

10 July 19xx

Dear Sheila,

I'm delighted to be able to tell you that I finally managed to persuade my parents to let me have a proper party for my sixteenth birthday, and you are invited.

We're having the party in my house. There'll be supper at 7 pm and then it's dancing until midnight. We have to get our own DJ, or at least someone to look after the music, and I'm hoping you can help me with that. All the gang from school are invited, together with some from the club and, of course, a few relations. You are welcome to bring along a friend if you wish.

Write soon and let me know whether you can come. I really hope you can – it's my first big party and I'll need your support!

Best wishes,

Anna

FORMAL INVITATION

Formal invitations are sent for events which are not so casual. They could be sent for a dinner party, a wedding reception or a special birthday or anniversary.

SAMPLE FORMAL INVITATION

Mr and Mrs William Murphy
request the pleasure of
Miss O'Brien's company
for dinner in the Abbey Hotel, Malahide,
on the evening of 5 October
at eight o'clock.
Dress informal.

20 September 19xx
19 Drury Street
RSVP

Note: RSVP is the abbreviation for the French phrase *Respondez s'il vous plait,* meaning *Please reply*.

SAMPLE ACCEPTANCE

Miss O'Brien is pleased to accept
Mr and Mrs Murphy's kind invitation
for 5 October at eight o'clock.

24 September 19xx
6 O'Connor Place

DECLINING A FORMAL INVITATION

Miss O'Brien regrets that a previous engagement prevents her acceptance of the kind invitation of Mr and Mrs Murphy for 5 October.

24 September 19xx
6 O'Connor Place

Letters to write

1. Your brother is coming home from America and you are organising a party for his homecoming. Write a letter to a friend inviting him or her to the party.

2. You have recently moved to a new house in a different part of town. Your parents have said you can throw a party for your friends. Write a letter of invitation to one of them.

3. Your family is going on a weekend holiday in the countryside. Write a letter to a friend living in that part of the country, inviting him or her to spend the weekend with you and your family.

4. You are going abroad on a summer holiday with your family. Your parents have given you permission to invite one of your friends to go with you. Write a letter of invitation to the friend you have chosen.

5. You are a member of a local sports club which is enrolling new members. Write a letter to a friend who has always wanted to join the club, inviting him or her to apply for membership.

LETTER OF CONGRATULATIONS

Some occasions
- A friend's success in some sport
- An engagement
- A wedding
- Good exam results
- Winning a prize
- Birth of a baby
- A holiday

A few ideas
- Express pleasure in your friend's success.
- Show appreciation for your friend's efforts.
- Express good wishes for the future.

Letters to write

1. Your friend has been chosen to be a member of a national team in some sport. Write a letter congratulating him or her on the good news.

2. A friend of yours has always been interested in drama. He/she has been given an important role in a play being produced by a local drama society. Write a letter to congratulate him or her.

3. Your friend's parents have scooped a big money prize in a television quiz show. You know that the father is unemployed and that the prize is going to be a great help to the family. Write a letter of congratulations to your friend.

SAMPLE LETTER OF CONGRATULATIONS

24 Brookwood
Dublin 4

26 October 19xx

Dear Alice,

Congratulations on the great results you got in the Junior Cert exams. I hope I can do half as well as you next year when my turn comes.

You really deserved those results. I know how hard you studied, and I know all the sacrifices you made, staying in evening after evening poring over your books.

Once again, my heartiest congratulations! Keep up the good work for the Leaving Cert.

All good wishes,

Emily

FUNCTIONAL LETTERS

Here is a list of functional letters – sometimes called business letters.

1. Letter to a newspaper – letter to the editor
2. Job application
3. Letter of enquiry
4. Letter of complaint
5. Lobbying letter

LETTERS TO THE EDITOR

Letters to the editor can deal with a wide range of subjects.
• In reply to a letter written earlier in the week.
• In protest against some decision that affects you.
• Complaining about a problem in a certain area (transport, litter, care of the young/elderly)
• Informing readers about an interesting event
• Commenting on a news item

Try this

Over the next week, make a collection of Letters to the Editor as they appear in the national press or in local newspapers. Put the letters into different categories. Have a class discussion about the kinds of letters which people write.

Guidelines

• Keep your letter as short as possible.
• Write neatly and legibly. Better still, type the letter if you can.
• State the topic of your letter in a short opening paragraph. Expand it in the second paragraph. Sum it up in a short third paragraph.
• When dealing with matters of fact, don't make wild general statements that you can't back up.
• Use a little humour if you can.
• When replying to a previously published letter, never use personal abuse.

Note: Your letter must include your address or telephone number so that the people in the newspaper office can check, if necessary, that your letter is genuine and not a hoax.

SAMPLE LETTER TO THE EDITOR

16 Jones Drive
Westbrook
Dublin 1

27 May 19xx

The Editor
'The Evening Chronicle'
Middle River Street
Dublin

Dear Sir,

It's summer again and once more Dublin City is looking dreadful. What must tourists think!

To judge by the number of holes being dug in the streets, a tourist might be forgiven for thinking that gangs of maniacs with picks and shovels are loose in the city searching for Viking gold. Or maybe the tourists think that these pits are for the use of anyone who wants a convenient place to dispose of their litter.

Considering the importance of tourism to the Irish economy, surely these problems should be sorted out once and for all.

Yours, etc.,

John Citizen

Letters to write

1. The authorities are planning to open a rubbish tip near your house. Write a letter of protest to the 'Morning Chronicle'.

2. A local councillor has made a speech criticising young people for the way they dress, for their hairstyles etc. Write a letter to the 'Evening Post' defending teenagers.

3. The chairperson of a local music society has written to the 'Evening Post' describing pop music as 'a load of rubbish'. Write a letter to the editor giving your views on this.

4. You have learned that your local school bus service is to be axed by the local council as part of a series of cutbacks. Write a letter to the editor arguing for the retention of the service.

5. Football hooliganism is giving sport a bad name, so that all soccer fans are thought of as thugs. Write a letter to the 'Morning Chronicle' in defence of soccer fans in general.

JOB APPLICATION

A letter applying for a job may turn out to be the most important letter you have ever written. The **presentation** and **contents** of your letter may lead to a personal interview and may help you get the job you want.

Guidelines

- Use unlined white paper with a matching envelope
- Your handwriting should be neat and legible (readable).
- If you're worried about your handwriting marching up or down hill on unlined paper, put a lined piece underneath for guidance.
- Leave a margin of about 3 cm on all four sides of the page.
- Write your address and your telephone number in the upper right-hand corner.
- Write the date on the left-hand side.
- Write the name and/or title of the addressee (the person to whom you are writing) on the left-hand side of the page.
- Start your letter at the left-hand margin with *Dear Sir/Madam/Mr/Mrs/Miss/Ms*, as appropriate.
- Directly below the first word after *Dear*, begin the letter proper.
- Four short, basic paragraphs are usually all you need to write.
  - ★**Name the job** you are applying for.
  - ★**Tell where and when** you saw the advertisement.
  - ★**Give all the information** about yourself that the potential employer will need to decide whether to call you for an interview. If, however, you are enclosing a Curriculum Vitae (CV), you will not need to do this.
  - ★**Supply the names, addresses and telephone numbers of your referees** (the people who will vouch for your character and abilities).
  - ★**Give the times** when you will be available for an interview.
  - ★**Close the letter** with *Yours faithfully* or *Yours truly*. As well as signing your name below this, it is a good idea to write your name in block letters below your usual signature.

SAMPLE OF A JOB APPLICATION

Evening Chronicle
19 October 19xx

Trainee shop assistant required for weekend work in small city-centre store. Successful applicant should have Junior Cert standard of education and be of tidy appearance. Character references essential. Apply in your own handwriting to Mr J. White, Good Value Store, O'Connell Street, Limerick.

72 James Avenue
Martinville
Limerick
Telephone 023-1234

20 October 19xx

Mr J. White
Good Value Store
O'Connell Street
Limerick

Dear Mr White,

I would like to apply for the vacancy of Trainee Shop Assistant advertised in the 'Evening Chronicle' of 19 October.

I am 16 years old and a student at St Mary's School in Martinville. I achieved good grades in this year's Junior Certificate Examination, obtaining Bs in both Maths and English. I am now studying four subjects for the Leaving Certificate at Higher Level.

Last year in school I was a Junior Prefect with responsibility for a first year class. For a month last year I worked in a small local drapery shop and I think my experience from that would help me in the position you have advertised.

The owner of that shop, Mrs Davis, and the principal of my school, Mr Loughran, have said that they will give me character references and that they will comment on my abilities. Their addresses and phone numbers are attached separately.

I can attend an interview any day after 4.30 pm, or on Saturday mornings or afternoons.

Yours faithfully,

Emma O'Reilly

EMMA O'REILLY

Letters to write

Answer the following advertisements which appeared in the 'Evening Chronicle' of 20 September.

1.

Motor trade. Part-time store person required for busy wholesaler. Experience not essential, but should have an interest in cars. Apply in writing to 'Evening Chronicle', Box T 628.

2.

Co. Dublin. Mini supermarket requires part-time staff. Must be good at sums. Reply to 'Evening Chronicle', Box 983.

3.

Supermarket. Busy suburban delicatessen requires counterhands. Must be interested in good food. Apply in writing to 'Evening Chronicle', Box T 736.

4.

Hairdressing. Part-time workers required. Must be willing to learn and interested in latest styles. Apply in writing to 'Evening Chronicle', Box T 948.

5.

Boutique. Southside suburbs, requires responsible part-time workers. No experience needed, but an interest in the latest fashions would be an advantage. Apply in writing to 'Evening Chronicle' Box T 295.

- -

LETTER OF ENQUIRY

Letters of enquiry are usually written in response to something which you have heard about or which was advertised in the paper. When you write, you should give precise details of the sort of information you need.

SAMPLE LETTER OF ENQUIRY

St. Mary's College
Tralee
Co. Kerry

10 November 19xx

The Secretary
French Embassy
Dublin

Dear Sir or Madam,

My class has been assigned a school project dealing with the most famous historic monuments in France.

Students have been given different French cities to research, and mine is Rouen.

I would appreciate any information you can send me on this subject, especially on the city's history and its monuments.

Thank you for your assistance.

Yours truly,

Emily Browne
(Third Year)

Letters to write

Write for further information about each of the following.

1.

Junior tennis clinics. Weekly, commencing 20 June. Expert coaching. Apply to 'Evening Post,' Box T746.

2.

Cavalier King Charles Spaniels, male and female. Beautiful markings. Adorable pets. Apply to 'Evening Post,' Box T569.

3.

I am Sooty, a collie-type mongrel. I need a good home because my owners are emigrating. I am very fond of children. If you are the right person, you can have me for nothing. Apply to 'Evening Post', Box T398.

4.

Want to join a small disco-dancing club? Apply to 'Evening Post,' Box T951.

5.

Stamps required. All countries. Must be in good condition. Apply to 'Evening Post', Box T837.

LETTER OF COMPLAINT

Letters of complaint are sometimes written in response to:
• A defective or shoddy product
• Inefficient service
• Bad manners on the part of a shop assistant, waiter, receptionist, civil servant etc.
• Receiving wrong information (price, dates, type of holiday accommodation etc.)

Guidelines

A product
• Where you bought the item (name and address of the shop)
• When you bought it
• Precisely what is wrong with it
• Your dissatisfaction
• Possible solution

A service
• When the incident took place
• The circumstances (where etc.) in which it took place
• The cause of your dissatisfaction

Letters to write

1. You had lunch at _____ restaurant on _____ date. You were charged _____ [price] for stale cheese and cold soup. Write a letter of complaint to the manager of the restaurant.

2. You were at a pop concert at which there were too many people and too few security personnel. As a result, there was a lot of confusion and fights broke out in which people were hurt. Write a letter of complaint to the organisers of the concert.

3. Your local park has been badly neglected by the authorities. It is strewn with litter, the grass hasn't been cut in ages and the lighting is very poor. Write a letter of complaint to the manager of public parks.

4. The new DJ on your favourite radio show is not playing enough of the kind of music you like. Write a letter of complaint to the producer of the show.

5. A rule of your local golf club prevents anyone under 18 from applying for membership. Write a letter of complaint to the president of the club. Argue the case for the age limit being reduced.

SAMPLE LETTER OF COMPLAINT

67 Ring Road
Sligo

7 July 19xx

Manager
Quality Control
The Chocolate Co.

Dear Sir,

On 5 July, I bought a box of chocolates [mention brand name] at the Corner Store, Patrick's Street, to give as a present to my mother. Yesterday was my mother's birthday, and when we opened the box we found that the chocolates were discoloured and had a very odd taste.

As you can imagine, it was a very embarrassing and disappointing experience for me. I am enclosing the chocolates as evidence of the truth of my complaint.

My mother has always liked your products, which is the reason I bought the gift. I hope you will be able to put things right as soon as possible.

Yours truly,

Jane Byrne

A LOBBYING LETTER

Lobbying means trying to influence someone, usually in some position of authority, to take your side and then to do something about a particular situation.

Some reasons for writing
- To influence someone to champion your cause
- To look for a change in a situation
- To try to improve something (such as public library hours)
- To stop something which you disapprove of

Try this
Local newspapers often carry articles about events which have to do with special-interest groups. Study the local press over a few weeks to see whether you can find examples of this. What kinds of lobbying letters might these groups want to write?

Guidelines
- Be courteous and firm.
- Don't be abusive.
- Use argument and persuasion.
- Know the interests of the person being lobbied.

Letters to write
1. There are no sports facilities in your area. Write a letter to a local politician asking him/her to do something about it.
2. The bus service on your route is very poor. Write a letter to the manager of the bus company making a case for improving the service.

SAMPLE LOBBYING LETTER

35 Tower Road
Waterford

9 October 19xx

Mr David O'Brien
County Council Offices
West Avenue
Waterford

Dear Mr O'Brien,

We have a small youth club in our area which has been in existence for the past two years. It answers a great need in our area, keeping young people out of trouble. Unfortunately, we have just heard that the County Council is planning to demolish the building in which we meet and no alternative meeting place has been offered to us.

We're sure that you will agree with us that this is most unfair. It may be that the officials of the County Council are not fully aware of what is involved in what they intend to do.

This area has always given you great support at election times, and you have generally been attentive and efficient in representing its interests. In this case, we hope you can exert whatever influence you have to get the County Council to change its mind about demolishing our youth club, or at least persuade it to provide us with alternative accommodation.

Yours sincerely,

James Dunne

on behalf of

Tower Road Youth Club

CRITICAL READING

WRITING A SUMMARY

A summary is a shortened version of a piece of writing. In a summary, only the most important details are included.

Most pieces of prose which a student will be asked to summarise contain **essential** information, as well as **additional** information. The real work in writing a good summary is recognising what is essential and what is additional. When writing a summary, leave out as much of the additional information as you can – such as the descriptive details in this example.

<u>There is a</u> large old beech <u>tree in my</u> beautiful front <u>garden</u>.

- **essential** = There is a tree in my garden.
- **additional** = large old beech ... beautiful front garden

Although the details have been left out, the reader still has the essential information – that there is a tree in the garden. Even in this short sentence, a great deal has been lost – that the tree is large and old; that it is a beech tree; that it is in the front garden. But the essential information is still understandable and it still makes sense.

- Keep your summary in one tense – present, past or future.
- A summary should be about one-third the length of the original.

Try these

Summarise each of these sentences. Underline the essential words first. Be sure to leave out any additional information. The example above will help you.

1. The vicious black dog from down the street chased the frightened cat.
2. It was a bleak, windy day when we set out in the rickety old car on our three-hour journey to the west coast.
3. The flashing red lights of the crowded disco made all the excited dancers look like weird spirits from a faraway planet.
4. The sleepy little town, with its dusty streets, nestled in the valley, far from the noise and bustle of the busy city.
5. The dirty-faced boy ignored the angry cries of the stooped old man as he scrambled down from the tree, his pockets filled to bursting with juicy red apples.

WRITING A SUMMARY – STEP-BY-STEP

• •

1. **Read** the passage carefully to get its overall meaning.
2. Give the passage a **title**. This will be your main guideline.
3. **Underline** the key words and phrases. **Note**: Check the section of this book that deals with clauses. Remind yourself of the differences between a principal clause and a subordinate clause. The principal clauses will contain the essential information. Spotting these clauses will help you to organise a good summary.
4. Make a **rough draft** first by jotting down the words and phrases you have underlined. At this stage, your summary will not read continuously because it will be made up of disconnected bits.
5. Now try **connecting** the words and phrases so that they begin to make sense.
6. Now **rewrite** the rough draft in continuous or connected prose. **Use your own words** as much as possible rather than just copying directly from the original passage.

A SAMPLE SUMMARY ASSIGNMENT

No unexplored region in our times, neither the heights of the Himalayas, the Antarctic wastes, nor even the hidden side of the moon, has excited quite the same fascination as the mystery of the sources of the Nile. For two thousand years at least the problem remained unsolved; every expedition that was sent up the river from Egypt returned defeated. By the middle of the nineteenth century – barely 100 years ago – this matter had become the greatest geographical secret after the discovery of America.

This was something more than an ordinary field of exploration. In these deserts the river was life itself. Had it failed to flow, even for one season, then all Egypt perished. Not to know where the stream came from, not to have any sort of guarantee that it would continue – this was to live in great insecurity.

But there is no record of the river's ever having failed. The great brown flood came pouring out of the desert for ever, and no one could explain why it was that it should rise and flow over its banks in the Nile Delta in September, the driest and hottest time of the year on the Mediterranean shore; nor how it was possible for the river to continue in its lower reaches for well over a thousand miles through one of the most frightful of all deserts without receiving a single tributary and hardly a drop of water.

By 1856, even the most determined of explorers on the White Nile had not been able to get beyond the neighbourhood of the present township of Juba, on latitude five degrees north. At that point they were still nowhere near the source of the river. Cataracts, vast forests of papyrus reeds, malarial fever, the fierce tropical heat, the opposition of the pagan tribes – all these combined to prevent any further progress south. By now that impenetrable blank space in the centre of the continent had become filled in imagination with a thousand monstrosities, dwarf men and cannibals with tails, animals as strange as the fabulous griffins and the salamander, huge inland seas, and mountains so high they defied all nature by bearing on their crests, in this equatorial heat, a mantle of perpetual snow.

It was <u>in order to find out</u> what the country was really like that <u>two explorers, Richard Francis Burton and John Hanning Speke</u>, set off for Africa in <u>1856</u>.

(from *The Source of the Nile* by Alan Moorehead)

TITLE
Exploring the sources of the Nile

ROUGH DRAFT
Now, change the underlined words and phrases into a list of sentences. Use your own words to clarify or simplify the original passage.

No unexplored region in our time has excited the same fascination as the mystery of the sources of the Nile.

For over two thousand years the problem remained unsolved.

Barely 100 years ago it was the greatest geographical secret.

It was more than an ordinary field of exploration.

All Egypt would perish if the river failed.

There is no record that the river had ever failed.

No one could explain why it rose and overflowed its banks in September, the driest period of the year.

It did not seem to have a single tributary and there was hardly any rain.

Exploration was hindered by high waterfalls, huge forests, fever, fierce heat and hostile natives.

People imagined that the unknown was filled with monsters and freaks of nature.

Two explorers, Robert Francis Burton and John Hanning Speke, set off for Africa in 1856 to solve the mystery of the sources of the Nile.

THE COMPLETED SUMMARY
Now use your rough draft to write the final summary. You should end up with a paragraph which makes sense and which gives any reader the main idea of the original piece.

The mystery of the sources of the Nile has fascinated people for more than two thousand years. Only 100 years ago it was considered the greatest geographical secret. There was something extraordinary about the Nile. Without any known tributaries and without any rainfall to speak of, the river rose and overflowed its banks in the driest part of the year. The whole of Egypt depended on this overflow of the Nile's waters for its survival. And it overflowed every year without fail. No one knew why. Exploration of the sources of the Nile was hampered by all kinds of difficulties: waterfalls, jungles, intense heat, disease and hostile natives. People imagined all sorts of strange stories about where the Nile rose. Finally, in 1856, two explorers, Robert Francis Burton and John Hanning Speke, set out for Africa to solve the mystery.

CRITICAL READING

In a critical reading assignment, students are asked to **think about** what they are reading. To do this, they must try to get inside the mind of the author to **discover** exactly what he or she is saying. The following questions will help you to do your critical reading more successfully.

- What is the **subject matter**?
- What is the **theme**?
- What is the author trying to do – the author's **intention**?
- What is the **tone** of the passage?
- What is the author's **attitude to the reader**?
- What special **language techniques** are being used by the author?
- How successful or **effective** is the author?
- What is **your impression** of the author?

THE SUBJECT MATTER

Authors can – and do! – write about many subjects. When reading a passage for the first time, try to discover what that subject is. This list will give you a few ideas about possible subjects – but there are many, many more.

- sport
- a particular period in history
- some aspect of the environment
- music
- life in a coal mining village
- life in the American Wild West
- a fisherman's life
- life in an imaginary world
- life on a modern housing estate
- school life
- life among gangsters
- the world of espionage
- a discovery
- life among the rich
- life in big business
- life in the army

Challenge time

Using short phrases like these, list ten more possibilities for an author's subject matter.

THE THEME

You should try to discover the difference between the subject matter and the theme of a passage. For example, the subject matter may be sport – and the theme may be what the writer thinks of the use of drugs by athletes.

- The **subject matter** is the raw material – the information in the passage.
- The **theme** is what the writer does with the raw material – the author's lesson or message.
- The **subject matter** of a potter is the clay. The **theme** is the vase which the potter makes out of the clay.

DISCOVERING THE SUBJECT MATTER

Read the following passage carefully. Then decide what its subject matter is.

A few days ago, the writer of a letter to a daily newspaper raised, in a new form, an old, well-known cry – that familiar cry of the elderly – that the country, to judge from the behaviour of the young, was going to the dogs. In this instance, the evidence was the spelling. Undergraduates, we were told, cannot spell their own native tongue; they are totally unfamiliar with its structure.

(Hugh Trevor-Roper)

The subject matter of this passage is the English language. The writer obviously wants to discuss if – and how – our knowledge of the English language has declined, which is what many older people seem to think. So his theme is whether younger people have a poor grasp of the English language.

It's your turn!

What is the **subject matter** of each of these passages?

1.

'It was some Englishman who came to Beiginis,' and he looked out to Beiginis as he spoke. 'They had a big boat and they used to spend the week there fishing. That is why the old ruin is to be seen on the Island still. Well, Maurice, one day we were going out to Mass – the King, Sean Fada and I – and we were rowing at our ease past Beiginis to the north when my oar caught in a rope ...'

(Maurice O'Sullivan, *Twenty Years A-Growing*)

2.

Yesterday I should have gone back to school, had I been a hundred years younger.
My most frequent dream nowadays – or nowanights I suppose I should say – is that I am back at school, and trying to construe difficult passages from Greek authors unknown to me. That they are unknown to me is my own fault, as will be pointed out to me sternly in a moment. Meanwhile I stand up and gaze blankly at the text, wondering how it is that I can have forgotten to prepare it.

(A.A. Milne)

3.

When William caught sight of the valley of the Boyne, he could not suppress an exclamation and a gesture of delight. He had been apprehensive that the enemy would avoid a decisive action, and would protract the war till the autumnal rains should return with pestilence in their train. He was now at ease. It was plain that the contest would be sharp and short.

(Lord Macaulay)

4.

When he first appeared, scarcely a foot long, his brow furrowed with loose wrinkles, as if he bore all the cares of the world upon him, Rufus looked like a bloodhound on an extremely reduced scale. Then he grew and grew longitudinally and emerged from the process as a dachshund of highly respectable pedigree and a pleasing brown colour. From his unpopularity with the other dogs in the village, it is believed that they do not recognise him as a fellow-dog and take him for some kind of rat.

(Bernard Darwin)

5.

The other day there was a ship that died. It was my own ship, and in a way I would it had not died. But die it had to, for it was mortal, having been made in this world: to be accurate, at Bembridge, in the Isle of Wight, nearly sixty years ago. Moreover, since boats also must die, it is right that they should die their own death in their own element; not violently, but after due preparation; for, in spite of modern cowardice, it is better to be prepared for death than unprepared.

(Hilaire Belloc)

Challenge time

Try to say what the theme is for each of the pieces you have just read.

THE AUTHOR'S INTENTION

In every piece you read, try to discover what the author is trying to do – his or her **intention**.

- Is the author giving us information **objectively** or **impartially** (without taking sides)?

If the passage is a *factual* or *non-fiction* piece, examine the writer's selection of facts. Ask if any information seems to be left out or distorted – the author's bias.

- Is the author trying to **persuade** the reader to accept a certain viewpoint?

- Is the writer **using emotive language** – language which works on one's feelings or emotions? Is this being done in order to persuade the reader to think about something in a certain way?

- Is the writer **manipulating** the connotations – or associations – of words and phrases to **influence** the reader's feelings?

Remember! Connotations are the meanings we associate with certain words. These are more than the meanings which we would find in a dictionary.

For example, the word 'tropical' may be used to suggest exotic things such as sunshine and sandy beaches, warm blue seas, palm trees, adventure, faraway places.

A writer may write 'He wallowed in self-pity'. This is meant to have unpleasant connotations or associations of a pig wallowing in the muck. Without actually saying so, the writer is probably trying to turn us against someone.

- Connotations are used to work on our feelings or emotions. They may be used to make us either like or dislike something. They may also be used to entertain or amuse.

Try these

The following words, on their own, have no particular connotations. Try to give each word a different 'feeling', as in the first example.

1. dog

   a positive connotation = the courageous, faithful dog

   a negative connotation = the vicious, wild dog

   an amusing connotation = the flop-eared, silly dog

2. fish
3. woman
4. bicycle
5. teacher
6. lifeguard
7. ship
8. explorer
9. bird
10. school-boy

THE TONE

What is **the writer's attitude** towards the subject matter? This attitude will give us the **tone** in which the piece is written.

Serious?
Humorous?
Confident?
Authoritative?
Hostile?
Uncertain?
Sympathetic?
Informative?
Sarcastic?
A combination of a few?

Discovering the tone

Read the following short piece and think about its tone.

> A few stars are known which are hardly bigger than the earth, but the majority are so large that hundreds of thousands of earths could be packed inside each and leave room to spare. Here and there we come upon a giant star large enough to contain millions of millions of earths. And the total number of stars in the universe is probably something like the total number of grains of sand on all the seashores of the world. Such is the littleness of our home in space when measured up against the total substance of the universe.
>
> (James Jeans)

The tone of this passage is both serious and informative. It is not heavy, however. The writer seems to know his subject matter very well. But he doesn't overpower the reader with confusing statistics and lots of technical information, although the reader feels that he could if he wished.

It's your turn

This is a longer passage. After you have read it, talk about whether you agree with the Comment about its tone which follows the piece.

St Francis of Assisi was very fond of birds, and often had his picture taken with them sitting on his shoulders and pecking at his wrists. That was all right, if St Francis liked it. We all have our likes and dislikes, and I have more of a feeling for dogs. However, I am not *against* birds as a class. I am just against pigeons.

I do not consider pigeons birds, in the first place. They are more in the nature of people; people who mooch. Probably my feeling about pigeons arises from the fact that all my life I have lived in rooms where pigeons came rumbling in and out of my window. I myself must have a certain morbid fascination for pigeons, because they follow me about so much – and with evident ill will. I am firmly convinced that they are trying to haunt me.

Although I live in the middle of a very large city (well, to show you how large it is – it is the largest in the world), I am awakened every morning by a low gargling sound which turns out to be the result of one, or two, or three pigeons walking in at my window and sneering at me. Granted I am a fit subject for sneering as I lie there, possibly with one shoe on or an unattractive expression on my face, but there is something more than just a passing criticism in these birds making remarks about me. They have some ugly scheme on foot against me, and I know it. Sooner or later it will come out, and then I can sue.

(Robert Charles Benchley)

Comment

The tone of this passage is humorous. It uses a device which is often described as *comic exaggeration*. St Francis, for instance, is portrayed as a sort of tourist posing for a photograph with the pigeons perched on his shoulders.

The main exaggeration portrays pigeons as in the nature of people. The writer develops further exaggerations out of this idea. These 'pigeon-people' are out to get the writer. They come to his window to sneer at him. They have some ugly scheme on foot against him. The writer even considers suing them!

THE WRITER AND THE READER

What is the attitude of the writer towards the reader?

Respectful?

Condescending (treating the reader as inferior)?

Intimidating or bullying?

Belligerent or aggressive?

Exploitative or manipulative?

> When a woman says 'I look a fright' she invariably adds, by way of explanation, 'My hair is a show.' She is referring, not to a worsening condition due to the ravages of time, but to a temporary set-back due to want of time. She seems to be making a statement, but she is really planning a campaign.
>
> (John D. Sheridan)

The writer's attitude towards his readers is sexist. Women are seen as comical creatures who don't know the difference between the serious side of life and something as trivial as a hairstyle. The writer seems sure that his male readers will share this view of women. Worse still, he seems unaware that this view is offensive to women. He is not trying to take women's feelings into account.

Challenge time

Read the last piece again. Then try to pick out its subject matter, its theme and its intention. Select any words or phrases which you think have particular connotations. Say what these connotations are. Describe the tone of the piece.

LANGUAGE TECHNIQUES

What **language techniques** are used to help the writer to achieve his or her objective – whether that is one of persuasion or simply to impart information?

Metaphors and **similes** are two important language techniques which are often used to influence the reader. Both are comparisons which bring certain images to mind.

- **metaphor**

He was so hungry, he wolfed his food down.

- **simile**

He was as ravenous as a wolf.

- A simile is introduced by the words **like** or **as**.
- A simile is a **more limited** comparison than a metaphor.

He fought like a lion.
(This comparison is a simile. It is limited to the bravery of the lion in fighting.)

He was a lion in the fight.
(This comparison is a metaphor. It makes us think not only of courage, but of wildness and strength as well.)

USING LANGUAGE TECHNIQUES

Read this short piece by Dylan Thomas. Then comment on the techniques he has used.

> But that was not the same snow. Our snow was not only shaken in whitewash buckets down from the sky. I think it came shawling out of the ground and swam and drifted out of the arms and hands and bodies of the trees; snow grew overnight on the roofs of the houses like a pure and grandfather moss, minutely ivied the walls, and settled on the postman, opening the gate, like a dumb, numb thunderstorm of white torn Christmas cards.
>
> (Dylan Thomas)

Dylan Thomas uses both metaphors and similes in this passage. Look at these colourful metaphors. The snow is <u>shaken in whitewash buckets</u>. It <u>shawls</u> and <u>swims</u> and <u>grows</u>. It <u>ivied the walls</u>. The trees have <u>arms and hands and bodies</u>. By using these metaphors, Thomas wants to convey the effect of countless white snowflakes swirling down from the sky and covering everything on which they fall.

Thomas also uses two similes. The snow covers the roofs of the houses <u>like a pure and grandfather moss</u>. And the postman, covered in snow, comes through the gate <u>like a dumb, numb thunderstorm</u>.

These metaphors and similes enrich the description by bringing numerous images of association into play. For example, saying that the snow grows like moss conveys a sense of softness and smoothness. It also reminds us of the way in which moss grows slowly, quietly, almost without our noticing it.

Try these

A. Say what the following **metaphors** add to each description.

1. He had a mountain of problems facing him.
2. He was a terrier in the ring.
3. The cold bit into their hands.
4. The sun was splitting the heavens.
5. It was raining cats and dogs.
6. The teacher is a mine of information.
7. The smoke snaked across the sky.
8. He was a fox among chickens.
9. To bring Mary into that company was to put a fox among chickens.
10. She is a dove of peace.

B. Say what the following **similes** add to each description.

1. She was as wise as an owl.
2. The old man was as sly as a fox.
3. The teacher was like a raging bull last Monday.
4. The dress was as white as snow.
5. Her hair shone like gold.
6. He roared like a lion.
7. The girl swam like a fish.
8. He ran like the wind.
9. She was like a fish out of water.
10. He is as stubborn as a mule.

Challenge time

Use metaphors and similes in a description of each of the following.

• Give each description a title.
• Think about both your subject matter and your theme.
• Decide on your intention and the types of connotations you want to use.
• What tone will you use?
• What is your attitude towards your readers?

1. a walk through a heavy downpour of rain
2. a night in a haunted house
3. a camel trek across the desert
4. dinner in an expensive restaurant
5. a wildlife safari in Africa
6. being lost in space
7. trying to cover up breaking your aunt's favourite vase
8. doing the weekly shopping on your own for the first time
9. giving up sweets for Lent
10. your first solo aeroplane flight

STEREOTYPING

A stereotype is an idea about a person, place or thing which becomes fixed in people's minds because of repeated use. Stereotypes are seldom based on facts or someone's personal experience. They usually rely on hear-say and are rarely true-to-life.

A few examples a stereotypes are:
- All Alsatians are vicious.
- All Americans are rich.
- All foreign food is greasy.
- All teenage drivers are careless.

Read the following stereotyped description of a soccer fan. Because of football hooligans, this is what many people think all soccer fans are like. What is your opinion of this stereotype?

Stereotype of a soccer fan

He stood before me in an aggressive pose, his hands tightly clenched. His hair was cut to within a centimetre of his scalp. A small silver ring pierced his right nostril, and rings also dangled from his ear lobes. The red and white scarf of his team was wrapped twice around his bull neck. His fingers glittered with I don't know how many thick rings. He didn't so much speak as make menacing guttural noises.

Try these

Write a short stereotyped description of each of the following.

1. a bully
2. a pop star
3. a miser
4. a football hooligan
5. a bored housewife
6. a vulgar millionaire
7. a nice old lady
8. a cranky shopkeeper
9. a yuppie
10. a coward

QUESTION AND ANSWER

What is the attitude of the London lawyer to the French as revealed in the following two paragraphs? Is there any evidence of stereotyping?

Our friend, the London lawyer, a man steeped in English reserve, was watching what he called 'the antics of the French' from the Fin de Siecle cafe in Cavaillon. It was a market day, and the pavement was a human traffic jam, slow-moving, jostling and chaotic.

'Look over there,' he said, as a car stopped in the middle of the street while the driver got out to embrace an acquaintance, 'they're always mauling each other. See that? Men kissing. Damned unhealthy, if you ask me.' He snorted into his beer, his sense of propriety outraged by such deviant behaviour, as alien to the respectable Anglo-Saxon.

Comment

The writer is using a stereotype of the English in describing the reactions of the London lawyer.

The Englishman is <u>steeped in English reserve.</u> He is very conservative and slow to show his feelings. He doesn't trust anyone who does not share his values and point of view. He likes order and organisation. He is intolerant of customs which are different from his own. He sees himself and his own behaviour as the acceptable 'norm'.

The French are portrayed as very emotional and delighted to show their emotions. Kissing each other on the cheek is a perfectly acceptable form of greeting for French men. For the London lawyer, kissing is only permissible among people of the opposite sex and should not be done in public. He sees it as something which is unhealthy.

THE AUTHOR'S SUCCESS OR FAILURE

How effective do you think the writer is? Has he or she been successful in presenting his/her point of view?

For example, a writer may have set out to describe a family holiday – only to end up telling us about a traffic accident which he/she witnessed. A writer who really makes us think about his or her point of view on a particular topic has been successful. If, however, we end up not caring about the author's point of view, then he/she has failed.

IMPRESSIONS OF THE WRITER

What kind of person comes across to you from the passage?

> Serious?
> Humorous?
> Cheerful?
> Optimistic?
> Depressing?
> Interesting?
> Boring?
> Snobbish?
> Prejudiced?
> Well informed?
> Uninformed?

CRITICAL READING

● ●

In this section, you will be reading a number of extracts from a variety of books. When you have read each passage and answered the questions which follow it, think about the aspects of critical reading which you have learned.

- Subject matter
- Theme
- The author's intention
- Use of language
- Attitude towards the reader
- Stereotyping
- The author's success or failure
- Your impression of the writer

A. Read the following passage carefully and then answer the questions which follow it.

The Visit

Early one morning Pa took his gun and went hunting. He had meant to make the bedstead that day. He had brought in the slabs, when Ma said she had no meat for dinner. So he stood the slabs against the wall and took down his gun.

Jack wanted to go hunting, too. His eyes begged Pa to take him, and whines came up from his chest and <u>quivered</u> in his throat till Laura almost cried with him. But Pa chained him to the stable.

'No, Jack,' Pa said. 'You must stay here and guard the place.' Then he said to Mary and Laura, 'Don't let him loose, girls.'

Poor Jack lay down. It was a disgrace to be chained, and he felt it deeply. He turned his head from Pa and would not watch him going away with the gun on his shoulder. Pa went farther and farther away, till the <u>prairies</u> swallowed him and he was gone.

Laura tried to comfort Jack, but he would not be comforted. The more he thought about the chain, the worse he felt. Laura tried to cheer him up to <u>frisk</u> and play, but he only grew more <u>sullen.</u>

Both Mary and Laura felt that they could not leave Jack while he was so unhappy. So all that morning they stayed by the stable. They stroked Jack's smooth, <u>brindled</u> head and scratched around his ears, and told him how sorry they were that he must be chained. He licked their hands a little bit, but he was very sad and angry.

His head was on Laura's knee and she was talking to him, when he suddenly stood up and growled a fierce, deep growl. The hair on his neck stood straight up and his eyes <u>glared</u> red.

Laura was frightened. Jack had never growled at her before. Then she looked over her shoulder, where Jack was looking, and she saw two naked, wild men coming, one behind the other, on the Indian trail.

'Mary! Look!' she cried. Mary looked and saw them, too.

They were tall, thin, fierce-looking men. Their skin was brownish–red. Their heads seemed to go up to a peak, and the peak was a tuft of hair that stood straight up and ended in feathers. Their eyes were black and still and glittering, like snakes' eyes.

(from Little House on the Prairie
by Laura Ingalls Wilder)

Think about it

1. How does the writer create a sense that something dangerous is about to happen? Refer to specific details from the passage.
2. Describe the relationship between Jack and the two girls.
3. Do you think that the writer portrays the Indians in a stereotyped way? Give reasons for your answer.
4. How would you describe the atmosphere of the passage? How do you think the writer creates that atmosphere?

5. Where does the writer use connotations in this passage? What is the purpose of these connotations?
6. Explain the meaning of the underlined words as they are used in the passage.

B. Read the following passage carefully. Then answer the questions which follow it.

Rockets

Though it seems that the Chinese were the first to build true rockets, the 'principle of reaction' dates back much further in history, even though it was not properly understood. About 360 years before Christ, the Greek scientist Archytas is said to have made a 'flying pigeon'. If our accounts of it are correct, the pigeon itself was made of wood, and did not fly in the real sense of the word. It was hung by means of a cord, and a <u>counterweight</u> was used to make it move in a circle round its point of suspension. What Archytas <u>apparently</u> did was to make use of steam, which was blown out from a hole in the wooden model and made the pigeon 'move'.

Much later, between AD 1700 and 1730, a Dutchman named Jacob s'Gravesande planned the first of all steam cars. This was made up of a metal container mounted on a small truck. The container was filled with water, and steam was produced when the water was heated by a fire underneath it. This steam was allowed to escape through an exhaust hole, and so once again we had a rush of hot gas, which was enough to move the whole vehicle. S'Gravesande seems to have built a model, and he may even have tried to make a full-size steam car, though we cannot be sure.

Of course, it would be easy enough nowadays to build a steam car of this sort, but it would be hopelessly clumsy and <u>inefficient,</u> so that it would be useful only to show the principle of the way in which it moved. Even rocket-engined cars have never been a real success.

Meanwhile, the war rocket was still being talked about, even though the Chinese themselves never developed it further. In a book published in 1405, Konrad von Eichstadt, a German, discussed military rockets in some detail; fifteen years later an Italian engineer, de Fontana, even planned a rocket torpedo. The torpedo was to be painted to look like the head of a sea-monster, and other de Fontana rockets were to be disguised as flying pigeons, running rabbits and floating fish. They were meant to set fire to enemy ships and defences, but it does not seem that de Fontana actually tried to make them, and nobody else followed up his idea.

(from *Rockets and Earth Satellites*
by Patrick Moore)

Think about it

1. Write a summary of this passage. Look back at the suggestions for writing a summary on page 100.
2. Explain how the 'flying pigeon' of Archytas is supposed to have worked.
3. Why does the writer think that it would not be worthwhile nowadays to build a steam car?
4. How would you describe the writer's attitude towards the early inventions he describes?
5. Explain the meanings of the underlined words as they are used in the passage.

C. Read the following passage carefully. Then answer the questions which follow it.

Two Romantic Figures

It's a figure that's known the world over. A man on a horse, wearing a high-crowned, wide-brimmed <u>felt</u> hat. Round his throat is a gay handkerchief, knotted to one side and surmounting the open-necked <u>checkered</u> shirt. Down the sides of the leather overalls that cover his legs and thighs there's a wide fringe, like a row of tiny <u>pennants</u>. There's a <u>glint</u> of spurs above the high-heeled boots. It's that <u>legendary</u> character, the cowboy of the Wild West.

His fame has been carried to every land in films and books, in songs and stories, in countless radio and television programmes. Through them we know of his strength and skill in looking after horses and cattle, and of his <u>prowess</u> in single combat with Indian braves or lawless <u>rustlers.</u> Yet every country has its men who look after horses and cattle. Why should so much romance have grown round the men who carried out these tasks in the western parts of the United States?

The answer is that nowhere in the world were there such opportunities for adventure, excitement and colourful incidents as there in the great open spaces of North America's Western states. They began when these territories were being opened up; and they continued with all the developments through the years. The story goes back to the days just before the early years of the nineteenth century. And it begins with that other romantic figure – the Redskin.

Cowboys and Indians! The names are inseparably linked in the history of the West. Long before the cowboy invaded the rolling plains, the American Indian roamed and hunted over them. But over the years the 'cattle-kingdoms' grew and the Red Man's hunting-grounds <u>diminished</u>. Today the Indians have their reservations, where they can keep up their ancestral customs. Many of them, of course, live the same life as other citizens of the United States. The pure Indian race, however, is dying out. But the stories of their battles and the legends of their tribes will continue to be told.

(from *The True Book about Cowboys*
by Ross Salmon)

Think about it

1. Write a summary of this passage.
2. Why does the writer think that the cowboy of the Wild West became a romantic figure?
3. What does the writer tell us about American Indians today?
4. The writer presents cowboys and Indians in slightly different ways. Do you think he is fair to both of them? Explain.
5. How do you think a modern North American Indian would react to this passage? Give reasons for your answer.
6. Explain the meanings of the underlined words as they are used in this passage.

D. Read carefully the following passage and then answer the questions which follow it.

An Adventure Begins

My story of Ben starts on the 22nd of June, 1890. Ben's own story had begun some four or five months earlier, in the den where his mother, who was a Black Bear, had spent the winter; but although I came to know Ben rather intimately later on, he never spoke of his early childhood to me and I never asked him about it. So we'll take that for granted.

Early in May of that year, three of us, Martin Spencer, Jack O'Brien and myself, had set out from Spokane, Washington, to hunt Grizzlies and prospect for gold in the rugged and, at that time, largely unexplored Bitter Root Mountains in Idaho. We had a small pack train and a large stock of enthusiasm, and we arrived at the foothills with both in good condition. But although it was well past the middle of the month when we reached the mountains, we soon found ourselves floundering in snowdrifts that increased in depth as we climbed, and when, for several days on end, we had cut our way with a two-handed saw through fallen trees that barred our progress and had dug the saddle and pack horses out of pot holes in the snow into which a misstep or an act of deliberate stupidity had sent them rolling, both men and horses had become exhausted. And so, when a cold storm had added itself to our other troubles, we had pitched camp in a little opening facing the south and settled down to wait for better days. And we had waited there three solid weeks.

Once, on the morning of the 19th of June, dawn had shown us a clear sky, against which, fifty miles to the east of us, we could see the main range of the jagged Bitter Roots; and after a cheerful breakfast we had hastily broken camp, packed our horses, and started for the summit of the ridge along which we proposed to travel. But here, roaring up out of the next valley, we had met another great storm of icy wind and swirling snow, and I had soon been forced to leave my companions with the horses while I stumbled down the mountain and hunted up another sheltered spot where we could take refuge from the huge storm. And so by noon we had once more found ourselves crowded under a hemlock bark lean-to, thankfully facing a blazing fire of logs and listening to the wind howling overhead. And it was not until the afternoon of the twenty-first that the storm had passed. Then at last the sun had come out hot and clear and had begun forcing the great masses of snow that clung to the limbs of the trees to loosen their grip so that the forest was filled with the splash of their falling, while laden bushes jerked their heads free from the weight that bore them down and the horses stood steaming with the warm air.

(from *A Century of Nature Stories*, edited by J.W. Robertson)

Think about it

1. Summarise the events described in this passage.
2. Why were the three prospectors delayed in their journey for three solid weeks?
3. What kind of life do you think prospectors had in those times?
4. How would you describe the attitude of the narrator towards his experiences?
5. Comment on the writer's use of words to convey the harshness of the life which he experienced.
6. What impression do you form of the narrator's personality? Cheerful? Pessimistic? Courageous? Give reasons for your answer.
7. Explain the meanings of the underlined words as they are used in the passage.

E. Read the following passage carefully. Then answer the questions which follow it.

The Birdman of Rushy Bay

Rushy Bay was forbidden territory to us, along with most of the west coast of Bryher. The pool under Gweal Hill and the beach on Pollestones beyond was as far as any of us children were allowed to go in that direction. We never asked why, for we did not have to. We all knew well enough that the west coast of the island was dangerous, far too dangerous for children, whatever the weather. Mother and father reminded me repeatedly about it, and they were right to do so. At Shipman's Head and Hell Bay there were black cliffs hundreds of feet high that rose <u>sheer</u> from the <u>churning</u> sea below. Here even on the calmest of days the waves could sweep you off the rocks and take you out to sea. I had been there often enough, but always with father. We used to go there for firewood, collecting the <u>driftwood</u> off the rocky beaches and dragging it above the high-water mark to claim it for our own; or we would go for the seaweed, piling the cart high with it before going back home to dress the flower pieces or the potato fields. But I never went alone over to that side of the island; none of us ever did.

There was another more <u>compelling</u> reason though why we children were warned away from Rushy Bay and Droppynose Point and the west coast of the island, for this was the side of the island most <u>frequented</u> by the Birdman of Bryher. He was the only one who lived on that side of the island. He lived in the only house facing out over the west coast, a long, low thatched cottage on Heathy Hill overlooking Rushy Bay itself. No one ever went near him and no one ever spoke to him. Like all the other children on the island, Daniel and I had learnt from the cradle that the Birdman was to be avoided. Some said the Birdman was mad. Some said he was the devil himself, that he fed on dogs and cats, and that he would put spells and curses on you if you came too close.

The little I saw of the Birdman was enough to convince me that all the stories we heard about him must be true. He was more like an owl, a flitting creature of the dark, the dawn and the dusk. He would be seen outside only rarely in the daylight, perhaps out in his rowing boat around the island or sitting high on his cart; and even in the hottest summers he would always wear a black cape over his shoulders and a pointed black <u>sou'wester</u> on his head. From a distance you could hear him talking loudly to himself in a strange, <u>unearthly monotone</u>. Maybe it was not to himself that he talked but to the <u>kittiwake</u> that sat always on his shoulder or to the black jack donkey that pulled his cart wherever he went, or maybe it was to the great woolly dog with the greying muzzle that loped along beside him. The Birdman went everywhere barefoot, even in winter, a stooped black figure that <u>lurched</u> as he walked, one step always shorter than the other. And wherever he went he would be surrounded by a flock of screaming seagulls that circled and floated above him, tirelessly <u>vigilant</u>, almost as if they were protecting him. He rarely spoke to anyone, indeed he scarcely even looked at anyone.

(from *Why the Whales Came*
by Michael Morpurgo)

Think about it

1. What is the gist of this passage?
2. How would you describe the boy's attitude towards the Birdman? Do you think the boy's attitude is the same as that of the adults?
3. What kind of community lifestyle do you think the writer conveys?
4. Invent a story which explains why people see the Birdman as they do.
5. What details (images, words etc.) does the writer use to convey the mystery of the Birdman?
6. How would you describe the atmosphere of the passage? How does the writer create that atmosphere?
7. Explain the meanings of the underlined words as they are used in this passage.

F. Read the following passage carefully. Then answer the questions which follow it.

Not a Typical Family

I'd better start by telling you a bit about our family. It's not a typical family — whatever that is. What I mean is we're not like my friend Morag's family which consists of her and her brother and wee sister and their mother and father. Her father lives at home all the time and has a job with a monthly <u>salary</u>, and they have two colour tellies, a video recorder, a home computer, a deep-freeze the size of a caravan, a microwave, and a dishwasher.

We don't have many of those things.

In our family there's me, Sam (short for Samantha), and my brother Seb (short of Sebastian) and our father Torquil who comes and goes and is employed off and on (mostly off) and our mother Isabella who runs a second-hand clothes shop in a basement across the road from our flat. As you can imagine, that doesn't bring in a fortune! We have one telly that's <u>on the blink</u> half the time and needs to be thumped to settle down, no video, no computer, no freezer, no microwave. And Seb and I are the dishwashers.

But we do have a granny. And she's certainly part of the family! She lives round the corner.

Well, *normally* she does. But things weren't quite normal at present, as she was staying in our flat to 'keep an eye on us' while our parents were away. Round the corner is a much better place for our grandmother, as far as Seb and I are concerned. Glasgow would be even better since it's more than forty miles from Edinburgh and not even she, with her long-range sight, would be able to see what we were up to from there. But perhaps I shouldn't wish her on Glasgow. I've nothing against the place after all.

Bella and Torquil had gone off to wander round the Greek islands. We'd had postcards from them from all over the Aegean Sea. It looked as if they were <u>lurching</u> about like a couple of drunken sailors, Granny said. They'd been gone for two months and in five days' time we were due to fly out to Athens to join them for half-term. We would then take a boat to one of the islands.

'I think Naxos could be OK,' I said.

OK! The very thought of it thrilled me. You see, Seb and I had never been abroad, unlike everyone else who's been to Spain,

Cyprus, Malta, Turkey ... You name it, somebody in my class has been there. I was torn between the islands of Ios and Naxos, was busy studying them on the atlas. Morag had said that Corfu was nice, she'd had a great time there, but it sounded rather <u>hectic</u> to me, with discos going non-stop and <u>lager louts</u> chucking their tins about, and although I like people and lots of things happening, I fancied a bit of quiet for our week's holiday. Our family can make enough noise on its own.

(from *Glad Rags* by Joan Lingard)

Think about it

1. What is your impression of the way of life described in this passage?
2. Do you think that the narrator accepts her own lack of advantages as compared with those of her friend Morag? Is she envious or does she not seem to care?
3. Is there any evidence of stereotyping by the writer, or do you think she is being true to life? Give reasons for your answer.
4. Comment on the conversational style of writing used. Do you think it adds to your enjoyment of reading? How?
5. What is the writer's attitude towards her parents? Do you find it convincing?
6. Humour is an important appeal of this passage. Show how this humour works.
7. Explain the meaning of the underlined words as they are used the passage.

G. Read the following passage carefully. Then answer the questions which follow it.

Mother and Son

I wanted a mouth-organ, I wanted it more than anything else in the whole world. I told my mother. She kept ignoring me but I still wanted a mouth-organ badly.

I was only a boy. I didn't have a proper job. Going to school was like a job, but nobody paid me to go to school. Again I had to say to my mother, 'Mum, will you please buy a mouth-organ for me?'

It was the first time now, that my mother stood and answered me properly. Yet listen to what my mother said. 'What d'you want a mouth-organ for?'

'All the other boys have a mouth-organ, Mum,' I told her.

'Why is that so important? You don't have to have something just because others have it.'

'They won't have me with them without a mouth-organ, Mum,' I said.

'They'll soon change their minds, Delroy.'

'They won't, Mum. They really won't. You don't know Wildo Harris. He never changes his mind. And he never lets any other boy change his mind either.'

'Delroy, I haven't got the time to argue with you. There's no money to buy a mouth-organ. I bought you new shoes and clothes for Independence Celebrations. Remember?'

'Yes, mam.'

'Well, money doesn't come on trees.'

'No, mam.' I had to agree.

'It's school-day. The sun won't stand still for you. Go and feed the fowls. Afterwards milk the goat. Then get yourself ready for school.'

She sent me off. I had to go and do my morning jobs.

(from *A Thief in the Village* by James Berry)

Think about it

1. How would you describe the boy's relationship with his mother? Support your answer with specific references to the passage.
2. What kind of setting and social background does the passage suggest to you? Give reasons for your answer.
3. Describe how you think Delroy gets on with his friends.
4. How effectively do you think the language or style of the passage suits the writer's subject matter?

H. Read the following passage carefully and then answer the questions which follow it.

Trial by Water

When the water came it was different from other times. I could hear a roaring of water approaching even above the noise of the wind in the trees and then suddenly it was rushing around the trunk of the tree and pouring over the lower branches. I mean, it didn't rise slowly like the other floods I'd seen; it was halfway up the trunk all at once and I was wet with <u>spray</u> in the highest branches. And then the whole tree seemed to be moving. Yes, I know the branches had been moving but now I had the feeling that everything was slowly <u>toppling</u>, and then I was in the water though I was still holding the branch. And now it was the water instead of the wind trying to <u>tear</u> me off the branch, even the rough bark was hurting the skin on my chest and arms as I clung for my life. I struggled and reached for branches above me, caught one and pulled myself clear of the water. There were great salt waves washing over the tree. I could taste them and my eyes stung as I tried to climb above them. The tree was lying right over on its side, and climbing it was different. I reached a branch that was clear of the waves and clung on with my arms and legs.

The water didn't seem to be rushing round the trunk as it had been and in the darkness the tops of the other trees seemed to be moving away. Then I knew I was afloat, and alone in the darkness and the storm.

How should I know how long I floated, or how far? All I knew was that I must hang on. Though the <u>current</u> didn't drag at the tree, now that we were floating along with it, the wind still tugged at me and the spray broke over me. The night seemed without end. I even thought that perhaps the sun had been washed away too and it would never return.

I don't know how I got the feeling that I was always moving through the water, <u>voyaging</u> like a ship through the night. I can only remember the darkness of the sky and the blacker darkness of the waves, but perhaps I did see solid things that stayed still while I moved past them. They must have been the tops of palm trees that were still hanging on to the earth with their roots while the water <u>swirled</u> around them.

Then I think I remember feeling I must be dead or that everything had come to an end, because the wind died down and the waves stopped tearing at me and when I looked up I saw the stars. But all around me was darkness and water and all I could do was lie exhausted on my branch. I was nowhere and there was nothing I could do.

(from *The Night the Water Came* by Clive King)

Think about it

1. How does the narrator convey the drama of his situation? Point to specific uses of language.
2. How effectively do you think the narrator describes his dilemma? Do you think he includes too many details in his description? Give reasons for your answer.

3. How convincing is the narrator's description of the storm?
4. In what kind of background do you think the storm is taking place? Give reasons for your answer.
5. Explain the meanings of the underlined words as they are used in the passage.

I. Read the following passage carefully. Then answer the questions which follow it.

Life on the Housing Estate

Monday March 30th

A terrible thing happened last night. My father and Mr Lucas had a fight in the *front* garden, and the whole street came outside to watch! My mother tried to separate them but they both told her to 'keep out of it'. Mr O'Leary tried to help my father, he kept shouting 'Give the smarmy bugger one for me, George'. Mrs O'Leary was shouting horrible things at my mother. By the sound of things she had been watching my mother's movements since Christmas. The civilised meeting broke up at about five o'clock when my father found out how long my mother and Mr Lucas had been in love.

They had another civilised meeting at about seven o'clock, but when my mother disclosed that she was leaving for Sheffield with Mr Lucas, my father became uncivilised and starting fighting. Mr Lucas ran into the garden but my father rugby-tackled him by the laurel bush and the fight broke out again. It was quite exciting really. I had a good view from my bedroom window. Mrs O'Leary said, ''Tis the child I feel sorry for', and all the people looked up and saw me, so I looked especially sad. I expect the experience will give me a trauma at some stage in the future. I'm all right at the moment, but you never know.

Tuesday March 31st

My mother has gone to Sheffield with Mr Lucas. She had to drive because Mr Lucas couldn't see out of his black eyes. I have informed the school secretary of my mother's desertion. She was very kind and gave me a form to give to my father; it is for free school dinners. We are now a single-parent family.

Nigel has asked Barry Kent to stop menacing me for a few weeks. Barry Kent said he would think about it.

(from *The Secret Diary of Adrian Mole Aged 13¾* by Sue Townsend)

Think about it

1. Comment on the humour of this passage. Do you think the humour depends on the style of writing?
2. What kind of social background does the passage suggest? Give reasons for your answer.
3. Does the picture of Adrian Mole in this passage give you the impression of a real–life character?
4. How would you describe the author's attitude towards her characters? Give reasons for your answer.
5. How does Adrian Mole's innocence and humour connect with the world in which he has to survive?

J. Read the following passage carefully. Then answer the questions which follow it.

Behind the Battle–lines

We are at rest five miles behind the front. Yesterday we were relieved, and now our bellies are full of beef and beans. We are satisfied and at peace. Each man has another meal-tin full for the evening; and, what is more, there is a double hand-out of sausage and bread. That does a lot for a man. We have not had such luck as this for a long time. The cook is begging us to eat. He does not see how he can empty his pan in time for coffee. Tjaden and Muller have produced two wash-basins and had them filled up to the top. In Tjaden, this is greed, in Muller, it is looking ahead. Where Tjaden puts it all is a mystery, for he is, and always will be, as thin as a bean-pole.

We have a mistake to thank for all this. Fourteen days ago we had to go up and relieve the front line. It was fairly quiet where we were, so the officer had ordered the usual quantity of food for the full company of one hundred and fifty men. But on the last day an astonishing number of English guns shot at our position, so that we suffered severely. And came back only eighty strong.

Last night we moved back and settled down to get a good sleep for once: Katczinsky is right when he says it would not be such a bad war if only one could get a little more sleep. In the line we have had next to none, and fourteen days is a long time at one stretch.

It was noon before the first of us crawled out of bed. Half an hour later, every man had his meal-tin and we gathered at the cook-house, which smelt good. At the head of the queue of course were the hungriest – little Albert Kropp, the clearest thinker among us; Muller, who still carries his school-books with him, and dreams of examinations; Leer, who wears a full beard, and is one for the women; and the fourth, myself, Paul Baumer. We are nineteen years of age, and all four joined up from the same class as volunteers for the war. Close behind us were our friends: Tjaden, the biggest eater of the company; Haie Westhus, who can hold a whole loaf in his hand and say: Guess what I've got in my hand; then Detering, who thinks of nothing but his farm, and his wife; and finally Stanislaus

Katczinsky, the leader of our group, cunning, tough-minded, forty years of age, with a face of the soil, blue eyes, bent shoulders, and a remarkable nose for bad weather, good food, and soft jobs.

We were growing impatient, for the cook paid no attention to us. Finally Katczinsky called to him: 'Open up the kitchen, Heinrich. Anyone can see the beans are done.'

He shook his head: 'You must all be there first.'

Tjaden grinned: 'We are all here.'

The cook took no notice: 'You might be,' he said. 'But where are the others?'

'They won't be fed by you today. They're either wounded or dead.'

The cook was quite put out as he learned the facts. He was amazed. 'And I have cooked for one hundred and fifty men.'

Kropp poked him in the ribs. 'Then for once we'll have enough. Come on, begin.'

Suddenly Tjaden went into a dream. His eyes grew small with cunning, and he whispered hoarsely: 'Then you got bread for one hundred and fifty men too, eh?'

The cook nodded absent-mindedly. Tjaden seized him by the clothes. 'And sausage?' The cook nodded again. 'Tobacco too?'

'Yes, everything.'

Tjaden beamed: 'What a feast! That's all for us! Each man gets – wait a bit – yes, almost double the amount!'

Then the cook stirred himself and said: 'That won't do. Eighty men can't have what is meant for a hundred and fifty.'

We got excited and began to crowd around. Katczinsky got angry. 'You might be generous for once. You haven't drawn food for eighty men. You've drawn it for the Second Company. Good. Let's have it then. We are the Second Company.'

We began to push the fellow. No one felt kindly towards him, for it was his fault that the food often came up to us in the line too late and too cold. There would certainly have been a fight if our Company Commander had not appeared. He learnt the facts of the argument, and only remarked: 'Yes, we did have heavy losses yesterday.' He glanced in the pot. 'The beans look good.' He looked at us. He knew what we were thinking. He lifted the lid again, and sniffed. Then passing on he said: 'Bring me a plateful. Serve it all out. We can do with it.'

(from *All Quiet on the Western Front* by Erich Maria Remarque)

Think about it

1. There is a sharp contrast between the horror of the war and the very human act of food-sharing which this scene describes. What effect do you think the writer is aiming at by doing this? Do you think he achieves his intention? Give reasons for your answer.
2. What kind of person do you think the narrator, Paul Baumer, is?
3. In supplying the reader with snippets of detail about the other characters who are his friends, what is the narrator trying to tell the reader?
4. What does the scene in this passage tells us about the effect of war on people?
5. In the last paragraph, the narrator remarks that the Company Commander 'knew what we were thinking'. What, in fact, did the Company Commander know? Give reasons for your answer.

K. Read the following passage carefully. Then answer the questions which follow it.

A Mysterious Character

In the late spring of 1930 Philip Rhayader came to the <u>abandoned</u> lighthouse at the mouth of the Aelder. He bought the light and many acres of marshland and salting surrounding it.

He lived and worked there alone the year round. He was a painter of birds and of nature, who, for reasons, had withdrawn from all human society. Some of the reasons were <u>apparent</u> on his fortnightly visits to the little village of Chelmbury for supplies, where the natives <u>looked askance</u> at his mis-shapen body and dark <u>visage</u>. For he was a hunchback and his left arm was crippled, thin and bent at the wrist, like the claw of a bird.

They soon became used to his queer figure, small but powerful, the massive, dark, bearded head set just slightly below the mysterious mound on his back, the glowing eyes and the clawed hand, and marked him off as 'that queer painter chap that lives down to lighthouse'.

Physical deformity often breeds hatred of humanity in men. Rhayader did not hate; he loved very greatly – man, the animal kingdom, and all nature. His heart was filled with pity and understanding. He had mastered his handicap, but he could not master the <u>rebuffs</u> he suffered, due to his appearance. The thing that drove him into <u>seclusion</u> was his failure to find anywhere a return of the warmth that flowed from him. He repelled women. Men would have warmed to him had they got to know him. But the mere fact that an effort was being made hurt Rhayader and drove him to avoid the person making it.

He was twenty-seven when he came to the Great Marsh. He had travelled much and fought <u>valiantly</u> before he made the decision to withdraw from a world in which he could not take part as other men. For all the artist's <u>sensitivity</u> and woman's tenderness locked in his barrel breast, he was very much a man.

(from *The Snow Goose* by Paul Gallico)

Think about it

1. How would you describe the attitude of the writer towards the character of Philip Rhayader?
2. What details does the writer use to create an atmosphere of mystery about his character?
3. Why do you think Philip Rhayader's heart was 'filled with pity and understanding'?
4. Why do you think Philip Rhayader might prefer nature to human society?
5. Explain the meanings of the underlined words as they are used in the passage.

L. Read the following passage carefully. Then answer the questions which follow it.

Who are the Borrowers?

At the time, Kate never doubted their existence – a race of tiny creatures, as like to humans as makes no matter, who live their secret lives under the floors and behind the wainscot of certain quiet old houses. It was only later that she began to wonder ...

The original story had smacked of hearsay: Mrs May admitted – in fact, had been at some pains to convince Kate – that she, Mrs May, had never actually seen a borrower herself; any knowledge of such beings she had gained at second hand from her younger brother, who she admitted was a little boy with not only a vivid imagination but well known to be a tease. So there you were, Kate decided – thinking it over afterwards – you could take it or leave it.

And, truth to tell, in the year or so which followed, Kate tended rather to leave it: the story of the borrowers became pushed away in the back of her mind with other childish fantasies. During this year she changed her school, made new friends, acquired a dog, took up skating, and learned to ride a bicycle. And

there was no thought of 'borrowers' in Kate's mind (nor did she notice the undercurrent of excitement in Mrs May's usually calm voice) when, one morning at breakfast in early spring, Mrs May passed a letter across the table, saying: 'This will interest you, Kate, I think.'

It didn't interest Kate a bit (she was about eleven years old at the time): she read it through twice in a bewildered kind of way but could make neither head nor tail of it. It was a lawyer's letter from a firm called Jobson, Thring, Beguid & Beguid; not only was it full of long words like 'beneficiary' and 'disentailment' but even the medium-sized words were arranged in such a manner that, to Kate, they made no sense at all (what, for instance, could 'vacant possession' mean? ...)

Names there were in plenty – Studdington, Goodenough, Amberforce, Pocklinton – and quite a family of people who spelled their name 'deceased' with a small 'd'.

'Thank you very much,' Kate had said politely, passing it back.

'I thought perhaps,' said Mrs May (and her cheeks, Kate noticed, looked slightly flushed as though with shyness), 'you might like to go down with me.'

'Go down where?' asked Kate, in her vaguest manner.

'My dear Kate,' exclaimed Mrs May, 'what was the point of showing you the letter? To Leighton Buzzard, of course.'

Leighton Buzzard? Years afterwards, when Kate described this scene to her children, she would tell them how, at these words, her heart began to bump long before her mind took in their meaning: Leighton Buzzard ... she knew the name, of course: the name of an English country town ... somewhere in Bedfordshire, wasn't it?

'Where Great-aunt Sophy's house was,' said Mrs May, prompting her. 'Where my brother used to say he saw the borrowers.' And before Kate could get back her breath she went on, in a matter-of-fact voice: 'I have been left a little cottage, part of the Studdington estate, and,' her colour deepened as though what she was about to say now might sound slightly incredible, 'three hundred and fifty-five pounds. Enough,' she added, in happy wonderment, 'to do it up.'

Kate was silent. She stared at Mrs May, her clasped hands pressed against her middle as though to still the beat of her heart.

'Could we see the house?' she said at last, a kind of croak in her voice.

'Of course, that's why we're going.'

(from *The Borrowers Afield* by Mary Norton)

Think about it

1. What impression do you form of the relationship between Kate and the old lady, Mrs May, who lives in her house?

2. How does the writer create a sense of mystery surrounding the 'borrowers'? Give examples from this extract.

3. How would you describe the tone of this passage? Does the writer have a particular readership in mind? Give reasons for your answer.

4. What impression do you form of Mrs May? Your answer should be based entirely on this passage.

5. How does the writer create a sense of suspense or a 'read-on' interest in her story?

6. Explain the meanings of the underlined words as they are used in the passage.

M. Read the following passage carefully. Then answer the questions which follow it.

Dr Livingstone's Mission

The buildings of the mission station at Kuruman, which Livingstone found upon his arrival there, stood in splendid contrast to their surroundings in a sparsely-populated, parched region of Bechuanaland, where little grew naturally except stunted thorn-bushes. The church was spacious and solid, and built of stone with high-pitched gables. Nearby stood the low, wide-eaved houses of the staff and the huts of the native servants. There were workshops, a forge and a cattle-pen, and an irrigated garden which produced fine crops of peaches, apricots, pomegranates, grapes, and such vegetables as the yellow soil of Kuruman could be made to produce.

To Dr Livingstone, however, such things meant little. With the zeal and impatience of a young man, he felt that with so much to be done in Africa it was a pity that so much effort was wasted on a thinly-populated area. His own thoughts dwelt upon the almost unknown regions to the north, where he remembered Robert Moffat telling him he had sometimes seen, in the morning-sun, the smoke of a thousand villages in which no missionary had ever set foot.

This region was the home of several Bechuana tribes and Livingstone was impatient to get to know them. He had, however, been given instructions to wait at Kuruman until Moffat, the superintendent of the mission at Kuruman, returned from leave. So, for a time, he busied himself with the affairs of the station. There was always a great deal to do, and, as his fame as a doctor spread, natives, whose tribal lore led them to believe that there was a 'medicine' for every kind of trouble, came from far and wide to seek his help.

(from *With Livingstone in South Africa* by George Morey)

Think about it

1. Why was Dr Livingstone not content to stay at the mission station of Kuruman?

2. What work did Dr Livingstone do at Kuruman that would be of great assistance to him in his later missionary work? Why do you think this was so?

3. Describe what you think Livingstone's attitude was towards the native Africans.

4. What details, if any, in this passage do you think might give offence to modern day Africans? Give reasons for your answer.

5. Write a summary of the above account of Dr Livingstone in about a third of its present length.

6. Explain the meanings of the underlined words as they are used in the passage.

N. Read the following passage carefully. Then answer the questions which follow it.

Boss Buck

Buck did not read the newspaper, or he would have known that trouble was brewing, not alone for himself, but for every tide-water dog, strong of muscle and with warm, long hair, from Puget Sound to San Diego. Because men, groping in the Arctic darkness, had found a yellow metal, and because steamship and transportation companies were <u>booming</u> the find, thousands of men were rushing into the Northland. These men wanted dogs, and the dogs they wanted were heavy dogs, with strong muscles by which to toil, and furry coats to protect them from the frost.

Buck lived at a big house in the sun-kissed Santa Clara Valley. Judge Miller's place, it was called. It stood back from the road, half hidden among the trees, through which glimpses could be caught of the wide cool <u>veranda</u> that ran around its four sides. The house was approached by gravelled driveways which wound about through wide-spreading lawns and under the <u>interlacing</u> boughs of tall <u>poplars.</u> At the rear, things were on an even more spacious scale than at the front. There were great stables, where a dozen <u>grooms</u> and boys held forth, rows of vine-clad servants' cottages, an endless and orderly array of outhouses, long grape arbours, green pastures, orchards, and berry patches. Then there was the pumping plant for the <u>artesian well,</u> and the big cement tank where Judge Miller's boys took their morning plunge and kept cool in the hot afternoon.

And over this great <u>demesne</u> Buck ruled. Here he was born, and here had lived the four years of his life. It was true, there were other dogs. There could not but be other dogs on so vast a place, but they did not count. They came and went, resided in the <u>populous</u> kennels, or lived obscurely in the <u>recesses</u> of the house after the fashion of Toots, the Japanese pug, or Ysabel, the Mexican hairless — strange creatures that rarely put nose out of doors or set foot to ground. On the other hand, there were the fox terriers, a score of them at least, who yelped fearful promises at Toots and Ysabel, looking out of the windows and protected by a legion of housemaids armed with brooms and mops.

But Buck was neither house-dog nor kennel-dog. The whole realm was his. He plunged into the swimming tank or went hunting with the Judge's sons; he escorted Mollie and Alice, the Judge's daughters, on long twilight or early morning rambles; on wintry nights he lay at the Judge's feet before the roaring library fire; he carried the Judge's grandsons on his back, or rolled them in the grass, and guarded their footsteps through wild adventures down to the fountain in the stable yard, and even beyond, where the paddocks were, and the berry patches. Among the terriers he stalked <u>imperiously,</u> and Toots and Ysabel he utterly ignored, for he was king – king over all creeping, crawling, flying things of Judge Miller's place, humans included.

(from *The Call of the Wild* by Jack London)

Think about it

1. What details in this passage help to establish the importance of Buck's position on Judge Miller's place?

2. Although the writer is writing about dogs, he seems to have some human types in mind as well. What kind of people do you think he has in mind? Do you think there is any sexist bias in his presentation of these characters?

3. Describe the writer's attitude towards Buck. Do you find it admiring or in any way critical? Use specific references to the passage in your answer.

4. Instead of instantly giving the reader a description of Judge Miller's place, the author first gives some details which prepare the plot and arouse the reader's interest. What are these details?

5. Explain the meanings of the underlined words as they are used in this passage.

O. Read the following passage carefully. Then answer the questions which follow it.

A Stranger in Ballinamore

The man chose a dark corner of the pub and pushed his knapsack under the table. He sat down quickly and <u>hunched</u> over his drink as if to <u>ward off</u> the curious stares of the townsmen. Strangers were seldom seen in Ballinamore but this man drew even more attention than most. Judging by the dusty state of his clothes and the small instrument cradled under his arm, he was a travelling musician; but though he was shabby

and <u>unkempt,</u> his face shone pale and intelligent beneath the black frame of his hair and beard. His eyes were a startling grey colour, <u>flickering</u> over the room like a candle, one moment cloudy and <u>withdrawn,</u> the next <u>luminous,</u> almost white, with a strange intensity.

The townsmen disliked him instantly, though they didn't really know why, and without so much as the <u>customary</u> nod or 'good-day' they turned their backs on him and <u>resumed</u> their conversations. Standing by the bar, Patsy shook his head a little sadly. He liked the look of the man and hoped there might be a song or a story to hear. Patsy's farm was more than a mile from the town but he would walk the distance after a day's work to have a quiet drink and collect the news. If he were lucky, something interesting might happen, something to think about when he was working in the fields all day. He nodded to the barman for two pints of beer and carried them over to the stranger. The man glared up at him, but Patsy placed the drinks on the table and sat down.

'You needn't talk to me if you don't want to,' he said easily. 'I'm on my way home soon enough.'

The stranger looked him over carefully, then relaxed, and Patsy knew he was accepted as company.

'You've been travelling, I'd say.'

'I have. For many years now,' the man said.

Patsy hardly had time to note the pleasant lilt of his voice, when the man suddenly stiffened and glared at the men at the bar.

'Fools!' he hissed. 'What do they think they are talking about?'

His face <u>contorted</u> with anger and the harsh change in his manner gave Patsy a start. The farmer leaned forward to listen to John-Joe McGovern's arguing with his friend.

'Go 'way now, Ben, you're coddin' yourself. The bull was brown like the old book says,' John-Joe repeated with his usual air of absolute knowledge.

'And I say it was red. Red as blood,' his friend contended.

'Oh do you now?' John-Joe said with a look of mischief. 'And would you say the Great Queen had a red bull to match the colour of her *hair*? Is that what you're saying?'

The other men burst out laughing even as Patsy did. He knew they were arguing about an old legend of the area, and that this particular subject was a favourite of John-Joe's and Ben's, a regular contest of wits that amused them and anyone else who listened.

Patsy turned back to the stranger in surprise.

'Sure it's only talk. A bit of crack.'

'Talk? They can make a joke of things they know nothing about? They laugh in their own ignorance, these little men of the house and pavement ...' He would have continued but for the slow hardening of Patsy's eyes.

'You're speakin' badly of people who have done you no harm,' the farmer said quietly.

The stranger turned away and <u>brooded</u> over his drink. He began to mutter under his breath. Patsy sat back feeling slightly annoyed with him, but after a while his annoyance switched to John-Joe and Ben. They *were* talking a lot of rubbish, he thought to himself, and the more it went on the more it bothered him. He began to feel restless, and he looked out the window at the darkening streets and decided to head home.

(from *The Druid's Tune* by Orla Melling)

Think about it

1. How does the writer create an air of mystery around the stranger?
2. What qualities distinguish Patsy from the other men at the bar?

3. What is it about the stranger that makes the townsmen dislike him instantly?
4. How well does the writer set the scene which is described in the passage?
5. How effective is the writer's use of dialogue to describe the characters and advance the plot?
6. Explain the meanings of the underlined words as they are used in the passage.

P. Read the following passage carefully. Then answer the questions which follow it

There's a fox on the prowl

A cold east wind blew in across the meadows, stirring the clumps of <u>withered</u> grass that rose above the patches of crisp snow. It whistled through the leafless trees at the top of the rise and ruffled the feathers of a <u>rook</u> that still preferred the top-most branches to a more friendly patch farther down. In the hedgerow beneath, a single robin bared his red breast to the wind for a moment before turning tail and hopping off about his business.

The wind curled through the dead leaves behind the hedge and around the foot of the trees, and now and then it flicked up a leaf and <u>impaled</u> it on a <u>scraggy</u> hawthorn branch or on a strand of barbed wire. For a moment a <u>yellowhammer</u> flitted through a clump of gorse, lending a flash of colour to a bush that wouldn't flower more fully until the approach of Easter. Then, sensing that the gorse was already occupied, it <u>beat a hasty retreat</u>.

The soft belly of the young dog fox rose and fell as he lay in the undergrowth. His legs were wet and muddy, for he had travelled far, and each panted breath <u>misted</u> warmly for a moment before being taken away by the cold wind. There was a lean, hungry look about him, a look not accounted for by his lack of years. It had been a hard year, and it was getting harder. His black ears twitched to every sound, and the sharp, vertical pupils of his eyes missed nothing as he looked across the bleak, wintry landscape.

'I could have told him he was wasting his time,' thought the young fox. Not that he would have. He just felt <u>resentful</u> that the big bird had gone off. He had been down there and he knew there was nothing in it for him. It was too cold and hard, so the <u>snipe</u> and the ducks hadn't come in to feed. If they didn't eat there, neither did he.

He was more interested in the house to the right. There was a stack of turf at the back, a line of washing, and a dog. There was always a dog. Not that it mattered, as the house had no hens that he could see. What held his attention was the brightly-lit room.

A fire was burning in the grate, and a man and a woman and several children were sitting around a table eating. The young fox licked his lips at the sight of the food, but it was the brightly-coloured lights flashing on and off that caught his eye. Tempting though the food was, the flashing lights stirred an even deeper <u>instinct</u> in his mind. Somewhere in his <u>sub-conscious</u> they awakened the realisation that the time of greatest danger had come. He may not have understood that for humans, the flashing red lights <u>signalled</u> peace and goodwill. He did know that for him, they heralded the days when man would deal out most death to his fellow creatures.

The young fox <u>eased</u> himself up, and with a flick of a tail that was tipped with black, turned around and headed for the high country.

(from *Run With the Wind* by Tom McCaughren)

Think about it

1. How does the writer create an effective setting for the story? Point out the words and images which you consider effective.
2. How well do you think the writer knows the countryside which he is describing? How can you tell this?
3. What do you think is the writer's attitude towards wildlife in general? Refer to specific details in the passage.
4. How convincing do you find the writer's understanding of the fox's behaviour? Give reasons for your answer.
5. Explain the meanings of the underlined words as they are used in the passage.

Q. Read the following passage carefully and then answer the questions which follow it.

School Life

The children ate lunch at their desks. The county had been promising Lark Creek a lunchroom for twenty years, but there never seemed to be enough money. Jesse had been so careful not to lose his <u>recess time</u> that even now he chewed his bologna sandwich with his lips tight shut and his eyes on the initialed heart. Around him conversations <u>buzzed</u>. They were not supposed to talk during lunch, but it was the first day and even Monster-Mouth Myers shot fewer flames on the first day.

'She's eating clabber.' Two seats up from where he sat, Mary Lou Peoples was at work being the second snottiest girl in the fifth grade.

'Yogurt, stupid. Don't you watch TV?' This from Wanda Kay Moore, the <u>snottiest</u>, who sat immediately in front of Jes.

'Yuk.'

Lord, why couldn't they leave people in peace? Why shouldn't Leslie Burke eat anything she durn pleased?

He forgot that he was trying to eat carefully and took a loud slurp of his milk.

Wanda Moore turned around, all <u>priss-face</u>. 'Jesse Aarons. That noise is pure repulsive.'

He glared at her and gave another slurp.

'You are disgusting.'

Brrrrring. The recess bell. With a yelp, the boys were pushing for first place at the door.

'The boys will all sit down.' Oh, Lord. 'While the girls line up to go out to the playground. Ladies first.'

The boys <u>quivered</u> on the edges of their seats like moths fighting to be freed of <u>cocoons</u>. Would she never let them go?

'All right, now if you boys ...' They didn't give her a chance to change her mind. They were halfway to the end of the field before she could finish her sentence.

The first two out began dragging their toes to make the finish line. The ground was rutted from past rains, but had hardened in the late summer <u>drought</u>, so they had to give up on sneaker toes and draw the line with a stick. The fifth-grade boys, bursting with new importance, ordered the fourth-graders this way and that, while the smaller boys tried to include themselves without being conspicuous.

(from *Bridge to Terabithia* by Katherine Paterson)

Think about it

1. What words and details in the passage point to an American location for this extract?
2. How convincing is the writer's picture of school life? Back up the points you make with specific references to the passage.
3. Do you think that Jesse's attitude towards the girls is typical of boys? Do you get a sense of approval or disapproval of this on the writer's part?
4. How effectively does the writer use dialogue to convey the impression of

character? Back up the points you make with specific references to the passage.
5. Explain the meanings of the underlined words as they are used in the passage.

R. Read the following passage carefully and then answer the questions which follow it.

A Sense of Ownership

I met a lady the other day who had travelled much and seen much, and who talked with great <u>vivacity</u> about her experiences. But I noticed one <u>peculiarity</u> about her. If I happened to say that I too had been, let us say, to Tangier, her interest in Tangier immediately faded away and she switched the conversation on to, let us say, Cairo, where I had not been, and where therefore she was quite happy. And her enthusiasm about the Honourable Ulick de Tompkins vanished when she found that I had had the honour of meeting that <u>eminent personage.</u> And so with books and curiosities, places and things – she was only interested in them so long as they were her <u>exclusive</u> property. She had the itch of possession, and when she ceased to possess, she ceased to enjoy. If she could not have Tangier all to herself, she did not want it at all.

And the chief trouble in this <u>perplexing</u> world is that there are so many people <u>afflicted</u> like her with the <u>mania</u> of owning things that really do not need to be owned in order to be enjoyed. Their experiences must be <u>exclusive</u> or they have no pleasure in them. I have heard of a man who <u>countermanded</u> an order for an <u>etching</u> when he found that someone else in the same town had bought a copy. It was not the beauty of the etching that appealed to him: it was the <u>petty</u> and childish notion that he was getting something that no one else had got, and when he found that someone else had got it, its value ceased to exist.

The truth, of course, is that such a man could never possess anything in the only sense that matters. For possession is a spiritual and not a material thing. I do not own – to take an example – that wonderful picture by Ghirlandajo of the bottle-nose old man looking at his grandchild. I have not even a good print of it. But if it hung in my own room I could not have more pleasure out of it than I have experienced for years. It is among the <u>imponderable</u> treasures stored away in the galleries of the mind with memorable sunsets I have seen and noble books I have read, and beautiful actions or faces that I remember. I can enjoy it whenever I like and recall all the tenderness and humanity that the painter saw in the face of that plain old Italian gentleman with the bottle nose as he stood gazing down at the face of his grandson long centuries ago. The pleasure is not <u>diminished</u> by the fact that all may share this spiritual ownership, any more than my pleasure in the sunshine, or the shade of a fine beech, or the smell of a hedge of sweetbrier, or the song of the lark in the meadow is diminished by the thought that it is common to all.

(from *Alpha of the Plough* by A.G. Gardiner)

Think about it

1. Write a summary of the writer's argument in about a third of its present length.
2. How does the writer use his encounter with the lady (described in the first paragraph) to develop his main argument?
3. From the various references in the passage, what impression do you form of the writer? Give reasons for your answer.
4. Do you agree or disagree with the writer's notion of 'possession' as defined in the passage?
5. Explain the meanings of the underlined words as they are used in the passage.

DRAMA

Nearly every civilisation in the world has produced some kind of drama. Theatre and drama were found in ancient China, ancient Greece and ancient Rome. Modern drama has been traced backed to ancient Rome and to the drama of the Middle Ages.

In this section, we will concentrate on the fundamentals (the basics) of drama as we understand and experience it now.

WHAT IS DRAMA?

Drama is some kind of play. It is the exploration and presentation of human conflict within the context of theatre. The word *human* gives us **characters** – the **actors** – who use **dialogue** in a particular **setting** of time and place. *Conflict* gives us **action** – the characters' response to situations of conflict in which they find themselves.

The drama and other literary forms, especially the novel, share a great deal. The main difference is that drama is a human conflict which is acted out in a theatre. Drama must have actors and an audience.

DIALOGUE IN DRAMA

Dialogue means people carrying on a conversation. It is easy to see the difference between dialogue in a novel and a piece of dialogue from a play. In a novel, the dialogue is meant to be read. In a play, the dialogue has been written to be performed or acted out.

Example

The following is the opening scene from Joe Orton's *Entertaining Mr Sloane*. Read it and look at the way in which it is presented. Then study the 'Things to note' and the 'Comments' which follow this extract.

A room. Evening.
　[KATH *enters followed by* SLOANE]

KATH: This is my lounge.
SLOANE: Would I be able to use this room? Is it included?
KATH: Oh, yes. [*Pause.*] You mustn't imagine it's always like this. You ought to have rung up or something. And then I'd've been prepared.
SLOANE: The bedroom was perfect.
KATH: I never showed you the toilet.
SLOANE: I'm sure it will be satisfactory. [*Walks around the room examining the furniture. Stops by the window.*]
KATH: I should change them curtains. Those are our winter ones. The summer ones are

more of a chintz. [*Laughs.*] The walls need re-doing. The Dadda has trouble with his eyes. I can't ask him to do any work involving ladders. It stands to reason.

[*Pause.*]

SLOANE: I can't give you a decision right away.

KATH: I don't want to rush you. [*Pause.*] What do you think? I'd be happy to have you.

[*Silence.*]

SLOANE: Are you married?

KATH: [*Pause.*] I was. I had a boy ... killed in very sad circumstances. It broke my heart at the time. I got over it though. You do, don't you?

[*Pause.*]

SLOANE: A son?

KATH: Yes.

SLOANE: You don't look old enough.

[*Pause.*]

KATH: I don't let myself go like some of them you may have noticed. I'm just over ... As a matter of fact I'm forty-one.

[*Pause.*]

SLOANE [*briskly*]: I'll take the room.

(from *Entertaining Mr Sloane* by Joe Orton)

Things to note

• The stage directions – the things which the actors should do – are written in *italics*. The setting – where the action occurs – and the time are also written in *italics*.

• The directions are also set apart from the speech with square brackets [ ].

• There are no quotation marks.

• Every time a new character speaks, a new line begins with that person's name in CAPITAL LETTERS.

Comments

• Two characters, KATH and SLOANE, enter a scene (the setting) which is simply described as *A room*. The time is *Evening*.

• With one brief exchange of dialogue, we are presented with a situation: Kath is the prospective landlady; Sloane is the prospective lodger. Kath is keen to impress Sloane. Sloane is not fussed, but is taking his time as he looks around at what is on offer.

• In just one small conversation, we are already wondering – Will Sloane take the room? Will he be put off by the landlady's chatter? What kind of relationship will develop between Kath and Sloane if Sloane decides to rent the room? Will Kath's dead son have anything to do with things?

• All of these things have become clear through the dialogue, the characters, and the setting. We can already see that something is going to happen. As this is the opening of the play, there is little or no tension, but an action of some sort is imminent.

Think about it

1. What is your impression of Kath?
2. What do you think makes Sloane decide to take the room?
3. What do you think the characters are thinking during the directions marked [*Pause*] and [*Silence*]?
4. What do the stage directions add to our understanding of what is happening?

Dialogue in a novel or short story

The following piece is from a short story. Like the play, it also contains dialogue. What differences do you note in its presentation?

'And what has become of Margaret?'

'Ah, didn't her mother send her to America as soon as the baby was born? Once a woman is waked here she has to go. Hadn't Julia to go in the end, and she the only one who ever said she didn't mind the priest?'

'Julia who?' said I.

'Julia Cahill.'

The name struck my fancy, and I asked the driver to tell me her story.

'Wasn't it Father Madden who had her put out of the parish, but she put her curse on it, and it's on it to this day.'

'Do you believe in curses?'

'Bedad I do, sir. It's a terrible thing to put a curse on a man, and the curse that Julia put on Father Madden was a bad one, the divil a worse. The sun was up at the time, and she on the hilltop raising both her hands. And the curse she put on the parish was that every year, a roof must fall in and a family go to America. That was the curse, your honour, and every word of it has come true. You'll see for yourself as soon as we cross the mearing.'

'And what has become of Julia's baby?'

'I never heard she had one.'

He flicked his horse pensively with his whip, and it seemed to me that the disbelief I had expressed in the power of the curse disinclined him for further conversation.

'But,' I said, 'who is Julia Cahill, and how did she get the power to put a curse upon the village?'

'Didn't she go into the mountains every night to meet the fairies, and who else could've given her the power to put a curse upon the village?'

'But she couldn't walk so far in one evening.'

'Them that's in league with the fairies can walk that far and much farther in an evening, your honour. A shepherd saw her; and you'll see the ruins of the cabins for yourself as soon as we cross the mearing, and I'll show you the cabin of the blind woman that Julia lived with before she went away.'

(from 'Julia Cahill's Curse' in *The Untilled Field* by George Moore)

Comments

This exchange of dialogue is between the two characters, the driver and the narrator (his passenger). The main purpose of the dialogue is a **device** by which the author can start telling his story. This will be the story of Julia Cahill.

Try this

Turn the dialogue in this short extract into a dramatic scene. Set the scene. Use stage directions. Write the dialogue in dramatic form.

CHARACTERS

Just as in a novel or a short story, a character in a play may be portrayed as an individual or a stereotype (a miser, for example). But in drama, the character must be thoroughly involved in developing the **action** of the drama and moving it forward. The **conflict** which is at the centre of the dramatic situation is usually between two or more characters. These characters will see the world differently and will have different values. They may have a personality clash, or there may be a clash in their interests. A miser will react differently from a generous person when confronted by a beggar. They will also react to one another if confronted by a beggar at the same time.

Dramatic characters must be seen in relation to the dramatic situation in which the characters are involved. For example, a character's age may or may not be important. This will depend on whether 'age' has any meaning in the context of the dramatic situation.

When discussing dramatic character, the key questions are:
• What values does the character stands for?
• How well has the playwright shown these values through this character? For example, a very vicious character may be chosen to represent the vice of greed.

It's your turn

Introduce the following pairs of characters. Then write a short dramatic scene which clearly shows the kind of people you want to introduce to the audience.

1. A greedy person and a generous person.
2. A cruel person and a compassionate (kind) person.
3. A bigoted person and a liberal person. (Talk about what *bigoted* and *liberal* mean first.)
4. A victim and a bully.
5. A strict teacher and an easy-going teacher.
6. A conventional mother and her rebellious daughter.

ACTION AND CHARACTER

In drama, the action – even a slight physical movement – is always tied up with character. Dramatic actions become meaningful when we see what is happening through the characters. It helps us to understand why people are behaving as they are.

Dialogue in drama must be meaningful. It must express a human experience in some way. It must also help the characters to perform some kind of action.

DRAMATIC THEME

We can discover the theme of a play by asking a few questions.
• What is the play about?
• What kind of conflict is being explored by the playwright? Love? Joy? Death? Loneliness? Fear? Hatred?

Try this

Create short dramatic scenes with the following themes.

1. The evils of war.
2. Love is more important than wealth.
3. Might is not always right.
4. The pain of loneliness.
5. Violence is bred of intolerance.
6. Action speaks louder than words.
7. The happiness of a reunion.

SUBJECT MATTER

Remember – do not confuse the subject matter with the theme.
• The subject matter of a play may be a social class (working class, middle class, the unemployed, drug addicts etc.), a feud about land in a rural community etc. The characters will be part of the subject matter – the material (setting of time and place, nature of characters etc.) which is used by the playwright in exploring the meaning of certain kinds of human behaviour.

Try this

What details (of character, setting etc.) do you think a play should have which deals with the following subject matter?

1. Unemployment in the family.
2. The death of a loved one.
3. Drug addiction.
4. Teenage pregnancy.
5. Family life.
6. Emigration.

MORE ABOUT CHARACTER

The audience forms an impression of a character in the context of a **theatrical production**. This context will include actors, scenery, dialogue, sound effects.

When students read of a play, they must depend on the written text or **script,** including stage directions and other written instructions.

Here is a brief list of things you should consider when you are asked to give your impression of a character from reading a printed extract from a play.

1. What, if anything, does the playwright tell us directly about the character?
   • Age?
   • Social class?
   • Personality type?
   • Physical appearance?
   • Past experience?
   • Temperament?
   • Prejudices?
   • Motivation?
2. What do we learn about the character from his or her behaviour, both alone and in the company of others?
3. What do we learn about the character from what he or she says? (People usually reveal themselves in their speech).
4. What do we learn about the character from what other characters say about him or her?
5. What do we learn about a character from other characters' attitudes towards him or her?

It's your turn

1. In the following excerpt from Arthur Miller's play, *All My Sons*, the playwright directly introduces three characters in some detail.

Read this excerpt carefully. Then show how the dialogue and actions (in the form of stage directions) are consistent with the playwright's introductory descriptions of the characters. In giving your impression of each of the characters, support your statement with references to the text.

The characters are: (a) Joe Keller; (b) Doctor Jim Bayliss; and (c) Frank Lubey.

2. Describe the attitude of KELLER and BAYLISS towards LUBEY.

KELLER *is nearly sixty. A heavy man of stolid mind and build, a business man these many years, but with the imprint of the machine-shop worker and boss still upon him. When he reads, when he speaks, when he listens, it is with the terrible concentration of the uneducated man for whom there is still wonder in many commonly known things, a man whose judgments must be dredged out of experience and a peasant-like common sense. A man among men.*

DOCTOR JIM BAYLISS *is nearly forty. A wry self-controlled man, an easy talker, but with a wisp of sadness that clings to his self-effacing humour.*

[*At curtain,* JIM *is standing at left, staring at the broken tree. He taps a pipe on it, blows through the pipe, feels in his pockets for tobacco, then speaks.*]

JIM: Where's your tobacco?
KELLER: I think I left it on the table. [JIM *goes slowly to a table on the arbour, finds a pouch, and sits there on the bench, filling his pipe.*] Gonna rain tonight.
JIM: Paper says so?
KELLER: Yeah, right here.
JIM: Then it can't rain.
[FRANK LUBEY *enters, through a small space between the poplars.* FRANK *is thirty-two but balding. A pleasant, opinionated man, uncertain of himself, with a tendency towards peevishness when crossed, but always wanting it pleasant and*

neighbourly. He rather saunters in, leisurely, nothing to do. He does not notice JIM *in the arbour. On his greeting,* JIM *does not bother looking up.*]

FRANK: Hya.

KELLER: Hello, Frank. What's doin'?

FRANK: Nothin'. Walking off my breakfast. [*Looks up at the sky.*] That beautiful? Not a cloud.

KELLER [*looking up*]: Yeah, nice.

FRANK: Every Sunday ought to be like this.

KELLER [*indicating the sections beside him*]: Want the paper?

FRANK: What's the difference, it's all bad news. What's today's calamity?

KELLER: I don't know, I don't read the news part any more. It's more interesting in the want ads.

FRANK: Why, you trying to buy something?

KELLER: No, I'm just interested. To see what people want, y'know? For instance, here's a guy is lookin' for two Newfoundland dogs. Now what's he want with two Newfoundland dogs?

FRANK: That is funny.

KELLER: Here's another one. Wanted – old dictionaries. High prices paid. Now what's a man going to do with an old dictionary?

FRANK: Why not? Probably a book collector.

KELLER: You mean he'll make a living out of that?

FRANK: Sure, there's lots of them.

KELLER [*shaking his head*]: All kind of business goin' on. In my day, either you were a lawyer, or a doctor, or you worked in a shop. Now –

FRANK: Well, I was going to be a forester once.

KELLER: Well, that shows you; in my day, there was no such thing. [*Scanning the page, sweeping it with his hand*] You look at a page like this you realise how ignorant you are. [*Softly, with wonder, as he scans page*] Pss!

DRAMATIC SITUATION

Drama would not be dramatic without **conflict** or a **dramatic situation**. It must be immediate, in the present time, though there may be references to the past which we need to make sense of the present. In the opening stage directions, the playwright often sketches out the dramatic situation.

Try this

1. Read carefully the following excerpt from the play *The Browning Version* by Terence Rattigan. Describe the dramatic situation in which the two characters find themselves. Identify the nature of the developing conflict.

2. Give your impression of the two characters and the way in which they interact with each other.

The characters

TAPLOW *is a student;* FRANK HUNTER *is a young schoolmaster of science;* ANDREW CROCKER-HARRIS (*who is only referred to at this point in the play*) *is a retiring schoolmaster of Latin.*

The setting is the rooms of CROCKER-HARRIS *in a public school in the South of England.*
TAPLOW *is in detention.* FRANK *does not know this. He enters the room.* TAPLOW *is distracting himself by pretending he is playing golf with a walking-stick.* FRANK *innocently becomes involved.*

FRANK: Roll the wrists away from the ball. Don't break them like that.

[*He walks over quickly and puts his large hands over the abashed* TAPLOW.] Now swing.

[TAPLOW, *guided by* FRANK'S *evidently expert hands, succeeds in hitting the carpet with more effect than before.*] Too quick. Slow back and stiff left arm. It's no good just whacking the ball as if you were the headmaster and the ball was you. It'll never go more than fifty yards if you do. Get a rhythm. A good golf swing is a matter of aesthetics, not of brute strength. [TAPLOW *is only half-listening, gazing at the carpet.*] What's the matter?

TAPLOW: I think we've made a tear in the carpet, sir. [FRANK *examines the carpet perfunctorily.*]

FRANK: Nonsense. That was there already. [*He puts the stick in a corner of the room.*] Do I know you?

TAPLOW: No, sir.

FRANK: What's your name?

TAPLOW: Taplow.

FRANK: Taplow! No, I don't. You're not a scientist, I gather?

TAPLOW: No, sir. I'm still in the lower fifth. I can't specialise until the next term — that's to say if I've got my remove [*i.e. promotion to the next form*] all right.

FRANK: Don't you know yet if you've got your remove?

TAPLOW: No, sir. Mr Crocker-Harris doesn't tell us the results like the other masters.

FRANK: Why not?

TAPLOW: Well, you know what he's like, sir.

FRANK: I believe there is a rule that form results should only be announced by the headmaster on the last day of term.

TAPLOW: Yes — but who else pays any attention to it — except Mr Crocker-Harris?

FRANK: I don't, I admit — but that's no criterion. So you've got to wait until tomorrow to know your fate, have you?

TAPLOW: Yes, sir.

FRANK: Supposing the answer is favourable — what then?

TAPLOW: Oh — science, sir, of course.

FRANK [*sadly*]: Yes. We get all the slackers.

TAPLOW [*protestingly*]: I'm extremely interested in science, sir.

FRANK: Are you? I'm not. Not at least in the science I have to teach.

TAPLOW: Well, anyway, sir, it's a good deal more exciting than this muck. [*Indicating his book.*]

FRANK: What is this muck?

TAPLOW: Aeschylus, sir. Agamemnon.

FRANK: And your considered view is that Agamemnon of Aeschylus is muck, is it?

TAPLOW: Well, no, sir. I don't think the play is muck — exactly. I suppose, in a way, it's a rather good plot, really: a wife murdering her husband and having a lover and all that. I only meant the way it's taught to us — just a lot of Greek words strung together and fifty lines if you get them wrong.

FRANK: You sound a little bitter, Taplow.

TAPLOW: I am rather, sir.

FRANK: Kept in, eh?

TAPLOW: No, sir. Extra work.

FRANK: Extra work — on the last day of school?

TAPLOW: Yes, sir — and I might be playing golf. You'd think he'd have enough to do anyway himself, considering he's leaving tomorrow for good — but oh no. I missed a day last week when I had 'flu — so here I am — and look at the weather, sir.

FRANK: Bad luck. Still, there's one consolation. You're pretty well bound to get your remove tomorrow for being a good boy in taking extra work.

TAPLOW: Well, I'm not so sure, sir. That would be true of the ordinary masters, all right. They just wouldn't dare not give a chap a remove after taking extra work — it would be such a bad advertisement for them. But those sort of rules don't apply to the Crock — Mr Crocker-Harris. I asked him yesterday out-right if he'd given me a remove and do you know what he said, sir?

FRANK: No. What?

TAPLOW [*mimicking a very gentle, rather throaty voice*]: 'My dear Taplow, I have given you exactly what you deserve. No less; and certainly no more.' Do you know, sir, I think he may have marked me down, rather than up, for taking extra work. I mean, the man's barely human. [*He breaks off quickly.*] Sorry, sir. Have I gone too far?

FRANK: Yes. Much too far.

THE PLOT
• •

The plot of a play, just as the plot of a novel or a short story, is the *development of the action* that evolves from a dramatic situation. In drama, plot is tied up with the movement or tempo of the action. Using suspense as much as possible, the action should move towards a peak of intensity. The plot should be interesting enough to hold our interest as the action unfolds.

TRAGEDY AND COMEDY
• •

• **Tragedy** refers to a human story involving suffering. This suffering may or may not make sense to the characters who are doing the suffering. The outcome of a tragedy always involves a 'sad ending'.

• **Comedy** has a 'happy ending'. A comedy may be a humorous entertainment which distracts us from a painful reality. It may be a way of teaching us about the foolishness of our attitudes and behaviour by making fun of them.

Try this

Adapt the following scene to dramatic form. Use introductory descriptions of the characters. Give stage directions where necessary. Leave out or add any material as you wish. The excerpt comes from Roddy Doyle's award-winning novel, *Paddy Clarke Ha Ha Ha*.

Paddy Clarke, the narrator-hero of Roddy Doyle's comic novel, has been reading about the life of Father Damien. He was the Belgian priest who, in the 19th century, devoted his life to caring for the outcast lepers on the leper colony of Molokai, one of the Hawaiian islands. The whole story of the saintly priest, who died from leprosy himself which he contracted from the lepers he cared for, has captured Paddy's imagination. He now wants to act out the role of Father Damien and use his pals as the lepers. (Note that Roddy Doyle uses dashes — instead of quotation marks to indicate his dialogue.)

I needed lepers. Sinbad wasn't enough. He kept running away. He told our ma that I was making him be a leper and he didn't want to be one. So I needed lepers. I couldn't tell Kevin because he'd have ended up being Father Damien and I'd have been a leper. It was my story. I got the McCarthy twins and Willy Hancock. There were four, the three of them. They thought it was great being with a big boy, me. I made them come into our back garden. I told them what lepers were. They wanted to be lepers.

— Can lepers swim? said Willy Hancock.

— Yeah, I said.

— We can't swim, said one of the McCarthys.

— Lepers can swim, said Willy Hancock.

– They don't have to swim, I said. – You don't have to swim. You only have to pretend you're lepers. It's easy. You just have to be a bit sick and wobble a bit.

They wobbled.

– Can they laugh?

– Yeah, I said. – They only have to lie down sometimes so I can mop their brows and say prayers on them.

– I'm a leper!

– I'm a leper! Wobble wobble wobble!

– Wobble wobble wobble!

– Wobble wobble wobble!

– Our Father who art in heaven hallowed by thy name –

– Wobble wobble wobble!

– Shut up a sec . . .

– Wobble wobble wobble.

They had to go home for their dinners. I heard them through the hedge on the path to their houses.

– I'm a leper! Wobble wobble wobble!

AN EXTRACT WITH SAMPLE QUESTIONS AND ANSWERS

The following extract is taken from Act Two, Scene Three of *The Field*, a play by John B. Keane.

Read the extract carefully. Then study the questions, comments and answers which follow it.

[*The action in this scene takes place on a lonely country road. The time is midnight. Two figures,* THE BULL McCABE *and his son* TADHG, *are huddled together in a gateway on the side of the road. They are waiting for William Dee, a character who outbid The Bull earlier in an auction for a field which The Bull feels should rightfully be his. They wish to give William Dee 'a bit of a beatin' in order to put* him off going through with the purchase of the field. While they wait they talk about the weather, the growing grass, crows and …*]

TADHG: Why don't yourself and Ma talk, Da?

BULL: Ah, hould your tongue!

TADHG: Ah, Da, come on! I always told you about my women.

BULL: Your mother is a peculiar woman, son. I won't account for her. She's led me a queer life all these years.

TADHG: How long has it been?

BULL: How long has what been?

TADHG: Since you spoke to her?

BULL: Eat your sandwich, can't you, and give us a rest. I'm addled from you.

TADHG: Ah, tell us, Da. [*Sits near him.*]

BULL: [*Rises, pauses and returns to* TADHG] Eighteen years since I slept with her or spoke to her.

TADHG: Who was the cause?

BULL: Who was the cause, but a tinker's pony … a hang-gallows piebald pony, a runty get of a gluttonous knacker with one eye. I was at the fair of Carraigthomond that day … and she gave permission to a tinker's widow to let the pony loose in one of the fields. The land was carryin' fourteen cows an' grass scarce. Fourteen cows, imagine, an' to go throwin' a pony in on top of them! Cripes, Tadhg, a tinker's pony would eat the hair off a child's head!

TADHG: He would, Dad, he would. But what happened between Ma and yourself?

BULL: God blast you! … that's what happened. Amn't I after tellin' you?

TADHG: But after the pony … what happened?

BULL: I was in bed when she told me. I had a share of booze taken. I walloped her more than I meant, maybe. I went out and looked at the pony … He had one eye, a sightful right eye. I shot him through the two eyes, the blind and the good ... a barrel at a time. It often played on my conscience. If 'twas an ass now, 'twouldn't matter, but a pony is a pony.

TADHG: An' she never spoke to you since?

BULL: Never a word. Not even a lone word, good or bad, in all that time. I tried to talk to her, to come around her. I put in electric light and bought the television. I built that goddamned bathroom ... for her ... all over a tinker's nag, a dirty one-eyed pony. You'd swear he was human.

TADHG: You had to do it, Da. Carrying fourteen cows. You had to do it.

BULL: Of course I had to do it, but she couldn't see it that way. You understand all right, Tadhg. You're a sensible fellow who knows the ropes.

TADHG: A tinker's pony would eat your finger nails.

BULL: A tinker's pony would eat your whiskers.

TADHG: Didn't you explain to her?

BULL: Aye! ... But you can't explain these things to women. It don't trouble them if the hay is scarce and the fields bare. I seen lonesome nights, Tadhg, lonesome nights. [*Comes suddenly upright*] Silence! What was that?

Question 1

'In this scene, The Bull McCabe portrays all the characteristics of a primitive man.'

Discuss this statement, supporting it by reference to the extract and the introduction.

Comment

This is a question about a person's character. The word 'primitive' is a pointer to the kind of aspects of the character which you should write about.

Answer

As the introduction informs us, The Bull McCabe is taking the law into his own hands and lying in ambush to attack someone. This points to a primitive quality in the man. The way he feels about his land is shown in his refusal to allow the tinker's widow to graze her pony in the field. This is very unreasonable. His savage and primitive nature is best revealed when he beats his wife for what was, on her part, an act of sympathy and kindness. His callous shooting of the innocent pony highlights The Bull's primitiveness. The gruffness of his conversation with his son, Tadhg, also shows up the crudeness of the man. But what is perhaps most revealing of The Bull's brutal and primitive nature is his inability to understand the savagery of his behaviour. He is also unable to understand his wife's response to what he has done. The Bull is a character beyond the law who ignores the need to be civilised and to live a decent life.

Question 2

From what you learn of her in this scene, what kind of a woman do you think The Bull McCabe's wife was? Would your sympathy be entirely with her?

Comment

This is also a question about character in which you are invited to offer your opinion on her behaviour.

Answer

In Bull's eyes, his wife's mistake was to let the tinker's widow graze her pony in his field. From this, we can guess that she was a kind person who took pity on the tinker's widow. As a countrywoman, she must have known that there would be a cost to this because of the amount of grass the pony would eat. But she still decided to give permission when she understood the widow's problem. Her husband's reaction was savage and very much out of proportion to what she had done. An ordinary farmer might simply have complained to his wife about what she done. However, she was badly beaten by the land-crazy Bull. His shooting of the pony was also inexcusable. Mrs McCabe was not a weak or simple person because it took courage for her to banish The Bull from their bedroom and her companionship for eighteen years. The impression of Mrs McCabe is of a person with great strength of character, kindness and compassion.

Question 3

What do the extract and introduction tell us about the relationship between The Bull McCabe and his son? How do their characters compare?

Comment

This is another character question. The focus of the answer must be on the relationship between the two men. Something has already been said about The Bull's character, so we must pay more attention to Tadhg.

Answer

The Bull's attitude towards his son is very domineering. Tadhg is a grown man, but his father treats him as a troublesome child. Tadhg is cowardly and immature because he accepts this humiliating role. He is also sly enough to flatter his brutal father in order to get the information he wants. Tadhg's spineless character is clearly shown in the lack of shock or horror which a normal son would show when he learns of the savage beating inflicted on his mother. Given Tadhg's spineless and cowardly nature, it is no wonder that The Bull can dominate him so easily. The Bull is a hateful character in every way. Tadhg is both hateful

and pathetic because of his moral and emotional weakness.

EXTRACTS WITH SAMPLE QUESTIONS

A. The following extract is from *Over The Bridge* by Sam Thompson. Study the extract carefully and then answer the questions which follow it.

[*The scene is a head foreman's office in the Belfast shipyard.* RABBIE WHITE *is leaning on the plan bench as he marks a football coupon.*]

RABBIE [*singing*]: 'Lead kindly light, amid the encircling gloom, Lead thou me on ...'
[WARREN BAXTER *quietly opens the office door and stands watching.*]
RABBIE [*to himself*]: Perm two groups of four from six groups of four. Fifteen lines at tuppence a line. Half a crown staked ...
[*he sings*] 'The night is dark, and I am far from home, Lead thou me on ...'
BAXTER: Man, you're a bloody ould hypocrite, too, Rabbie. Singing hymns while you mark your football coupon in the firm's time.
RABBIE [*startled*]: For Pete's sake, you whistle before you come in, Baxter. Do you want to give me a heart attack?
BAXTER: Relax, Rabbie, relax.
RABBIE: I thought you were ould Fox.
BAXTER: No such luck. It's only the poor shop steward, here on official business – public doormat number one, for bosses and workmates alike.
RABBIE: Don't take yourself so seriously, Baxter. Better men than you has been shop stewards and survived it. Have you broke the news to him yet?
BAXTER: To Fox?
RABBIE: About last night's decision of the District Committee?

BAXTER: I tried to tell him out there a minute ago, but he waved me away and told me to wait for him here.

RABBIE [*after a pause*]: The way you go about things at times, Warren, makes me wonder whether you're a shop steward or just plain shop stupid.

BAXTER: What's biting you?

RABBIE: The middle of the workshop is no place to tackle your head foreman about union matters.

BAXTER: Now just a minute ...

RABBIE: How many times have I to tell you that tackling Fox in front of the men about union matters only gets his back up? Do you need it in writing?

BAXTER: So what do you want me to do?

RABBIE: Always wait till you get him in here, in his office. [*sarcastically*] That's why a head foreman has an office. It's the place where he can discuss his business in private.

BAXTER [*grudgingly*]: I suppose you're right. You ould hands always think you are anyway.

RABBIE: Now, just keep your eye down that shop and make sure Fox doesn't walk in and catch me doing *my* business in his office. I just want to fill in this postal order ...

[WARREN *walks to the office door and looks down the shop.* RABBIE *sings another snatch or two of 'Lead Kindly Light' as he completes the postal order.* WARREN *lights a cigarette butt.*]

RABBIE: 'Lead thou me on...' You know, Warren, hymn singing is about the only thing that touches the depths of any bit of a soul I've got; it's the only time you'll get people together in loving harmony. Then after the 'Amen', they're at each other's bloody throats again. Have you still ould Fox in your sights?

BAXTER: He's down the shop gabbing to John Welsh.

RABBIE: What, again? You can relax. They'll be there to the blow.

BAXTER: I say, Fox has fairly taken Welsh under his wing this last while back ...

RABBIE: You can say that again.

BAXTER: I wonder if there's any truth in the rumour that Fox is going to make him a gaffer?

RABBIE: It looks like it. [*He pauses thoughtfully.*] Still, it's hard to believe that Welsh will make a gaffer: he's too intelligent.

BAXTER: You know, I've often wondered why ould Fox never made you a gaffer, Rabbie. Sure you've been marking-off him for years.

RABBIE: Any ambition I had, Warren, I lost it during the big depression. I was just about your age then, and very eager to build boats – only there was no boats to build. [*He holds up the football coupon.*] That's my ambition now, Warren – a first dividend on the treble chance for Martha and me. Then I'd tell ould Fox on Monday morning what he could do with his plans. [*He slips the postal order and football coupon into an envelope, takes out a stamp from his cigarette case, licks it and presses it on.*]

BAXTER: Sure you've been marking them things for years and got nothing out of them. I doubt you don't mark the right teams, Rabbie.

RABBIE: That's where you're wrong, sonny. I always mark them right; but the buggers don't *play* right. [*Having sealed the envelope and put it in his pocket, he walks to the office door and takes a cautious glance down the shop.*] Well now, seeing as we have a minute or two to spare, I want to mark your card about this meeting Davy's called for the meal hour.

BAXTER: Aye, just what does Davy think he's playing at anyway? It's not official.

RABBIE: Davy Mitchell has a lot more experience of trade union procedure than you have, sonny ...

BAXTER: I'm against any kind of unofficial meeting outside the branch room.

RABBIE: No more than Davy is against any
kind of religious bigotry being dragged into
the branch room.

BAXTER: So that's what we're up against –
religion!

RABBIE: Correct, Warren. Religion. And you
know the kind I mean. The kind that makes
them want to kick the other fellow's bowels
in to let him know his is different from theirs.

Questions

1. Give your impression of Rabbie. Is your
   attitude towards him sympathetic? Give
   reasons for your answer.

2. Describe the nature of the relationship
   between Rabbie and Baxter.

3. From this extract alone, what theme is
   beginning to emerge? Refer to the extract
   to support your answer.

4. How does the playwright create the
   atmosphere of the shipyard setting? Use
   details from the extract to support your
   answer.

B. The following extract is from the Sean
O'Casey play, *The Plough and the Stars*. Study the
extract carefully and then answer the questions
which follow it.

[NORA CLITHEROE *hates politics and the Irish
nationalism in which her husband has been involved.
She has seemingly succeeded in getting him to lose
interest in these things, but in fact his disengagement
is the result of his belief that he has been passed over
for promotion in the Irish Citizen Army of which he
was a member.*

Just before the scene presented in this extract,
NORA CLITHEROE *and her husband* JACK
*have been in a romantic mood. That romantic mood
has been rudely shattered by a knock at the door.*]

CLITHEROE: I wonder who can that be, now?

NORA [*a little nervously*]: Take no notice of it,
Jack; they'll go away in a minute. [*Another
knock, followed by a voice.*]

VOICE: Commandant Clitheroe, Commandant
Clitheroe, are you there? A message from
General Jim Connolly.

CLITHEROE: Damn it, it's Captain Brennan.

NORA [*anxiously*]: Don't mind him, don't
mind, Jack. Don't break our happiness ...
Pretend we're not in. Let us forget everything
tonight but our two selves!

CLITHEROE [*reassuringly*]: Don't be alarmed,
darling; I'll just see what he wants, an' send
him about his business.

NORA [*tremulously*]: No, no. Please, Jack; don't
open it. Please, for your own little Nora's sake!

CLITHEROE [*rising to open the door*]: Now
don't be silly, Nora.

[CLITHEROE *opens the door, and admits a young
man in the full uniform of the Irish Citizen Army
– green suit; slouch green hat caught up at one side
by a small Red Hand badge; Sam Browne belt,
with a revolver in the holster. He carries a letter in
his hand. When he comes in he smartly salutes*
CLITHEROE. *The young man is* CAPTAIN
BRENNAN.]

BRENNAN [*giving the letter to* CLITHEROE]:
A dispatch from General Connolly.

CLITHEROE [*reading. While he is doing so,*
BRENNAN'S *eyes are fixed on* NORA, *who
droops as she sits on the lounge.*] 'Commandant
Clitheroe is to take command of the eighth
battalion of the ICA. which will assemble to
proceed to the meeting at nine o'clock. He is
to see that all units are provided with full
equipment; two days' rations and fifty rounds
of ammunition. At two o'clock a.m. the army
will leave Liberty Hall for a reconnaissance
attack on Dublin Castle. – Com. Gen.
Connolly.' I don't understand this. Why does
General Connolly call me Commandant?

BRENNAN: Th' Staff appointed you Commandant, and th' General agreed with their selection.

CLITHEROE: When did this happen?

BRENNAN: A fortnight ago.

CLITHEROE: How is it word was never sent to me?

BRENNAN: Word was sent ... I meself brought it.

CLITHEROE: Who did you give it to, then?

BRENNAN [after a pause]: I think I gave it to Mrs Clitheroe, there.

CLITHEROE: Nora, d'ye hear that? [NORA makes no answer.]

CLITHEROE [there is a note of hardness in his voice]: Nora ... Captain Brennan says he brought a letter to me from General Connolly, and that he gave it to you ... Where is it? What did you do with it?

NORA [running over to him, and pleadingly putting her arms around him.]: Jack, please, Jack, don't go out tonight an' I'll tell you; I'll explain everything ... Send him away, an' stay with your own little red-lipp'd Nora.

CLITHEROE [removing her arms from around him.]: None o' this nonsense, now; I want to know what you did with th' letter?

[NORA goes slowly to the lounge and sits down.]

CLITHEROE [angrily]: Why didn't you give me th' letter? What did you do with it? ... [He shakes her by the shoulder] What did you do with th' letter?

NORA [flaming up]: I burned it, I burned it! That's what I did with it! Is General Connolly an' th' Citizen Army goin' to be your only care? Is your home goin' to be only a place to rest in? Am I goin' to be only somethin' to provide merry-makin' for you? Your vanity'll be th' ruin of you an' me yet ... That's what's movin' you: because they've made an officer of you, you'll make a glorious cause of what you're doin', while your little red-lipp'd Nora can go on sittin' here, makin' a companion of th' loneliness of th' night!

CLITHEROE [fiercely]: You burned it, did you? [He grips her arm.] Well, me good lady –

NORA: Let go – you're hurtin' me!

CLITHEROE: You deserve to be hurt ... Any letter that comes to me for th' future, take care that I get it ... D'ye hear – take care that I get it!

Questions

1. Describe the nature of the conflict in this scene between Nora and her husband Jack.

2. Give your impression of Clitheroe from his reaction to the fact that his wife has burned the letter informing him of his promotion.

3. Are there any details in his presentation of this scene which reveal the playwright's sympathies? Or do you find the presentation is impartial? Give reasons for you answer.

4. It has been said that the different viewpoints and values of Nora and her husband are the differences between men and women. Would you agree or disagree with this statement? Either way, argue your case, referring to the extract to support your view.

C. The following is an extract from John Millington Synge's *Riders to the Sea*. Study the extract carefully. Then answer the questions which follow it.

[*The setting is an island off the West Coast of Ireland. The old woman* MAURYA *and her two daughters,* CATHLEEN *and* NORA, *have just received news that the body of Michael, Maurya's son who was lost at sea, has been found. Maurya has already lost her husband and four other sons at sea. Her one remaining son, her youngest,* BARTLEY, *has set off, despite the old woman's efforts to stop him, to take a boat to a fair on the mainland.*

The door opens softly and OLD WOMEN *begin to come in, crossing themselves on the threshold and kneeling down in front of the stage with red petticoats over their heads.*]

MAURYA [*Half in a dream, to* CATHLEEN.]: Is it Patch, or Michael, or what is it at all?

CATHLEEN: Michael is after being found in the far north, and when he is found there how could he be here in this place?

MAURYA: There does be a power of young men floating round in the sea, and what way would they know if it was Michael they had, or another man like him, for when a man is nine days in the sea, and the wind blowing, it's hard set his own mother would be to say what man was in it.

CATHLEEN: It's Michael, God spare him, for they're after sending us a bit of his clothes from the far north.

[*She reaches out and hands* MAURYA *the clothes that belonged to Michael.* MAURYA *stands up slowly, and takes them in her hands.* NORA *looks out.*]

NORA: They're carrying a thing among them, and there's water dripping out of it and leaving a track by the big stones.

CATHLEEN [*In a whisper to* THE WOMEN *who have come in.*]: Is it Bartley it is?

ONE OF THE WOMEN: It is, surely, God rest his soul.

[*Two younger women come in and pull out the table. Then men carry in the body of* BARTLEY, *laid on a plank, with a bit of a sail over it, and lay it on the table.*]

CATHLEEN [*To the women as they are doing so.*]: What way was he drowned?

ONE OF THE WOMEN: The grey pony knocked him over into the sea, and he was washed out where there is a great surf on the white rocks.

[MAURYA *has gone over and knelt at the head of the table. The women are keening softly and swaying themselves with a slow movement.* CATHLEEN *and* NORA *kneel at the other end of the table. The men kneel near the door.*]

MAURYA [*Raising her head and speaking as if she did not see the people around her.*]: They're all gone now, and there's isn't anything more the sea can do to me ... I'll have no call now to be up crying and praying when the wind breaks from the south, and you can hear the surf is in the east, and the surf is in the west, making a great stir with the two noises, and they hitting one on the other. I'll have no call now to be going down and getting Holy Water in the dark nights after Samhain, and I won't care what way the sea is when the other women will be keening. [*To* NORA.] Give me the Holy Water, Nora; there's a small sup still on the dresser.

[NORA *gives it to her.*]

MAURYA [*Drops* MICHAEL'S *clothes across* BARTLEY'S *feet, and sprinkles the Holy Water over him.*]: It isn't that I haven't prayed for you, Bartley, to the Almighty God. It isn't that I haven't said prayers in the dark night till you wouldn't know what I'd be saying; but it's a great rest I'll have now, and it's time surely. It's a great rest I'll have now, and great sleeping in the long nights after Samhain, if it's only a bit of wet flour we do have to eat, and maybe a fish that would be stinking.

[*She kneels down again, crossing herself, and saying prayers under her breath.*]

CATHLEEN [*To an old man.*]: Maybe yourself and Eamon would make a coffin when the sun rises. We have fine white boards herself bought, God help her, thinking Michael would be found, and I have a new cake you can eat while you'll be working.

THE OLD MAN [*Looking at the boards.*]: Are there nails with them?

CATHLEEN: There are not, Colum; we didn't think of the nails.

ANOTHER MAN: It's a great wonder she wouldn't think of the nails, and all the coffins she's seen made already.

CATHLEEN: It's getting old she is, and broken.

[MAURYA *stands up again very slowly and spreads out the pieces of* MICHAEL'S *clothes beside the body, sprinkling them with the last of the Holy Water.*]

NORA [*In a whisper to* CATHLEEN.]: She's quiet now and easy; but the day Michael was drowned you could hear her crying out from this to the spring well. It's fonder she was of Michael, and would anyone have thought that?

CATHLEEN [*Slowly and clearly.*]: An old woman will be soon tired with anything she will do, and isn't it nine days herself is after crying and keening, and making great sorrow in the house?

MAURYA [*Puts the empty cup downwards on the table, and lays her hands together on* BARTLEY'S *feet.*]: They're all together this time, and the end is come. May the Almighty God have mercy on Bartley's soul, and on Michael's soul, and on the souls of Sheamus and Patch, and Stephen and Shawn [*bending her head*]; and may He have mercy on my soul, Nora, and on the soul of everyone is left living in the world.

[*She pauses, and the keen rises a little more loudly from the women, then sinks away.*]

MAURYA [*Continuing.*]: Michael has a clean burial in the far north, by the grace of the Almighty God. Bartley will have a fine coffin out of the white boards, and a deep grave surely. What more can we want than that? No man at all can be living for ever, and we must be satisfied.

[*She kneels down again and the curtain falls slowly.*]

Questions

1. 'For all the weakness of her age and her simplicity, old Maurya has a strength of character that is truly heroic.' Discuss this statement in relation to this extract.

2. Describe the tragic atmosphere of this scene. Refer to specific details in the playwright's creation of this atmosphere.

3. Describe the attitude of the other characters in the scene towards Maurya.

4. Discuss Maurya's attitude towards life, especially as she expresses it in the final lines she speaks.

5. What in your opinion do the stage directions add to this scene? Support your answer by quoting from the text.

6. 'Maurya's tragedy is not only the loss of her husband and her six sons. It is also the tragedy of life itself, in the sense that human beings can never avoid pain but must come to terms with it.' Discuss this statement in reference to the above scene.

D. The following extract is from John B. Keane's *The Year of the Hiker*.

Read the extract carefully. Then answer the questions which follow it.

[*The action takes place in the kitchen of the Lacey farmhouse. The time is the present – early morning of a September day. There is much bustle and activity, as a daughter of the house – Mary – is about to be married this morning. In the kitchen is* FREDA, *sister to the woman of the house.* FREDA *is a woman of fifty, austere and capable. Busily she sets the table for a brief tea before the family departs.*

Mr Lacey, the Hiker of the play's title, walked out on his wife and family twenty years before the scene of the following extract. His name is coming up now because his daughter Mary is getting married this morning. In the following scene, the Hiker's son

SIMEY *and his sister-in-law* FREDA *are discussing the Hiker.*]

SIMEY: Do you like Willie, Freda?

FREDA: He'll suit Mary.

SIMEY: Not as dashing as me, though!

FREDA: When you propose to a sensible girl, you'll find out how dashing you are.

SIMEY: Did anyone ever propose to you, Freda?

FREDA: I could have been married, if that's what you means. A healthy, respectable farmer from Kiskean was mad about me.

SIMEY: What happened?

FREDA: Nothing happened! I just wouldn't marry him. I saw enough of marriage in my time. Too much of it to want any part of it.

SIMEY: Ah, we're back to my Da! What did he run away from? From reality, Freda? From responsibility? From you, Freda?

FREDA: If you don't hurry up and shave, you'll be left behind.

SIMEY: That why you're not coming to the wedding today?

FREDA: Somebody has to mind the house. Do you want us to be robbed ... and what about the cows? Will they work the milking-machine themselves?

SIMEY: Freda ... you remember my father well, of course. I don't remember him at all. What kind of a fellow was he? ... I mean, had he any good points at all, or was he just the lousy bum I think he was?

FREDA: Oh, he was worse than a bum! He was a wanderer born and bred. We were often at the height of the harvest here, and if he heard of a coursing meeting or a football match, he was gone. God only knew when he'd show up then. I remember once, the hay was down in the big meadow and your mother was carrying Mary ... he went off to a race-meeting in Mallow and didn't come back for four days. Another time – I think it was a ploughing-

match – he made off with the milk cheque ... and the rates overdue! He was away a week that time. He came back broke to the ropes. We had to sell two cows to pay the bills.

SIMEY: No explanation for it?

FREDA: He was no good!

SIMEY: How did you get on with him?

FREDA: I couldn't stand him, and he couldn't stand me. He broke our hearts. He was always breaking our hearts.

SIMEY: Whose heart?

FREDA: I never spoke to him, or answered him if he spoke to me, not after he went away on his first hike. He was all life and bustle. That was the Hiker. He'd wear a person out, he was that full of whims. He was always going – moving, moving, moving – the entire night and day. He couldn't sit still! He couldn't sit by the fire and smoke his pipe like a sensible man. It was always off with him to have a look at this or have a look at that. He wasn't steady and you could never depend on him – not for anything.

SIMEY: Strange man!

FREDA: Try to picture a man the exact opposite of Joe and you have him. He'd leave here three days before a big hurling match in Dublin and walk the whole way in stages. That's how they gave him the name 'The Hiker'. He never thought of his family, not when he got the fit to be moving.

SIMEY: You didn't like him?

FREDA [*laughs grimly*]: I hated him!

SIMEY: Maybe that's why he left. I mean, if my mother hated him and you hated him, he saw no future in hanging around.

FREDA: That's not true! We didn't hate him at first.

SIMEY [*sarcasm*]: Maybe if there was no understanding ...

FREDA: Don't make me laugh! He wasn't born to stay in a place. It's not uncommon. There are others like him. It's in the blood ... a constant calling to be up and away. No sense of responsibility, wife and family all forgotten when the humour catches them. Didn't you ever see birds migrating? Well, like the birds or the fish, these people get uneasy and restless when their time for moving comes. It's a disease – like tuberculosis or pneumonia. Wandering is God's greatest curse!

SIMEY: Well, you can't blame him so! The thing was in him and he couldn't do much about it.

Questions

1. Give your impression of The Hiker as portrayed by Freda. Do you think that Freda's hatred of him is justified by what she says about him?

2. Describe Simey's attitude towards his father as portrayed by Freda. Do you find any sympathy for The Hiker in Simey's responses to Freda's account of The Hiker? Refer to the text in your answer this question.

3. From this scene, what do you think is the nature of the conflict that is developing? Support your answer by referring to the extract.

4. How would you describe the relationship between Simey and Freda? How does the dialogue bring this across?

5. To judge by this extract alone, do you think there is more to Freda's hatred of The Hiker than she is prepared to admit? Argue your viewpoint.

EXERCISES ON PLAYS YOU HAVE STUDIED

1. In any play you have studied, give your impression of two of its main characters. Give the title of the play and the name of the author.

2. In relation to any play you have studied, describe the dramatic situation out of which the play evolves. Give the title of the play and the name of the author.

3. Describe the atmosphere of any play you have studied and explain how the playwright has created that atmosphere. Give the title of the play and the name of the author.

4. Summarise the plot of any play you have studied.

5. Outline a situation of conflict: (a) between two characters; (b) between a character and his or her environment (social etc.); (c) between a character and his or her conscience.

6. Referring to any play you have studied, analyse a dialogue between two or more characters which reveals the kind of people they are. Give the title of the play and the name of the author.

7. Describe the theme of any play you have studied, distinguishing carefully between the theme and the subject matter. Give the title of the play and the name of the author.

8. Give a brief outline of any tragedy or comedy you have studied. Give the title of the play and the name of the author.

9. Take any short story you have read and adapt it to the form of a dramatic scene.

10. Taking the Shakespeare play you have studied, give a sketch of its main characters and describe the nature of the conflict out of which the play evolves.

POETRY

WHAT IS POETRY?

At different times and in different places around the world, poetry has done many things.
- It has told stories.
- It has recorded family histories (genealogy).
- It has told of simple, everyday happenings and world–shattering events
- It has been used to pass on information.

The ancient Greeks wrote many kinds of beautiful poetry. Like the ancient Celts, they passed on poetic thought from person to person, by word of mouth. The Greek goddess of the arts was called Mnemosyne, which means 'memory'. To these ancient people, poetry was something memorable, a memorable way of saying something. This idea gives us a good way of defining poetry.

> *Poetry is a memorable way of saying, singing or writing something which is worth remembering.*

Poetry = memorable speech

Speech is memorable because of
- *what* is said = **subject matter/theme**
- *the way* in which something is said
= **technique**

SUBJECT MATTER AND THEME

WHAT'S THE DIFFERENCE?

The subject matter is the raw material of the poem.
- its *setting* (city or countryside, past or present)
- the source and *nature* of its *imagery* (the sea, dreams, experiences of all kinds, both public and private)
- the concrete *details* of the poem

The subject matter of the poem is usually fairly obvious. It is only difficult when it involves something with which the reader is not familiar, such as classical mythology, with its many gods and goddesses, or some area of science.

The theme of the poem is the way in which the poet organises and shapes the subject matter. Imagine a piece of clay as the subject matter, and the wine jar into which the potter makes it as the theme. The theme may be:
- a moral or a message
- a thought
- the expression of a particular feeling or experience
- the evocation of a scene or a mood

The theme of a poem is not always obvious. It may need to be worked out or analysed by the reader. Teasing out the poem's theme will involve a reader's own interpretation and the exercise of judgment. This is a kind of critical reading which helps us find the proper appreciation of any poem.

Example

To illustrate the difference between subject matter and theme, read this poem by the American poet, Robert Frost.

THE HILL WIFE

The Impulse

It was too lonely for her there,
And too wild,
And since there were but two of them,
And no child,

And work was little in the house,
She was free,
And followed where he furrowed field,
Or felled tree.

She rested on a log and tossed
The fresh chips,
With a song only to herself
On her lips.

And once she went to break a bough
Of black alder.
She strayed so far she scarcely heard
When he called her.

And didn't answer – didn't speak –
Or return.
She stood, and then she ran and hid
In the fern.

He never found her, though he looked
Everywhere,
And he asked at her mother's house
Was she there.

Sudden and swift and light as that
The ties gave,
And he learned of finalities
Besides the grave.

Robert Frost

Some comments on the poem

The *subject matter* of this poem is the countryside. It is set in farmland which seems to be very remote from the rest of society.

The poem presents the farmer and his wife going about their daily chores of housework and farm work. There are images of woodland, fern and furrowed field, all of which seem very peaceful. But the absence of a child points to unhappiness.

> And since there were but two of them,
> And no child,
> And work was little in the house,
> She was free...

Despite the charming country setting, something terrible happens. The farmer's wife suddenly runs away and is never found.

> He never found her, though he looked
> Everywhere...

What happened? The absence of the child may be a hint. It seems to have caused a great deal of unhappiness for the wife, though she may never have spoken of this to her husband. This lack of a child has made life unbearable for her, and then one day she snaps because she can take no more.

> She strayed so far she scarcely heard
> When he called her.
> And didn't answer – didn't speak –
> Or return...

Perhaps she had a nervous breakdown. Perhaps she simply decided she could not stand being in this quiet countryside any more. Whatever the reason, she has left the farmer's life forever. And as he realises this, the farmer understands that death is not the only final separation – final separations can occur in life in many other ways.

> And he learned of finalities
> Besides the grave.

Once we have given it some thought, the theme of the poem begins to emerge. Death is not the only thing to dread. In life, we may also experience all the pain of being separated from someone we have loved or who we thought loved us. People we love may leave us forever. Life can be a fragile and painful business. And that should make us cautious about expecting too much from it.

It's your turn

Read the following poem carefully.

(a) Describe its subject matter.

(b) State what you believe to be its theme.

A GARDEN ON THE POINT

Now it is Easter and the speckled bean
Breaks open underground, the liquid snail
Winces and waits, trapped on the lawn's light
  green;
The burdened clothes-line heaves and barks in
  the gale,
And lost in flowers near the garage wall
Child and mother fumble, tidy, restrain.

And now great ebb tides lift to light of day
The sea-bed's briny chambers of decay.

Thomas Kinsella

The **subject matter** of a poem may be:
- Local or Universal
- Topical or Perennial
- Everyday or Exotic
- Romantic or Realistic
- Personal/Private or Public
- Political
- Philosophical
- National or International
- Urban or Rural
- Past/Present/Future. . .

The **theme** of a poem may be:
- Love or Hate
- Greed or Generosity
- Good or Evil
- Justice or Injustice
- War or Peace
- Love of nature
- Childhood
- Youth
- Old Age
- Happiness or Sadness. . .

Try these

1. Using the suggested categories for *subject matter*, select *any two poems* you have studied which share a common subject matter. Show how the subject matter is common to both poems. In both cases, give the title of the poem and the name of the poet.

2. Using the suggested categories for *theme*, select *any two poems* you have studied which share a common theme. State this theme, and compare and contrast the poets' handling of it. In both cases, give the title of the poem and the name of the poet.

TONE

The *tone* of a poem refers to the poet's *attitude* towards:
- the subject matter
- the reader
- the poet himself or herself

Attitudes towards the subject matter may be:
- serious
- humorous
- sympathetic
- hostile
- inquisitive. . .

Attitudes towards the reader may be:
- confidential
- distant
- respectful
- condescending
- angry
- resentful
- cynical . . .

Attitudes of the poet towards himself or herself may be confident or assertive, doubting or sceptical, self-indulgent, self-pitying. . .

Tone and theme are inter-related. The tone of a poem shows the reader the poet's intention, which is usually shown in the theme.

Example
This is an excerpt from a poem by the English nature poet, John Clare.

Little trotty wagtail, he went in the rain,
And tittering, tottering sideways he ne'er got
    straight again,
He stooped to get a worm, and looked up to
    get a fly,
And then he flew away ere his feathers they
    were dry.

Comments on the tone
The tone of this poem is light and humorous. It conveys the poet's observant, caring and sympathetic attitude towards nature, especially as represented by the wagtail.

It's your turn
Select poems in your anthology which you think will illustrate each of the following tones. Support your choices with references to the poems. In all cases, give the title of the poem and the name of the poet.
1. A serious tone
2. A sympathetic tone
3. An angry tone
4. An inquisitive tone
5. A self-doubting tone
6. A self-pitying tone
7. A cheerful tone

MOOD

The mood of a poem may be:
- cheerful
- depressed
- angry
- critical
- comical
- playful
- mysterious
- puzzled. . .

It's your turn
Select poems in your anthology which you think convey a definite mood. Describe that mood with reference to the poems you select. In all cases, give the title of the poem and the name of the poet.

HOW TO ANSWER TYPICAL QUESTIONS
The following poem, 'Does It Matter'?, was written by Siegfried Sassoon. He is one of the most famous poets to write about his experiences during the First World War (1914-18). First, read this poem carefully a few times. Think about what Sassoon is trying to say — and the way in which he is saying it. Then, study the sample questions/comments/answers.

DOES IT MATTER?

Does it matter? – losing your legs? ...
For people will always be kind,
And you need not show that you mind
When the others come in after hunting
To gobble their muffins and eggs.

Does it matter? – losing your sight? ...
There's such splendid work for the blind;
And people will always be kind,
As you sit on the terrace remembering
And turning your face to the light.

Do they matter? – those dreams from the
   pit? ...
And you drink and forget and be glad,
And people won't say that you're mad;
For they'll know that you've fought for
   your country
And no one will worry a bit.

             Siegfried Sassoon

Question 1 (a)

What picture of English country life do you find in this poem? What class in society are we talking about?

Comment on the question

These two questions are connected because the country life suggested by the poet is also the setting for the social class portrayed in the poem.

Answer

The class referred to in the poem is the English upper middle-class. Although these people may work in the city or live on their inherited money, they prefer to live in their country houses. Their lives are leisurely and they enjoy such pleasant pastimes as hunting, relaxing on the terrace and admiring the countryside, and enjoying evening cocktails.

Question 1 (b)

Describe the attitude of the people in the poem to the central person (the 'you') in the poem.

Comment on the question

Focus your answer on 'attitude'. Describe the ways in which this attitude is implied (hinted at) rather than stated openly in the silly and insensitive suggestions which these people come up with.

Answer

The attitude of these people is flippant (off-hand) and non-caring. The narrator is a returned soldier with whom the poet identifies, but he may be regarded as any wounded soldier who has returned from the war. The soldier himself is probably a product of this upper middle-class, since he seems so familiar with it.

The soldier has experienced the horrors of the First World War in which countless thousands lost their lives. Many thousands of others were dreadfully maimed and some were driven mad. These men thought they were fighting for love of country – at least that's what they were told in the propaganda of the time.

When these soldiers came back from the war, people like those in the poem, who had not experienced the horrors of the war, simply dismissed all the horrors of the war. Their attitude was insensitive and callous. It revealed a terrible indifference to human suffering. Their ideas of how the soldier might forget what he has been through reveal a cruel hollowness.

Question 2

Imagine you are the central person (the 'you') in the poem. Basing your answer ON THE DETAILS IN THE POEM, write an entry for your diary in which you talk about your physical and mental condition and say what you think about the people that surround you now.

Comment on the question

Remember your impressions of the people when you wrote about question 1 (a). Keep to the diary-entry format as the question requires.

Answer

Friday. Evening.

I am spending the weekend with Uncle James and his family in Hazel Thorpe, his country residence. Uncle James tells me that things here are pretty much as they were when I used to visit the place before the war. But I really can't say. Just one of the things I'll never see again!

This afternoon I heard the baying of the hounds in the distance. That, too, is part of a past that can never be re-lived by me.

But any self-pity I may want to feel is stifled by the anger that Uncle James and his social set arouse in me by their attitude towards us returned soldiers. They refuse to accept the horrors of the war we have been through, even though they must surely see it in our mangled bodies and minds. They are unmoved by the sight of us. They seem to think that a pat on the back and expressions like 'Brave lad!' will somehow wipe away everything that's happened.

Was it for this insensitive and uncaring society that I became what I am now? Is this the reward for fighting for your country? How little I thought things would turn out like this!

Question 3

'The attitude of the poet towards war is powerfully conveyed in this poem.' Discuss this statement.

Comment on the question

This is a discussion question. It means that you are not tied down as much in your answer. However, you should still concentrate on the poet's attitude towards war. This is expressed indirectly in his attitude towards the people in the poem.

Answer

The poet refers to the loss of legs and of sight and the madness into which the war plunged so many people. These sufferings were both physical and mental and were to be endured for the sake of one's country. But how did this privileged society react to so much suffering? The poet pictures it as a shallow, unfeeling society which is indifferent to the sufferings of those who fought and died. What, then, would justify the sufferings of war? Certainly not that 'love of country' which the men were told they were fighting for! To the poet, war seems like a horrible and futile (useless) business. The humiliation of the returned soldiers just makes the war seem even more senseless. A mood of anger simmers beneath the poem's understatements.

HOW TO ANSWER TYPICAL QUESTIONS

The following poem, 'Considering The Snail', is by Thom Gunn. Study the poem itself, then the questions/comments/answers which follow it.

CONSIDERING THE SNAIL

The snail pushes through a green
night, for the grass is heavy
with water and meets over
the bright path he makes, where rain
has darkened the earth's dark. He
moves in a wood of desire,

pale antlers barely stirring
as he hunts. I cannot tell
what power is at work, drenched there
with purpose, knowing nothing.
What is a snail's fury? All
I think is that if later

I parted the blades above
the tunnel and saw the thin
trail of broken white across
litter, I would never have
imagined the slow passion
to that deliberate progress.

Thom Gunn

Question 1 (a)

Suggest an alternative title for the poem.
Explain your choice.

Comments on the question

The title of a poem usually indicates the theme of the poem. (Poems without titles are usually 'named' by the first line in the poem.) To retitle this poem, we must first have some idea of what the poem is really about.

Answer

The poet focuses on the hugeness of this tiny creature's efforts to make its way to where it is going. The snail lives in a world in which the smallest of things (from a human point of view) are gigantic obstacles. The poet is amazed at the energy which drives the creature on. This energy is a mystery to him, as the power in all of nature is a mystery to human beings. If this reading of the poem is correct, then the poem might be retitled 'Slow Passion'. This new title is from the second-last line of the poem. It points to the passion which all creatures have for survival, no matter how slow the expression of that passion may be.

Question 1 (b)

Having considered the snail, what does the poet conclude?

Comments on the question

This question requires a statement of the poet's thoughts on what he has observed. In answering this question, do not simply repeat your answer to Question 1 (a).

Answer

The poet has observed the slow and steady progress of the snail as it goes out in search of food. He finds himself wondering at the energy of this simple creature which acts entirely on instinct. What the poet knows is that such energy drives living things ever onwards, helping them to overcome all obstacles to their survival. Even in such a 'lowly' creature as the snail, life makes a steady 'deliberate progress' towards survival.

Question 1 (c)

How does the poet succeed in making us view the snail in a new light? What words and phrases are particularly effective?

Comments on the question

A question like this refers to the use of language. It is important to support any statement you may make by quoting from the text.

Answer

By observing the snail closely, the poet sees it as through a magnifying glass. The grass through which the snail travels becomes a forest ('a wood of desire'). The projections on the snail's head give it the appearance of a large creature such as a deer (with 'pale antlers'). The poet describes the snail as pushing 'through a green night', which is the dark green world it inhabits. The poet gives us the idea that the snail is a mysterious and fabulous creature.

ELEMENTS OF POETIC TECHNIQUE

RHYTHM AND METRE

The rhythm of poetry is like the rhythm of music. It is the beat or the sound pattern of the words. When the rhythm has a regular pattern, we can measure this beat. The term given to this poetic beat is **metre**. An appreciation of metre gives us a better understanding of a great deal of poetry.

During the twentieth century, poets began to break with the traditional use of metre. But until then, most poetry in the English language used a measure called the **iambus** to regulate rhythm.

An iambus consists of two syllables, or parts. The first syllable is unstressed. The second is stressed or accented. Look at these words, which have an unstressed first syllable and a stressed second syllable.

begin = be GIN

attempt = at TEMPT

design = de SIGN

This is an example of a line written in iambic metre.

When I consider how my light is spent

To measure this line, we can first divide it into syllables. We can then mark the stressed and unstressed syllables. The unstressed syllable is marked ◡. The stressed syllable is marked ⎯.

When I con sid er how my light is spent

This line has five iambic feet. It is the most common kind of line in English-language poetry. It is the rhythm in which all of Shakespeare's plays are written and is called an **iambic pentameter**. (A pentagon has five sides; pentameter has five feet.)

Poets can vary the rhythm by substituting other kinds of metric feet for iambic feet. The most common substitute is the **trochee**. It consists of two syllables – the first stressed, the second unstressed. The following words are examples.

butter = BUT ter

garden = GAR den

flower = FLOW er

The **spondee** is another kind of metric variation. It has two stressed syllables, as in these examples.

headline

heartbreak

154

Common metric feet in English-language poetry

⏑ = **unstressed syllable**

— = **stressed syllable**

• • • • • • • • • •

iambus = ⏑ —

again = a GAIN

pretend = pre TEND

• • • • • • • • • •

trochee = — ⏑

apple = AP ple

lantern = LAN tern

• • • • • • • • • •

spondee = — —

doghouse

night-time

• • • • • • • • • •

dactyl = — ⏑ ⏑

beautiful = BEAU ti ful

organise = OR gan ise

• • • • • • • • • •

anapaest = ⏑ ⏑ —

apprehend = ap pre HEND

introduce = in tro DUCE

• • • • • • • • • •

amphibrach = ⏑ — ⏑

attracted = at TRACT ed

delivered = de LIV ered

• • • • • • • • • •

cretic = — ⏑ —

Amsterdam = AM ster DAM

Even though we may be able to measure the metre of a poem, poetry is not meant to be read with mechanical regularity. The speaking voice interprets the rhythm or beat, constantly creating variety.

Marking out of the metrical pattern is called **scansion**. We can **scan** the first four lines of a famous sonnet by Shakespeare like this.

⏑ — ⏑ — ⏑ — ⏑ — ⏑ —
That time of year thou mayst in me behold

⏑ — ⏑ — ⏑ — ⏑ — ⏑ —
When yellow leaves, or none, or few, do hang

⏑— ⏑ — ⏑ — ⏑ — ⏑ —
Upon the boughs which shake against the cold,

⏑ — ⏑ — ⏑ — ⏑ — ⏑ —
Bare ruined choirs, where late the sweet birds sang.

Questions about such poetic techniques as metre and rhythm are sometimes quite challenging. So it is a good idea to remember the following functions of rhythm.

- It helps to create *memorable language*.
- It *emphasises* important words and ideas.
- It helps to create *mood and atmosphere* (suspense, terror, joy, humour. . .).
- It is expresses *emotion* (happiness, sadness, anger. . .).

Example

To illustrate this, we will study another poem by Siegfried Sassoon, 'Base Details'.

BASE DETAILS

If I were fierce, and bald, and short of breath,
   I'd live with scarlet Majors at the Base,
And speed glum heroes up the line of death.
   You'd see me with my puffy, petulant face,
Guzzling and gulping in the best hotel,
   Reading the roll of Honour. 'Poor young chap,'

I'd say – 'I used to know his father well;
   Yes, we've lost heavily in this last scrap.'
And when the war is done and youth stone dead,
   I'd toddle safely home and die – in bed.

Siegfried Sassoon

Some comments on the rhythm

1. The pauses before the two *ands* in the first line are indicated by commas. These pauses enable the poet to emphasise 'fierce', 'bald' and 'short of breath'.
2. The rhythm of 'puffy, petulant face' expresses the poet's feeling of contempt.
3. Look at the lax (less definite) rhythm of
   'I used to know his father well;
      Yes, we've lost heavily in this last scrap.'
   This highlights the insincerity of the statement and the moral emptiness of the speaker.
4. There is an important pause before 'in bed' in the last line.
      I'd toddle safely home and die – in bed.
   This is an anti-climax which prepares the reader for the poet's judgment on the inhuman shallowness of the Majors of the poem.
5. Make a comment on the title of the poem.

It's your turn

1. (a) Scan (mark out) the metrical feet of the following lines.

   He clasps the crag with crooked hands;
   Close to the sun in lonely lands,
   Ringed with the azure world, he stands.
   The wrinkled sea beneath him crawls;
   He watches from his mountain walls,
   And like a thunderbolt he falls.

(from 'The Eagle', by Tennyson)

(b) Make three comments on the rhythm of these lines.

2. (a) Scan the following lines.

   I leant upon a coppice gate
   When Frost was spectre-grey,
   And winter's dregs made desolate
   The weakening eye of day.
   The tangle bine-stems scored the sky
   Like strings of broken lyres,
   And all mankind that haunted nigh
   Had sought their household fires.

(from 'The Darkling Thrush'
by Thomas Hardy)

(b) Make three comments on the rhythm of the lines.

3. (a) Scan the following lines.

   Whose woods these are I think I know.
   His house is in the village though;
   He will not see me stopping here
   To watch his woods fill up with snow.

(from 'Stopping by Woods on
a Snowy Evening' by Robert Frost)

(b) Make three comments on the rhythm of the lines.

4. (a) Scan the following lines.

   The trees are in their autumn beauty,
   The woodland paths are dry,
   Under the October twilight the water
   Mirrors a still sky;
   Upon the brimming water among the
      stones
   Are nine-and-fifty swans.

(from 'The Wild Swans at Coole'
by W.B. Yeats)

(b) Make three comments on the rhythm of the lines.

5. (a) Scan the following lines.

Now leave the check-reins slack,
The seed is flying far today –
The seed like stars against the black
Eternity of April clay.
        (from 'To the Man after the Harrow'
                by Patrick Kavanagh)

(b) Make three comments on the rhythm of the lines.

NON-METRICAL POETRY – FREE VERSE

In the early years of the 20th century, some poets began to feel that poetry was becoming too mechanical and dull. Too many untalented poets were producing monotonous and meaningless rhythms just by mechanically measuring out their lines.

In reaction to this, some people such as the American poet, Ezra Pound, claimed that the rhythm of poetry should be controlled by the ear and not just by syllable-counting. Modern poets thought that poetry should be free of traditional metrical patterns, and poets should be allowed to use whatever rhythms they felt were pleasing or appropriate.

Since then, many modern poets have paid little or no attention to traditional metre. Their poetry contains no regular beat. It requires great skill to write this kind of poetry successfully. Without such skill, poetry can easily become chopped-up prose. Then, part of the attraction of poetry – its memorable effects of rhythm – may be lost.

The reader must be especially careful in reading free verse. Questions like these have to be asked.
• Does the poem read smoothly or awkwardly?
• Does the rhythm enrich the sense of the poem?
• Does the rhythm contribute to the mood of the poem?

Example

The following is a poem in free verse by the English poet and novelist, D.H. Lawrence.

SORROW

Why does the thin grey strand
Floating up from the forgotten
Cigarette between my fingers,
Why does it trouble me?

Ah, you will understand;
When I carried my mother downstairs,
A few times only, at the beginning
Of her soft-foot malady,

I should find, for a reprimand
To my gaiety, a few long grey hairs
On the breast of my coat; and one by one
I watched them float up the dark chimney.
              D.H. Lawrence

Some comments on the rhythm

1. Line 1: The slow rhythm of 'the thin grey strand' suggests the slowly rising curl of the cigarette smoke.
2. Line 4: 'Why does it trouble me?' moves at a quicker pace. This suggests the suddenness of the poet's disturbance.
3. Lines 5-8: The very plain rhythm of these lines is in keeping with the ordinariness of the chore which the poet is describing.
4. Line 10: 'a few long grey hairs' has a slow, long-drawn-out rhythm which suggests the feeling of sadness.

RHYME

· ·

Words rhyme when they end in the same sound, apart from the initial consonant.

> deer/ fear
> munch/crunch
> head/bed
> cot/plot

These words involve only one syllable. More than one syllable can be involved, however.

> heather/ feather
> better/sweater
> honey/funny

Rhyming schemes – patterns of rhyme – are marked out by using the letters A, B, C, D etc. to indicate the different rhymes. Look at this example by William Wordsworth. Lines 1 and 3 rhyme – they are marked A. Lines 2 and 4 rhyme – they are marked B

She dwelt among the untrodden ways	A
Beside the springs of Dove,	B
A maid whom there were none to praise	A
And very few to love.	B

SPECIAL RHYMING FORMS
The heroic couplet

This is the name given to two rhyming lines of iambic pentameter.

u — u – u – u – u –
A fool, with more of wit than half mankind,   A
u — u – u – u – u –
Too rash for thought, for action too refined.   A

The ballad form

This is a typical example of the rhyme in ballad form.

u — u – u – u –
There lived a wife at Usher's Well   (4 stresses)

u u — u – u —
And a wealthy wife was she;   A (3 stresses)

u — u – u – u —
She had three stout and stalwart sons   (4 stresses)

u — u – u —
And sent them o'er the sea.   A (3 stresses)

The sonnet form

• The Shakespearean sonnet

This is a poem of fourteen lines of iambic pentameter. These lines are divided into three **quatrains** (groups of four lines) and a **couplet** (two lines). A Shakespearean sonnet usually follows this rhyming scheme.

ABAB CDCD EFEF GG

Here is the complete sonnet – Sonnet 73 – which you studied earlier in this chapter.

That time of year thou mayst in me behold	A
When yellow leaves, or none, or few, do hang	B
Upon those boughs which shake against the cold,	A
Bare ruined choirs, where late the sweet birds sang.	B
In me thou see'st the twilight of such day	C
As after sunset fadeth in the west;	D
Which by and by black night doth take away,	C
Death's second self, that seals up all in rest.	D
In me thou see'st the glowing of such fire,	E
That on the ashes of his youth doth lie,	F
As the deathbed whereon it must expire	E
Consumed with that which it was nourished by.	F
This thou perceiv'st, which makes thy love more strong,	G
To love that well which thou must leave ere long.	G

• **The Petrarchan** or **Italian sonnet**

This is a much less common type of sonnet because of the difficulty of finding two rhymes for eight lines. Like the Shakespearean sonnet, it consists of fourteen lines of iambic pentameter. However, it is divided instead into an **octet** (a group of eight lines) and a **sestet** (a group of six lines). Its rhyming scheme is:

ABBA ABBA (fixed) CDE CDE (variable).

ALLITERATION

Alliteration is the use of words beginning with the same consonant.

> Full fathom five thy father lies.

Alliteration lends a musical effect to the verse and makes it more memorable. It may also help to give emphasis to certain words and phrases.

It's your turn

Using your anthology, find ten examples of alliteration. In all cases, give the title of the poem and the name of the poet.

ASSONANCE

Assonance is vowel rhyme without any rhyme in the consonants.

> cap/hat
> feel/seen
> flatten/ladder
> fall/saw

Like alliteration, assonance is a means of creating musical effects which make the verse memorable and help to emphasise certain words and phrases.

It's your turn

Select ten lines of poetry which show assonance. In all cases, give the title of the poem and the name of the poet.

METAPHORS AND SIMILES

Both metaphors and similes involve comparisons. The purpose of comparison is to create a more vivid picture of a subject .

A **simile** is a direct comparison introduced by the word 'like' or 'as'. A **metaphor** does not use 'like' or 'as'. For instance, we could say

> Her eyes twinkled *like* stars. (**simile**)
> Her eyes *were* twinkling stars. (**metaphor**)

In the simile, the association is strictly confined to the twinkling appearance of the stars. With the metaphor, it is not only the image of the twinkling stars which comes to mind – there are other associations which the word 'star' may have. . . mystery. . . romance. . . magic. . .

Similes are more controlled and more limited in their associations. Metaphors are less controlled and more suggestive.

Metaphors are not meant to be understood literally. A person's eyes are *not* really stars. Both writer and reader know this, but the writer wishes to give certain images and feelings to what he or she is describing.

WHAT IS A GOOD METAPHOR?

Metaphors should add to the meaning of what the writer wishes to express. They should help to give us a picture which is much more vivid and interesting. The following is a good example of an effective metaphor.

As I walked out one evening,
  Walking down Bristol Street,
The crowds upon the pavement
  Were fields of harvest wheat.
(from 'As I walked out one evening'
                by W.H. Auden)

The theme of this poem is the fragile and temporary nature of individual life. In describing the crowds on the pavement as 'fields of harvest wheat', the poet wishes to draw our attention to the inevitability of death – the approach of autumn is unstoppable and then the fields of wheat are cut down in the harvest.

WHAT IS A BAD METAPHOR?

Metaphors should be consistent and not confusing. A common mistake in the use of metaphor is to mix them and cause confusion. The following examples of mixed metaphors should illustrate this error.

• When he let the cat out of the bag, I smelled a rat.
(The writer wishes to say: 'When he revealed the secret, I became suspicious.' But the metaphor begins by referring to a cat, and ends up with an image of a rat.)

• He hits below the belt when he flies off the handle.
(The writer wishes to say: 'He resorts to foul play when he loses his temper.' Starting with an image of boxing, the writer then goes off the track by ending with an image of something else entirely.)

Try these

Look at these mixed metaphors. What is the writer trying to say? What images are being mixed up in each?
1. They bounced the idea around but they were flogging a dead horse.
2. He put his foot in his mouth and jumped off the deep end.
3. The teacher blew his stack and hit the road.
4. The drinks were on the house, so we didn't have to put our hands in our pockets.
5. We thought he'd put down roots, but he flew the coop.

It's your turn

1. Find ten examples of mixed metaphors in your anthology. Say why they are bad.
2. Find five examples of what you consider to be good metaphors in the poems in your anthology. Give the reasons why you think they are good. In all cases give the title of the poem and the name of the poet.

POETIC FORMS

• •

FOLK SONGS AND BALLADS

The earliest forms of poetry are probably the ballad and the folk song (the word 'ballad' comes from the French word meaning 'to dance'). Genuine ballads and folk songs are anonymous (we don't know who wrote them). They were usually composed to record events (usually local, or with local colour) and to express feelings (of joy, sadness, surprise, terror. . .) Because they were passed on *orally*, by word of mouth, the survival of ballads and folk songs depended on their *memorability* and their *relevance* to human existence: love of life, fear of sickness and death, desire for a better world, the need for companionship etc. Ballads and folk songs often express a sense of rebellion or resentment against the established order.

CHARACTERISTICS OF A BALLAD OR FOLK SONG

1. They use *direct and simple language*.
2. They *tell a story*, or sketch the outline of a story.
3. They are *impersonal* – the composer does not speak directly to the audience.
4. The lines are in *groups of four* (called quatrains).
5. There is a definite *rhyming scheme* – line 2 usually rhymes with line 4.
6. These is a *dramatic treatment* of the subject matter, often with great *exaggeration*.
7. The use of *repetition* helps the reciter or singer to remember the lines. Repetition can also be used to heighten tension by slowing down the narrative or story. It can also help the communication of the ballad or folk song in a noisy atmosphere of talk and movement.
8. *Dialogue or conversation* are often used to heighten the dramatic effect.

Example

The following is part of the famous ballad, 'Robin Hood and the Three Squires'.

There are thirteen months in all the year,
    As I hear many men say.
But the merriest month in all the year
    Is the merry month of May.

Now Robin Hood is to Nottingham gone,
    With a link-a-down and a-day,
And there he met a silly old woman,
    Was weeping on the way.

'What news? What news, thou silly old woman?
    What news, I do thee pray?'
Said she: 'Three squires in Nottingham town
    Are condemned to die this day.'

A few comments

1. There are no long, complicated words. Instead, the words are the words of everyday speech, although some, like 'link-a-down', seem very strange to us. The poem was composed many years ago, however, when such little rhyming bits were common.
2. A story is going to be told about one of Robin Hood's adventures. It will have a local setting – Nottingham in England.
3. The poet presents the story directly without introducing himself or herself to the audience.
4. The poem is written in quatrains.
5. In each quatrain, lines 2 and 4 rhyme.
6. The story is dramatic. It involves the meeting of Robin Hood and the 'silly old woman'.
7. There are the repetitions of 'in all the year' in lines 1 and 3, and 'What news?' in lines 9 and 10.
8. The poem contains dialogue between Robin Hood and the old woman.
9. There is a hint that Robin Hood will spring into action and help someone who is in trouble.

Try this

These lines are from an American folk song, 'The Ballad of Joe Hill', which was written in the 1920s when working people were fighting for their rights. Joe Hill was a union organiser who was killed because he led the fight for these rights.

Look back at what you have learned about ballads and folks songs. Discuss the ways in which this short verse follows these ideas.

> I dreamed I saw Joe Hill last night,
> Alive as he could be.
> Says I, 'But Joe, you're ten years dead!'
> 'I never died,' said he.
> 'I never died,' said he.

QUESTIONS OFTEN ASKED ABOUT BALLADS

1. In your opinion, how effective is the ballad's use of simple language?

Suggestions

The language of ballads is usually simple because the people by whom and for whom they were composed were usually not educated people and they would not have understood long 'hard' words. Uneducated listeners could more easily identify with the characters who appeared in the ballad if these characters spoke in a language which was like their own. When something can be expressed in simple language, it often means that the feelings and ideas involved are universal – they are feelings and ideas that everyone has at some time or other.

2. Sketch out the story which the ballad tells.

Suggestions

Identify the characters (say who they are). Describe the incident(s) in which they are involved and say how they are involved. A story usually involves an action: describe how the action began, how it developed and how it ended.

3. What are the dramatic qualities of the ballad?

Suggestions
• Comment on the *setting* – the place in which the action occurs. Is it spooky or mysterious? Is it familiar or strange? Is it ordinary or fantastic? Does it belong to a time past?
• Comment on the *atmosphere*. Is the atmosphere happy or sad? Is it comforting or frightening? Give reasons for your comments.
• Comment on the *characters*. Are they kind or cruel, scoundrels or heroes?
• Comment on the *dialogue*. Does it bring the characters to life for you? What does it tell you about them?
• Comment on the *action*. Does the action move quickly or slowly? Is it interesting or boring? Does it make sense to you?
• Give reasons for all your comments.

4. What message, moral or theme do you think the ballad is concerned with?

Suggestions

A ballad may have one of these messages. Good always triumphs over evil. Courage and loyalty are to be admired. Disobedience is always punished in the end. A greedy person always meets a bad end. It is wrong to be cowardly. It is good to be kind and charitable. It is a noble thing to give up one's life for a good cause. War is evil. Power corrupts even good people. Life without love is unbearable.

It's your turn
Study the following ballad and then answer the questions which follow it.

A KNIGHT AND A LADY

> A knight and a lady
>   Went riding one day
> Far into the forest,
>   Away, away.

'Fair knight,' said the lady
  'I pray, have a care,
This forest is evil –
  Beware, beware!'

A fiery red dragon
They spied on the grass;
The lady wept sorely,
  Alas! Alas!

The knight slew the dragon,
  The lady was gay.
They rode on together,
  Away, away.

      (Anonymous)

1. In your opinion, how effective is the ballad's use of simple language?
2. Sketch out the story which the ballad tells.
3. What are the dramatic qualities of the ballad?
4. What message or moral do you think the ballad points out? Give reasons for your answer.

Try these

1. Select a ballad in the anthology you are using and point out its ballad characteristics.
2. Study the following ballad. Then answer the questions which follow it. (The words marked with an asterisk are explained in the margin.)

THE TWO CORBIES*   *crows

As I was walking all alone,
Down a down a down hey down
I heard twa* corbies making a moan;   *two
The one unto the other say,
'Where shall we gang* and dine today?'   *go

'In behind yon auld* fail* dyke   *old *turf
I wot* there lies a new slain knight;   *know
And nobody kens* that he lies there,   *knows
But his hawk, his hound, and his lady fair.

'His hound is to the hunting gane*,   *gone
His hawk to fetch the wild-fowl hame*,   *home
His lady's ta'en* another mate,   *taken
So we may make our dinner sweet.

'Ye'll sit on his white hause-bane*,   *neckbone
And I'll pike out his bonny blue een*;   *eyes
And with one lock of his golden hair
We'll theek* our nest when it grows bare.   *line

'Many a one for him makes moan,
Down a down a down hey derry
But none shall ken where he is gone;
O'er his white banes*, when they are bare,   *bones
The wind shall blow for evermain*.'   *evermore
With a down a down derry derry derry down.

163

1. In your opinion, how effective is the ballad's use of simple language?
2. Sketch out the story which the ballad tells.
3. What are the dramatic qualities of the ballad?
4. What message, moral or theme do you think is the concern of the ballad?

THE EPIC

An epic is a long poem dealing with the exploits of a great hero. The earliest epic poems expressed the values of the societies which produced them. For this reason, they provide us with important expressions of the national or tribal culture from which they have come.

- Homer's *Iliad* and *Odyssey* are expressions of classical Greek society.
- Virgil's *Aeneid* is the expression of imperial Rome.
- The *Táin* is seen as the expression of pre-Christian Irish society.

From the Middle Ages onwards, writers of epics – Dante (Italy: *The Divine Comedy*), Milton (England: *Paradise Lost*) and Camoens (Portugal: *The Lusiads*) – set out to produce great national poems to represent and celebrate their societies.

Try this

Using your school or local public library, or perhaps even your school anthology, read about any of the above epics. Give your impressions of the societies which they describe.

THE LYRIC

In a lyric, the personal voice of the poet can be heard. We have a sense that a specific individual is speaking to us, telling us about his or her experiences of life. Most poetry of the present century can be described as lyric poetry.

Here is a well-known lyric by the great English poet William Blake. It is titled 'The Poison Tree'.

THE POISON TREE

I was angry with my friend:
I told my wrath, my wrath did end.
I was angry with my foe:
I told it not, my wrath did grow.

And I watered it in fears,
Night and morning with my tears;
And I sunnéd it with smiles,
and with soft deceitful wiles.

And it grew both day and night,
Till it bore an apple bright;
And my foe beheld it shine,
And he knew that it was mine,

And into my garden stole
When the night had veiled the pole:
In the morning glad I see
My foe outstretched beneath the tree.

William Blake

Think about it

1. What experience of life do you think the poet is describing in this poem?
2. Select any poem in your anthology which you think can be described as a lyric. Give reasons for your choice.

QUESTIONS TO ASK WHEN STUDYING A POEM

SUBJECT MATTER AND THEME

- Is the voice speaking in the poem that of the poet himself or herself – or is the poet speaking through the voice of another character or person (as in a play)?

- To whom is the poet speaking?
- Does the poem have a specific setting in time and place? What are these?
- Has the poem a moral or a lesson? If so, what is it?
- Is the form of the poem dramatic, narrative, descriptive, argumentative?
- What feelings are expressed in the poem?
- Does the poem create a distinctive atmosphere (for example, of suspense, terror, joy etc.)?
- Does the poem have a level of meaning which is deeper than the apparent or obvious one?

POEMS THAT USE REGULAR METRE

- What metre does the poem use?
- What is the rhyming scheme of the poem?
- What musical qualities does the poem have (with reference to alliteration and assonance etc.)?
- What comments can you make about the relation between the poem's musical qualities and its meaning?
- Is the poem written in a strict metrical form such as the sonnet or the ballad?
- What comments can you make on the poem's use of line-breaks?

LANGUAGE OF POETRY

- Is the language of the poem simple or complicated?
- Do the words of the poem appeal to our senses? Which words and images appeal to which sense?
- Does the poem use similes and metaphors? If so, to what purpose and to what effect are they used?
- Does the language have any unusual features that make the poem distinctive?

TYPICAL QUESTIONS ABOUT POEMS

The following two poems deal with childhood. Read each poem carefully. Then answer the questions which follow each one.

LONG JOHN

Under the balcony, in the dry brown earth,
he hid the stolen coins while I looked on.
In no treasure chest or even paper bag,
the coins mingled with the earth that added
mystery to their metallic clink. A solemn oath,
fearful with threat, devised by him, bound
    the pact.

    The air was dense with menace.

Was it days or weeks later he left me
alone, a five-year-old, deep below
the riverbank, while the level
of the tidal-river rose inch by inch?
Briefly he looked down from the parapet,
his face contorted with glee.

    He answered nothing to my desperate plea.

Down the years of his crimes since then,
that I have merely read or heard about,
his devilish face has often come again,
to grin at my childish helplessness,
recalling stolen coins, my abandonment,
and, most of all, my silence then.

              M.J. Smith

Think about it

1. Why do you think the poet has entitled the poem 'Long John'? A clue: Long John Silver is the name of a villainous character in the classic children's novel, *Treasure Island*, by Robert Louis Stevenson.

2. What is the poet's attitude towards this experience of his childhood as he looks back on it now?

3. What do you think was the relationship between the poet and the other character in the poem?

4. Referring to the details of the poem, recreate the incident in which you think the two boys were involved.

5. Why do you think the incident made such a deep impression on the poet? Argue your point of view.

6. Comment on the words and images that suggest 'menace'. How effectively does the poet create an atmosphere of menace?

7. This poem is written in a fairly regular metre. Mark out the metre of the first seven lines.

• •

COUMEENOLE

For Owen

Dig! you cried

We dug out great trenches
and extended the abyss
down into utter darkness
that stopped the heart with its cold

We fought off monstrous beasts
that nudged and butted us with their blunt heads
and from those regions of terror we brought back
massive rocks and curious shells

We threw up huge walls
and ramparts to repel
the encroaching forces
of chaos and disorder

We took all the boulders and all the sand
in the world and ranged up
mountains into clouds
against the combing winds and the hard sea

And in the territories we had created
we established order
we set up high towers riveted with light
and we built roads, castles and cities

At evening as we left
looked back and saw whole continents dissolve
under the flood and heard
the soft collapse of walls and boundaries

you cried

Trevor Joyce

Think about it

In a note on this poem, the poet explains that Coumeenole 'is the name of a strand at the western end of the Dingle Peninsula, opening out onto the Atlantic from under Slea Head.'

1. Describe the attitude of the poet towards his young son as suggested by the details of the poem.

2. The elaborate castle made by the poet and his son means something different to each of them. Explain what you think this difference is.

3. In your opinion, what is the difference in meaning between the word 'cried' in the first line and 'cried' in the last line? Give reasons for your answer.

4. The poem has many images of menace and threat. Identify these images and explain how they work.

5. What do you think is the theme of this poem? (In your answer, do not confuse theme with subject matter.)

6. Comment on how rhythm is used to emphasise what is being said. Illustrate your answer with quotations from the poem.

MEDIA

FOCUS ON ADVERTISING

Advertising is big business all over the world. A huge industry in itself, it provides a service to huge industries of every sort. Advertising can also be a small business which caters for small and even personal businesses.

No matter where we are, we are bombarded by advertisements. We see them on billboards along the road, on television, on radio, at the cinema. In this section, we will focus on the advertising which appears in newspapers and magazines and on posters.

Try this

During the next week, compile a list of all the places in which you have seen or heard advertisements. Make a class list of all these places.

WHAT IS ALLOWED?

Because advertising has such a huge impact on our lives, it is regulated, or controlled. What advertising can and cannot do is stated by various laws and monitored, or watched, by certain agencies.

- Advertising in certain areas – tobacco, medicines and medical services, credit agencies (banks etc.) and employment is controlled by the law. Advertisers who break the law can be fined and suffer penalties.
- For all other consumer items and services, advertising is controlled by the *Advertising Standards Authority of Ireland* (ASAI).
- The ASAI is a watchdog committee funded by the advertising and media agencies. It operates a code of *advertising standards*. Its job is to see that advertisements are not deliberately misleading and that they respect the rules of fair play and competition. The ASAI is independent of the government; it is not enforced by the law and it exercises its power by influencing its members.
- The *Complaints Committee* of ASAI consists of eleven members. It listens to and investigates complaints from the public. If necessary, it invites the advertisers to consider the complaints very seriously. It is clearly in the interest of advertisers not to be involved in any complaints because of the possibility of bad publicity.

Think about it

Have you ever had any reason to complain about a product or a service? Discuss the reasons for making a complaint with your class. Look at the section on Letters for ideas about writing a letter of complaint.

A CRITICAL GRID

●●●●●●●●●●●●●●●●●●●●●●●●●●●●

We should always respond critically to any advertisement. The following question grid will help us to do this. This grid will teach us how to 'read' advertisements. The questions give us a way of analysing an advertisement to make sure we are not deceived or misled.

> **WHO?**
> **IS SELLING**
> **WHAT?**
> **HOW?**
> **AND**
> **TO WHOM?**

WHO?
• The client
The client is the customer. The client may be a small local firm such as a shop. It may also be a huge international industry such as a car manufacturer or a soft drink business. The advertising client may be a service industry such as a bank. Charities, political parties, religions, airlines – all of these and more are advertising clients.

• The advertising agency
An advertising agency is the company which is hired by the client to *promote a product, an idea or a message.* Some 'ad agencies' are themselves big international companies; others are small local businesses. Big ad agencies will charge a client millions of pounds to promote their product.

is selling. . .
The word 'selling' does not only mean 'selling'. An extremely important part of advertising is *persuading* people to buy a product, join a religion, contribute to a charity, believe in a message.

WHAT?
This is the product or idea or service which is being promoted.

HOW?
The way in which something is promoted will usually depend on the client's budget. Big firms like car manufacturers will want ads on TV and in glossy colour magazines. Small businesses will only be able to afford ads in local newspapers. Along with the client, the ad agency will
• choose *the place* in which the advertisement will appear.
• *design* an effective advertisement to appear in that place.

TO WHOM?
Every advertisement has a *target audience* – the people at whom the advertisement is aimed.

THE TARGET AUDIENCE
Once a budget – whether large or small – has been agreed, the advertising agency decides *how* to sell the product and to *whom.* Knowing the target audience helps the ad agency to decide where the advertisement will appear (in which paper or magazine) and how the advertisement will be designed.

If the product is a rock CD and the target audience is teenagers, there is no point in putting an advertisement in an interior decorating magazine. An advertisement designed for *The News of The World* will be different from one designed for *The Irish Times.*

It is extremely important for the advertising agency to analyse the product – whether it is a consumer item such as denim jeans or a 'message' such as 'Save the Whale'. It must then decide what kind of people are likely to be persuaded to 'buy'. To help to them in working this out, people have been divided into several groups, according to income, interests and lifestyle. These are called *socio-economic groups*. They are given ratings from A to E, with A as the highest group and E standing for the lower end of the income scale.

A = The well-to-do
B = The middle class
C = The lower middle class
D = The working class
E = The poor

Here is another way of describing groups for target audiences.

1. Universal mass market: men and women, all areas, all age groups.
2. Upper class market: men and women, all areas, all age groups, in upper third of the population.
3. Well-to-do market: men.
4. Well-to-do market: women.
5. Housewives: mass appeal.
6. Housewives: upper middle class appeal.
7. Young people (men and women aged 16-24): mass appeal.
8. Young women (aged 16-25).
9. Specialist groups: professional, retail trade, occupational, hobby etc.
10. Older people (over 40, men and women): mass appeal.

Try this
Using these ten groupings, compile a list of products/services/messages which would be aimed at each of these groups.

How?
ADVERTISING TECHNIQUES
Every advertising agency employs a number of specialists who look after different aspects of an advertisement. The most important aspects are the *copy* (the words), the *visuals* (any pictures or images) and the *relationship* between these two.

The copy – the written material
These are just a few of the ways in which words are used in advertisements.
- headlines
- slogans – rhymes, puns, punchy sayings
- statistics – various numbers and figures
- factual information
- endorsements or testimonials
- emotive language

The visuals – what it looks like
All the punchy sayings in the world are useless if the advertisement does not first attract attention. Ad agencies use many ways to attract attention with clever *design and layout*.
- photographs
- artwork and drawings
- logos – symbol of client company or product
- typography – the style of print – large, small, *italics*, **bold**, CAPITAL (upper case) letters, (small letters are called lower case), different type-faces

The **relationship** between the copy and the visuals is worked out by the experts until a pleasing combination is achieved.

ADVERTISING COPY

THE DETAILS

You may be asked to write about advertisements and to judge their effectiveness. Let's take a look at a few of the things which contribute to advertising copy.

The headline

A good advertising headline or slogan fixes that ad in the memory of the reader. To do this, the *copy-writer* often uses rhymes or puns (words that play on two or more meanings). For example, someone working on the advertising copy for a company called Luxury Luggage might come up with this slogan.

> *For an open and shut case, choose Luxury.*

Alliteration – words beginning with the same consonants – is also used effectively

> *We take the trouble. . . You take the trip.*

An effective headline should:

- be memorable or catchy

> *A Mars a day helps you work, rest and play.*

- make an offer of some kind

> *Fifty-fifty cash back*

- offer some immediate benefit (by responding now, you get something for nothing)

> *Book now and one passenger goes free!*

- indicate the price (if it is tempting)
- have some kind of tie-in with the advertisement's artwork

Of course, not all headlines do all of these things. But these are the points which copy-writers keep in mind.

Typography – the print

Readability is the main aim of good typography. The choice and arrangement of the print should help the reader to 'get the message' – the reason for the advertisement in the first place. For example, it has been proved that text or copy which is set completely in capital letters is more difficult to read than copy which uses both capital and lower case type. Large type may be striking to the eye, but it must also pass the test of readability.

Large blocks of type are usually avoided. No reader wants to wade through loads of text to 'get the message'. So advertising designers usually break up the copy – using small paragraphs, subheads (headings in different type), easy-to-see one-line statements.

Well-designed type is used to make things stand out. But it may also be used to conceal or play down something as well. This is especially true for conditions which might apply to a special offer. This is what people mean when they say 'Don't forget to check the small print'. Have you ever seen ads like this?

FREE VOUCHER
with purchases over £15.00

ONLY £199.95
VAT is extra.

Advertisement like these remind us that we must always be extremely careful when responding to special offers. Tricky typography may be very eye-catching, but to be really effective it needs to do more than attract attention: it must also communicate.

STATISTICS

Statistics are numerical facts. They can be very effective in persuading people to buy a product or agree with a viewpoint. Since statistics are used in science, we may feel that they have the authority of science behind them.

However, statistics can be misused. So it is always important to enquire about the source of the statistics – where the statistics came from. Who has compiled them? What interest does that person or company have in the findings of the statistics? For example, an advertisement for a dairy product may quote a set of statistics which indicate that there is no connection between the consumption of dairy products and heart attacks. The reader must find out if the dairy industry itself carried out the survey or whether it was carried out by an impartial or independent body such as a university medical department.

We often see statistics which say something like this.

52% of dogs prefer Woofer!

What we have to remember about such a statistic is that 48% of dogs *do not* prefer Woofer.

Try this

Make a collection of advertisements which quote statistics. Discuss these statistics with your class. What are they trying to tell us? Is anything hidden in the statistics – like the Woofer example?

FACTUAL INFORMATION

A fact is somewhat different from a statistics. It may contain numerical information, but it is not based on some kind of survey. For example, it is a fact that there are 26 counties in the Republic of Ireland.

Factual information, like statistics, can be very influential in persuading the potential consumer. The advertiser, however, is legally bound not to tell lies or deliberately misrepresent the product being advertised. An advertisement for a lotion claiming that it can cure baldness is stating a fact. This would be misleading, however, since it is well known that hair cannot be regrown except by a process of hair-transplanting. Many advertisements for cars state the fact that the car can travel so many kilometres per litre. What such advertisements deliberately fail to mention is that such fuel consumption depends on a traffic-free road *and* a head-wind which has a below-average speed.

In judging the factual content of an advertisement, the rule is that it should tell 'the truth, the whole truth and nothing but the truth.' Telling half the truth may be a lie. Leaving out some factual information may be a distortion of the truth, which could also be seen as a lie.

The key question to ask in judging the factual content of an advertisement is its reliability. On whose authority is the factual information based? Is that authority a respected one? People often believe what they want to believe, contrary to their common sense.

ENDORSEMENTS OR TESTIMONIALS

Endorsements or testimonials are statements, usually from celebrities, which say that they believe in a particular product or point of view. This advertising technique can be very effective. If your favourite rock group says that they approve of a certain soft drink, this will obviously help to convince you to drink it too.

One of the great figures of modern advertising is David Ogilvy. This is what he had to say about testimonials.

'Testimonials from celebrities get high recall scores, but I have stopped using them because readers remember the celebrity and forget the product. What's more, they assume that the celebrity has been *bought* , which is usually the case. On the other hand, testimonials from *experts* can be persuasive – like having an ex-burglar testify that he had never been able to crack a Chubb safe.'

The testimony of the non-expert celebrity helps to keep the brand name in the public mind. But it is the qualification of that expert which finally persuades the consumer to buy a product. The endorsement of a car by a famous Formula One driver is likely to be more persuasive than that of a film star who has no expert knowledge on cars.

EMOTIVE LANGUAGE

Every word has a particular dictionary meaning. But words can also have associated meanings – or connotations. The dictionary will give us the meaning of the word 'dog'. For one person, the word will be accompanied by images of a poodle or a dearly-loved black and white mongrel. For someone else, it will paint a picture of a fierce German shepherd dog that once scared him or her half to death.

Writers of advertising copy, just like poets and novelists, give careful thought to the connotations or associations of words. Their intention is to associate the product with very pleasant things or with unpleasant things, depending on the point they want to make.

This copy was written by the famous advertiser, Charles Saatchi. The subject is the importance of food hygiene. Saatchi wanted to associate poor hygiene with unpleasantness.

This is what happens
when a fly lands on your food.

Flies can't eat solid food,
so to soften it up they vomit on it.
Then they stamp the vomit in
until it's a liquid, usually stamping in
a few germs for good measure.
Then when it's good and runny,
they suck it all back again, probably
dropping some excrement at the
same time.
And then, when they've finished eating,
it's your turn.

WRITING ABOUT ADVERTISEMENTS

THINGS TO CONSIDER

When responding to an advertisement in a newspaper, a magazine or on a poster, you should consider the following points. (Not all of these apply to every advertisement.)

1. Identify the **target audience** of the advertisement.
2. Write comments of the advertising **copy** under the following headings:
   • **headline**
   • **typography**
   • **design or layout**
   • **statistics**
   • **factual information**
   • **endorsement or testimonial**
   • **emotive language**

3. Comment on the **visual image**.
4. Write three or more sentences on the way the copy, layout and visual image combine to achieve a certain purpose. Say what that purpose is.
5. In your opinion, what is the value of the **endorsement**?

Try this

Collect as wide a variety of advertisements as you can. Arrange them into categories – cars and related products, clothing, food, 'messages', banks etc.

Respond to these advertisements using the headings in the list above.

BOOK LIST

The following book list for children aged 13-15 is selected from *Books for Teenagers* complied by Senior Librarian, Rosemary Walton, and the staff of the Children's and Schools' Library, Dublin Corporation Public Libraries, 1 Wellington Quay, Dublin 2. Our thanks for their kind permission to use it here.

pbk = paperback
hb = hardback

ISBN = book identification number
★ = award-winning author

ADVENTURE

BANVILLE, Vincent
Hennessy
Poolbeg, 1991
ISBN 1853 711322 (pbk)

Hennessy Goes West
Poolbeg, 1992
ISBN 1853 711357 (pbk)

Hennessy in Africa
Poolbeg, 1992
ISBN 1853 712310 (pbk)

BRANFIELD, John
The Falklands Summer
Gollanz, 1987
ISBN 0575 039272 (hb)
Armada, 1989
ISBN 0006 72888X (pbk)

BRUNNER, Hans
Survivors
Firefly, 1989
ISBN 0333 492692 (pbk)

COBURN, Ann
The Granite Beast
Bodley Head, 1991
ISBN 0373 315456 (hb)

Red Fox
1992
ISBN 0099 85970X (pbk)

DILLON, Eilis
Island of Horses
Faber, 1991
ISBN 0571 161979 (pbk)

DUNLOP, Eileen
A Flute in Mayferry Street
Drew, 1987
ISBN 0862 671833 (pbk)

The House on the Hill
O.U.P., 1987
ISBN 0192 715658

★GALT, Hugh
Bike Hunt: A Story of Thieves and Kidnappers
O'Brien Press, 1988
ISBN 0862 781574 (pbk)
(Winner of the Irish Book Award,
Young People's Books, 1988)

GARFIELD, Leon
The December Rose
Viking Kestrel, 1986
ISBN 0670 810541 (hb)
Puffin, 1986
ISBN 0140 320709 (pbk)

GILMORE, Kate
Of Griffins and Graffiti
Puffin, 1987
ISBN 0140 321349 (pbk)

HALL, Willis
Vampire's Revenge
Bodley Head, 1993
ISBN 0370 317729 (hb)

HUGHES, Monica
Spirit River
Methuen, 1988
ISBN 0416 114423 (hb)

Teens Mandarin, 1989
ISBN 0749 70019X (pbk)

McMAHON, Sean
The Three Seals
Poolbeg, 1991
ISBN 1853 711489 (pbk)

MAGORIAN, Michelle
In Deep Water
Viking, 1992
ISBN 0670 837385 (hb)

PAULSEN, Gary
Hatchet
Macmillan, 1989
ISBN 0333 492811 (hb)
Pan, 1991
ISBN 0330 310453 (pbk)

The Return
Piper, 1992
ISBN 0330 324780 (pbk)

PEARCE, Colin
One Minute Dream
Armada, 1990
ISBN 0006 93594X (pbk)

PEYTON, K.M.
The Boy Who Wasn't There
Doubleday, 1992
ISBN 0385 402481 (hb)

STONE, G.H.
Reel Trouble
Armada, 1991
ISBN 0006 939449 (pbk)

STORR, Catherine
The Underground Conspiracy
Faber, 1987
ISBN 0571 148778 (hb)

TREASE, Geoffrey
Aunt Augusta's Elephant
Macmillan, 1991
ISBN 0333 550765 (hb)

Calabrian Quest
Walker, 1990
ISBN 0744 515289 (hb)

Shadow Under the Sea
Walker, 1990
ISBN 0744 515270 (hb)
Walker, 1991
ISBN 0744 514509 (pbk)

Song for a Tattered Flag
Walker, 1993
ISBN 0744 524121 (pbk)

USHER, Frances
Maybreak
Methuen, 1990
ISBN 0416 149928 (hb)
Mammoth, 1990
ISBN 0749 70411X (pbk)

WILSON, Jacqueline
Lonely Hearts
Armada, 1987
ISBN 0006 928080 (pbk)

Supersleuth
Armada, 1987
ISBN 0006 928072 (pbk)

CAMPBELL, Eric
The Place of Lions
Pan, 1991
ISBN 0330 319779 (pbk)

CONSIDINE, June
View from a Blind Bridge
Poolbeg, 1992
ISBN 1853 712442 (pbk)

FREWER, Glyn
Fox
P. Hardy Books, 1984
ISBN 0744 40052X (hb)

STEINBECK, John
The Red Pony
Pan, 1980
ISBN 0330 289365 (pbk)

STEWART, Paul
Adam's Ark
Viking, 1990
ISBN 0670 832812 (hb)
Puffin, 1992
ISBN 0140 344225 (pbk)

TAYLOR, Theodore
Sniper
Bodley Head, 1990
ISBN 0370 314654 (hb)

WILSON, A.N.
Stray
Walker, 1987
ISBN 0744 508010 (hb)
Walker, 1989
ISBN 0744 508428 (pbk)

WRIGHTSON, Patricia
Moon-dark
Hutchinson, 1987
ISBN 0091 725593 (hb)

★FINE, Anne
Goggle Eyes
Hamish Hamilton, 1989
ISBN 0241 126177 (hb)
Puffin, 1990
ISBN 0140 340718 (pbk)
(Winner of the Carnegie Medal, 1989)
(Winner of the Guardian Children's
Fiction Award, 1989)

FORD, Adam
The Cuckoo Plant
Mammoth, 1991
ISBN 0749 706139 (pbk)

LINGARD, Joan
The Guilty Party
Hamish Hamilton, 1987
ISBN 0241 120810 (hb)
Puffin, 1989
ISBN 0140 325026 (pbk)

MASTERS, Anthony
Battle for the Badgers
Hippo, 1990
ISBN 0590 763520

Sad Song of the Whale
Hippo, 1990
ISBN 0590 763482 (pbk)

NIMMO, Jenny
Ultramarine
Mammoth, 1992
ISBN 0749 709278 (pbk)

FAMILIES

ADLER, C.S.
Fly Free
Piper, 1989
ISBN 0330 309013 (pbk)

ALCOCK, Vivien
A Kind of Thief
Methuen, 1991
ISBN 0416 155626 (hb)

ALLEN, Judy
Between the Moon and the Rock
Julia MacRae, 1992
ISBN 1856 810631 (hb)

ASHLEY, Bernard
High Pavement Blues
Puffin, 1990
ISBN 0140 325891 (pbk)

ANIMALS

ADAMS, Richard George
Watership Down
Puffin, 1973
ISBN 0140 306013 (pbk)

★ARMSTRONG, William H.
Sounder
Puffin, 1973
ISBN 0140 305947 (pbk)
(Winner of the Newbery Medal 1970)

BYARS, Betsy
The Midnight Fox
Puffin, 1976
ISBN 0140 30844X (pbk)

ENVIRONMENTAL ISSUES

★ALLEN, Judy
Awaiting Developments
Walker, 1988
ISBN 0744 513219 (pbk)
(Winner of the Whitbread Award, 1988)
(Winner of the Earthworm Award, 1989)

DUANE, Diane
Deep Wizardry
Corgi, 1991
ISBN 0552 526460 (pbk)

BAWDEN, Nina
The Outside Child
Gollancz, 1989
ISBN 0575 046015 (hb)
Puffin, 1991
ISBN 0140 343040 (pbk)

BETANCOURT, Jeanna
Crazy Christmas
Macmillan, 1991
ISBN 0330 319841 (pbk)

BRESLIN, Theresa
Different Directions
Puffin, 1989
ISBN 0140 342818 (pbk)

BYARS, Betsy
Cracker Jackson
Bodley Head, 1985
ISBN 0370 30859X (hb)
Puffin, 1986
ISBN 0140 31881X (pbk)

*CONLON-McKENNA, Marita
The Blue Horse
O'Brien Press, 1992
ISBN 0862 783054 (pbk)
(Winner of the Children's Book Trust
Bisto Book of the Year Award, 1992)

DANZIGER, Paula
Can you sue your parents for malpractice?
Heinemann, 1986
ISBN 0434 965707 (hb)
Pan, 1987
ISBN 0330 300199 (pbk)

The Divorce Express
Heinemann, 1986
ISBN 0434 965715 (hb)
Piccolo, 1987
ISBN 0330 296574 (pbk)

It's an aardvark-eat-turtle world
Heinemann, 1987
ISBN 0434 93143 (hb)
Piper, 1988
ISBN 0330 303759 (pbk)

Make like a Tree and Leave
Heinemann, 1990
ISBN 0434 934127 (hb)

The Pistachio Prescription
Heinemann, 1986
ISBN 0434 965766 (hb)
Piccolo, 1987
ISBN 0330 300180 (pbk)

DESAI, Anita
The Village by the Sea
Heinemann, 1982
ISBN 0434 934364 (hb)
Puffin, 1988
ISBN 0140 325050 (pbk)

DOHERTY, Berlie
White Peak Farm
Methuen, 1984
ISBN 0416 470203 (hb)
Armada, 1986
ISBN 0006 724310 (pbk)

DUBOSARKY, Ursula
High Hopes
Puffin, 1990
ISBN 0140 343806 (pbk)

*FINE, Anne
The Book of the Banshee
Hamish Hamilton, 1991
ISBN 0241 131146 (hb)

Flour Babies
Hamish Hamilton, 1992
ISBN 0241 132525 (hb)

Goggle Eyes
Hamish Hamilton, 1989
ISBN 0241 126177 (hb)
Puffin, 1990
ISBN 0140 340718 (pbk)
(Winner of the Carnegie Medal, 1989)
(Winner of the Guardian Children's
Fiction Award, 1989)

Madame Doubtfire
Hamish Hamilton, 1987
ISBN 0241 120012 (hb)
Puffin, 1989
ISBN 0140 326332 (pbk)

FISK, Pauline
Telling the Sea
Collins, 1992
ISBN 0745 920616 (hb)

FITZHUGH, Louise
Nobody's Family is Going to Change
Lions, 1978
ISBN 0006 713513 (pbk)

FOX, Paula
One-eyed Cat
Dent, 1985
ISBN 0460 061860 (hb)
Pan, 1988
ISBN 0330 296469 (pbk)

GLEITZMAN, Morris
Misery Guts
Blackie, 1991
ISBN 0216 929598 (hb)
Piper, 1992
ISBN 0330 324403 (pbk)

Worry Warts
Blackie, 1992
ISBN 0216 932750 (hb)

HINTON, Nigel
Buddy
Dent, 1982
ISBN 0460 060899 (hb)
Puffin, 1984
ISBN 0140 315713 (pbk)

Buddy's Song
Dent, 1987
ISBN 0460 062611 (hb)
Puffin, 1989
ISBN 0140 326405 (pbk)

*HOWKER, Janni
Isaac Campion
Julia MacRae, 1986
ISBN 0862 032709 (hb)
Lions, 1987
ISBN 0006 727905 (pbk)

The Nature of the Beast
Julia MacRae, 1985
ISBN 0862 03194X (hb)
Lions, 1986
ISBN 0006 725821 (pbk)
(Winner of the Whitbread Award, 1985)
(Winner of the Young Observer Teenage
Fiction Prize, 1985)

KEANEY, Brian
If This is the Real World
O.U.P., 1991
ISBN 0192 716611 (hb)

KEMP, Gene
No Place Like
Faber, 1983
ISBN 0571 130631 (hb)
Puffin, 1988
ISBN 0140 317732 (pbk)

LINGARD, Joan
The Gooseberry
Hamish Hamilton, 1978
ISBN 0241 100232 (hb)
Beaver, 1984
ISBN 0099 340909 (pbk)

Snake Among the Sunflowers
Red Fox, 1991
ISBN 0099 865009 (pbk)

Strangers in the House
Hamish Hamilton, 1981
ISBN 0241 106710 (hb)

Rags to Riches
Puffin, 1990
ISBN 0140 328416 (pbk)

Glad Rags
Hamish Hamilton, 1990
ISBN 0241 130158 (hb)
Puffin, 1992
ISBN 0140 346333 (pbk)

MacBRATNEY, Sam
Put a Saddle on the Pig
Methuen, 1993
ISBN 0416 190324 (hb)

MARK, Jan
A Can of Worms and Other Stories
Bodley Head, 1990
ISBN 0370 314697 (hb)

MASTERS, Anthony
Streetwise
Methuen, 1987
ISBN 0416 024025 (hb)
Methuen, 1988
ISBN 0416 101526 (pbk)

O'NEAL, Zibby
In Summer Light
Lions, 1988
ISBN 0006 727972 (pbk)

PATERSON, Katherine
Park's Quest
Gollancz, 1989
ISBN 0575 04487X (hb)
Puffin, 1990
ISBN 0140 340769 (pbk)

PENDERGRAFT, Patricia
Miracle at Clement's Pond
Gollancz, 1988
ISBN 0575 04330X (hb)
Puffin, 1990
ISBN 0140342400 (pbk)

PFEFFER, Susan Beth
The Year without Michael
Bantam, 1991
ISBN 0553 403273 (pbk)

PILLING, Ann
Our Kid
Viking Kestrel, 1989
ISBN 0670 825840 (hb)
Puffin, 1991
ISBN 0140 329749 (pbk)

SPENCE, Eleanor
Another Sparrow Singing
O.U.P., 1992
ISBN 0195532457 (hb)

★TAYLOR, Andrew
The Coal House
Collins, 1986
ISBN 0001 848437 (hb)
Lions, 1987
ISBN 0006 728626 (pbk)
(Winner of the Whitbread Award, 1986)

★VOIGT, Cynthia
Building Blocks
Armada, 1988
ISBN 006 729290 (pbk)

Dicey's Song
Collins, 1984
ISBN 0001 841475 (hb)
Collins, 1984
ISBN 0001 841483 (pbk)
(Winner of the Newbery Medal, 1983)

Tree by Leaf
Collins, 1989
ISBN 0001 844350 (hb)
Collins, 1990
ISBN 0006 737692 (pbk)

FANTASY

AIKEN, Joan
Dido and Pa
Cape, 1986
ISBN 0224 023640 (hb)

ALLEN, Judy
The Dream Thing
Julia MacRae, 1990
ISBN 0862 034418 (hb)
Walker, 1990
ISBN 0744 52084 (pbk)

BURGESS, Melvin
An Angel for May
Anderson Press, 1992
ISBN 0862 643988 (hb)

COONTZ, Otto
The Shape-Shifters
Methuen, 1987
ISBN 0416 061524 (hb)
Magnet, 1988
ISBN 0416 10262X (pbk)

DUANE, Diane
Deep Wizardry
Corgi, 1991
ISBN 0552 526460 (pbk)

FISK, Pauline
Midnight Blue
Lion, 1990
ISBN 0745 919251 (hb)
Lion, 1992
ISBN 0745 918484 (pbk)

FORD, Adam
The Cuckoo Plant
Mammoth, 1991
ISBN 0749 706139 (pbk)

GARNER, Alan
The Owl Service
Collins, 1967
ISBN 0001 846035 (hb)
Armada Lions, 1972
ISBN 0006 706932 (pbk)

GORDON, John
The Quelling Eye
Bodley Head, 1986
ISBN 0370 31011X (hb)
Lions, 1988
ISBN 0006 728413 (pbk)

HALAN, Ann
Transformations
Orchard, 1988
ISBN 1852 131195 (hb)
Puffin, 1990
ISBN 0140 341862 (pbk)

HUGHES, Ted
The Iron Man
Faber & Faber, 1985
ISBN 0571 136753 (hb)
Faber & Faber, 1989
ISBN 0571 141498 (pbk)

JACQUES, Brian
Mariel of Redwall
Hutchinson, 1991
ISBN 0091 76405X (hb)

JONES, Diana Wynne
Fire and Hemlock
Mammoth, 1990
ISBN 0749 702834 (pbk)

Howl's Moving Castle
Methuen, 1986
ISBN 0416 615902 (hb)
Methuen, 1988
ISBN 0416 074421 (pbk)

Castle in the Air
Mammoth, 1990
ISBN 0749 704756 (pbk)

KELLEHER, Victor
To the Dark Tower
Julia MacRae, 1992
ISBN 1856 810860 (hb)

MAHY, Margaret
Dangerous Spaces
Hamish Hamilton, 1991
ISBN 0241 130662 (hb)
Puffin, 1992
ISBN 0140 34571X (pbk)

O'SHEA, Pat
The Hounds of the Morrigan
O.U.P., 1985
ISBN 0192 715062 (hb)
Puffin, 1987
ISBN 0140 322078 (pbk)

RODGERS, Frank
The Drowning Boy
Andre Deutsch, 1992
ISBN 0590 540726 (pbk)

RUSH, Alison
Adam's Paradise
Macmillan, 1989
ISBN 0333 462688 (hb)

SLEATOR, William
The Spirit House
Heinemann, 1992
ISBN 0434 960489 (hb)

VOIGT, Cynthia
Jackaroo
Collins, 1988
ISBN 0001 911120 (hb)
Lions, 1990
ISBN 0006 736114 (pbk)

GHOSTS AND THE SUPERNATURAL

FARMER, Penelope
Thicker than Water
Walker, 1989
ISBN 0744 512468 (hb)
Walker, 1991
ISBN 0744 513339 (pbk)

HOROWITZ, Anthony
Groosham Grange
Methuen, 1988
ISBN 0416 024629 (hb)
Methuen, 1988
ISBN 0416 101720 (pbk)

JACQUES, Brian
Seven Strange and Ghostly Tales
Hutchinson, 1991
ISBN 0091 763648 (hb)

KLEIN, Robin
Games
Viking Kestrel, 1987
ISBN 0670 814032 (hb)

MASTERS, Anthony
Scary Tales to Tell in the Dark
Puffin, 1992
ISBN 0140 361758 (pbk)

*MAHY, Margaret
The Changeover: A Supernatural Romance
Dent, 1984
ISBN 0460 061534 (hb)
Magnet, 1985
ISBN 0416 52270X (pbk)
(Winner of the Carnegie Medal, 1984)

PILLING, Ann
The Witch of Lagg
Armada, 1990
ISBN 0006 924581 (pbk)

PRINCE, Alison
A Haunting Refrain
Methuen, 1988
ISBN 0416 05322X (hb)
Mammoth, 1989
ISBN 0749 700696 (pbk)

RICHARDSON, Jean (Editor)
Beware! Beware! Chilling Tales
Lightning, 1989
ISBN 0340 500964 (pbk)

Cold Feet
Hodder, 1989
ISBN 0340 429631

SCOTT, Hugh
The Haunted Sand
Walker, 1990
ISBN 0744 514274 (pbk)

STOKER, Bram
Dracula
Armada, 1987
ISBN 0006 926738 (hb)

HISTORICAL

BURGESS, Melvin
Burning Issy
Anderson Press, 1992
ISBN 0862 643813 (hb)

*CARTER, Peter
The Sentinels
O.U.P., 1980
ISBN 0192 714384 (hb)
Drew, 1987
ISBN 0862 671957 (pbk)
(Winner of the Guardian Children's
Fiction Award, 1981)

CHEETHAM, Ann
The Pit
Armada, 1987
ISBN 0006 925316 (pbk)

CONLON-McKENNA, Marita
Under the Hawthorn Tree
O'Brien Press, 1990
ISBN 0862 782066 (pbk)

Wildflower Girl
O'Brien Press, 1991
ISBN 0862 782759 (hb)
O'Brien Press, 1992
ISBN 0862 78283X (pbk)

CONRAD, Pam
My Daniel
O.U.P., 1991
ISBN 0192 716484 (pbk)

DARKE, Marjorie
A Rose from Blighty
Collins, 1990
ISBN 0001 846868 (hb)
Lions, 1992
ISBN 0006 735436 (pbk)

GARFIELD, Leon
Revolution!
Lions, 1989
ISBN 0006 7344448 (pbk)

KILWORTH, Garry
The Drowners
Methuen, 1991
ISBN 0416 176828 (hb)
Mammoth, 1992
ISBN 0749 710497 (pbk)

LAIRD, Elizabeth
Kiss the Dust
Heinemann, 1991
ISBN 0434 947032 (hb)

LLYWELYN, Morgan
Brian Boru
O'Brien Press, 1990
ISBN 0862 782309 (pbk)

Strongbow
O'Brien Press, 1992
ISBN 0862 782740 (pbk)

MacLACHÁN, Mairí
The River Tree
Swallow Books, 1988
ISBN 0862 672198 (pbk)

PILLING, Ann
Black Harvest
Armada, 1990
ISBN 0006 926037 (pbk)

ROBERTSON, Wendy
Lizza
Hodder, 1987
ISBN 0340 391197 (hb)
Hodder, 1988
ISBN 0340 414219 (pbk)

ROSTKOWSKI, Margaret
After the Dancing Days
Pan, 1991
ISBN 0330 309536 (pbk)

*SPEARE, Elizabeth George
The Witch of Blackbird Pond
Puffin, 1970
ISBN 0140 303278 (pbk)
(Winner of Newbery Medal, 1959)

TOMALIN, Ruth
Long Since
Faber, 1989
ISBN 0571 152066 (hb)

TOMLINSON, Theresa
The Rope Carrier
Julia MacRae, 1991
ISBN 1856 812413 (hb)

TREASE, Geoffrey
The Arpino Assignment
Walker, 1988
ISBN 0744 50810X (hb)
Walker, 1989
ISBN 0744 513332 (pbk)

White Nights of St Petersburg
Drew, 1987
ISBN 0862 671965 (pbk)

VOIGT, Cynthia
On Fortune's Wheel
Lions, 1992
ISBN 0006 742882 (pbk)

WALSH, Jill Paton
Grace, a Novel
Viking, 1991
ISBN 0670 838209 (hb)
Puffin, 1993
ISBN 0140 347291 (pbk)

WILLARD, Barbara
The Keys of Mantlemass
MacDonald, 1989
ISBN 0356 131823 (hb)
MacDonald, 1989
ISBN 0356131831 (pbk)

HUMOUR

BYARS, Betsy
The Burning Questions of Bingo Brown
Bodley Head, 1988
ISBN 0370 311868 (hb)
Puffin, 1990
ISBN 0140 343199 (pbk)

Bingo Brown and the Language of Love
Bodley Head, 1989
ISBN 0370 314700 (hb)
Puffin, 1991
ISBN 0140 341412 (pbk)

Bingo Brown, Gypsy Lover
Bodley Head, 1991
ISBN 0370 315537 (hb)
Puffin, 1992
ISBN 0140 347658 (pbk)

Bingo Brown's Guide to Romance
Bodley Head, 1992
ISBN 0370 318005 (hb)

FINE, Anne
Flour Babies
Hamish Hamilton, 1992
ISBN 0241 132525 (hb)

GLEITZMAN, Morris
Misery Guts
Blackie, 1991
ISBN 0216 929598 (hb)
Piper, 1992
ISBN 0330 324403 (pbk)

Worry Warts
Blackie, 1992
ISBN 0216 932750 (pbk)

KLEIN, Robin
*The Lonely Hearts Club/Robin Klein and
Max Dann*
O.U.P., 1988
ISBN 0195 546482 (hb)

LILLINGTON, Kenneth
Jonah's Mirror
Faber, 1988
ISBN 0571 149618 (hb)

LIMB, Sue
China Lee
Orchard, 1987
ISBN 1852 130318 (hb)
Lions, 1989
ISBN 0006 733727 (pbk)

LINGARD, Joan
Rags to Riches
Puffin, 1990
ISBN 0140 328416 (pbk)

Glad Rags
Hamish Hamilton, 1990
ISBN 0241 130158 (hb)
Puffin, 1992
ISBN 0140 346333 (pbk)

TOWNSEND, Sue
The Secret Diary of Adrian Mole aged 13 ¾
Methuen, 1982
ISBN 0413 508900 (hb)
Methuen, 1982
ISBN 0403 592502 (pbk)

IRISH INTEREST

BANVILLE, Vincent
Hennessy
Poolbeg, 1991
ISBN 1853 711322 (pbk)

Hennessy Goes West
Poolbeg, 1992
ISBN 1853 711357 (pbk)

Hennessy in Africa
Poolbeg, 1992
ISBN 1853 712310 (pbk)

BAYLIS, Sarah
The Tomb of Reeds
Julia MacRae, 1987
ISBN 0862 032792 (hb)
Swallow, 1988
ISBN 0862 672252 (pbk)

CARTER, Peter
Under Goliath
O.U.P., 1977
ISBN 0192 714058
Puffin, 1980
ISBN 0140 311327 (pbk)

CASEY, Maude
Over the Water
Women's Press, 1987
ISBN 0704 349051 (pbk)

*CONLON-McKENNA, Marita
The Blue Horse
O'Brien Press, 1992
ISBN 0862 783054 (pbk)
(Winner of the Children's Book Trust
Bisto Book of the Year Award, 1992)

Under the Hawthorn Tree
O'Brien Press, 1990
ISBN 0862 782066 (pbk)

Wildflower Girl
O'Brien Press, 1991
ISBN 0862 782759 (hb)
O'Brien Press, 1992
ISBN 0862 78283X (pbk)

CONSIDINE, June
View from a Blind Bridge
Poolbeg, 1992
ISBN 1853 712442 (pbk)

DEVLIN, Polly
*The Far Side of the Lough: Stories from an
Irish Childhood*
Gollancz, 1983
ISBN 0575 032448 (hb)
Magnet, 1985
ISBN 0416 518206 (pbk)

DILLON, Eilis
Island of Horses
Faber, 1991
ISBN 0371 161979 (pbk)

*GALT, Hugh
Bike Hunt
O'Brien Press, 1988
ISBN 0862 781574 (pbk)
(Winner of the Irish Book Award, Young
People's Books, 1988)

JARVIE, Gordon (Editor)
The Genius and Other Irish Stories
Puffin, 1988
ISBN 0140 324550 (pbk)

LEACH, Bernadette
I'm a vegetarian
Attic Press, 1992
ISBN 1855 94040X (pbk)

LINGARD, Joan
The File of Fraulein Berg
Beaver, 1985
ISBN 0099 382903 (pbk)

The Twelfth Day of July
Hamish Hamilton, 1970
ISBN 0241 019842 (hb)
Puffin, 1973
ISBN 0140 306358 (pbk)
(Kevin and Sadie Series)

Across the Barricades
Hamish Hamilton, 1972
ISBN 0241 021677 (hb)
Puffin, 1975
ISBN 0140 306374 (pbk)

Into Exile
Hamish Hamilton, 1973
ISBN 0241 023165 (hb)
Puffin, 1974
ISBN 0140 307028 (pbk)

A Proper Place
Hamish Hamilton, 1975
ISBN 0241 891701 (hb)
Puffin, 1978
ISBN 0140 310363 (pbk)

Hostages to Fortune
Hamish Hamilton, 1976
ISBN 0241 894964 (hb)
Puffin, 1988
ISBN 0140 326251 (pbk)

LLYWELYN, Morgan
Brian Boru
O'Brien Press, 1990
ISBN 0862 782309 (pbk)

Strongbow
O'Brien Press, 1992
ISBN 0862 782740 (pbk)

MacBRATNEY, Sam
Put a Saddle on the Pig
Methuen, 1993
ISBN 0416 190324 (hb)

McCAUGHREN, Tom
Rainbows of the Moon
Anvil Books, 1989
ISBN 0947 96245X (hb)
Anvil Books, 1990
ISBN 0947 962514 (pbk)

McMAHON, Sean
The Three Seals
Poolbeg, 1991
ISBN 1853 711489 (pbk)

MELLING, Orla
The Druid's Tune
O'Brien Press, 1992
ISBN 0862 782856 (pbk)

The Singing Stone
Viking Kestrel, 1986
ISBN 0670 808172 (hb)

MITCHELL, Geraldine
Welcoming the French
Attic Press, 1992
ISBN 1855 94054X (pbk)

O'DONNELL, Joe
The Big Push
Children's Press, 1982
ISBN 0900 068671 (hb)
Children's Press, 1982
ISBN 0900 068663 (pbk)

O'SHEA, Pat
The Hounds of the Morrigan
O.U.P., 1985
ISBN 0192 715062 (hb)
Puffin, 1987
ISBN 0140 322078 (pbk)

PILLING, Ann
Stan
Viking Kestrel, 1988
ISBN 0670 817708 (hb)
Puffin, 1989
ISBN 0140 323880 (pbk)

*QUINN, John
The Summer of Lily and Esme
Poolbeg, 1991
ISBN 1853 712086 (pbk)
(Winner of the Children's Book Trust
Bisto Book of the Year Award, 1991)

REGAN, Peter
Urban Heroes
O'Brien Press, 1992
ISBN 0947 96262X (pbk)

SCOTT, Mike
Judith and the Traveller
Wolfhound, 1991
ISBN 0863 272991 (pbk)

SEFTON, Catherine
Along a Lonely Road
Hamish Hamilton, 1991
ISBN 0241 131367 (hb)

Shadows on the Lake
Hamish Hamilton, 1987
ISBN 0241 119979 (hb)
Methuen, 1988
ISBN 0416 09452X (pbk)

RELATIONSHIPS AND FRIENDSHIPS

*ALDRIDGE, James
The True Story of Spit MacPhee
Viking Kestrel, 1986
ISBN 0670 812137 (hb)
Puffin, 1988
ISBN 0140328017 (pbk)
(Winner of the Guardian Children's
Fiction Award, 1987)

BLUME, Judy
Otherwise known as Sheila the Great
Bodley Head, 1979
ISBN 0370 301706 (hb)
Piccolo, 1980
ISBN 0330 260510 (pbk)

BRANFIELD, John
The Fox in Winter
Lions, 1981
ISBN 0006 719325 (pbk)

COPPARD, Yvonne
Copper's Kid
Red Fox, 1991
ISBN 0099 638800 (pbk)

CORMIER, Robert
Other Bells for Us to Ring
Lions, 1990
ISBN 0006 740499 (pbk)

DANZIGER, Paula
Remember Me to Harold Square
Heinemann, 1988
ISBN 0434 93416X (hb)
Piper, 1989
ISBN 0330 309021 (pbk)

FOX, Paula
Monkey Island
Orchard, 1992
ISBN 1852 133929 (hb)

*MAGORIAN, Michelle
Goodnight Mister Tom
Puffin, 1983
ISBN 0140 315411 (pbk)
(Winner of the Guardian Children's
Fiction Award, 1982

*MARK, Jan
Handles
Viking Kestrel, 1985
ISBN 0670 80536X (hb)
Puffin, 1985
ISBN 0140 31587X (pbk)
(Winner of the Carnegie Medal, 1983)

Man in Motion
Viking Kestrel, 1989
ISBN 0670 826707 (hb)
Puffin, 1991
ISBN 0140 340297 (pbk)

MITCHELL, Geraldine
Welcoming the French
Attic Press, 1992
ISBN 1855 94054 (pbk)

MOONEY, Bel
A Flower of Jet
Puffin, 1990
ISBN 0140 345736 (pbk)

NEWBERY, Linda
Hard and Fast
Armada, 1989
ISBN 0006 932495 (pbk)

O'NEAL, Zibby
In Summer Light
Lions, 1988
ISBN 0006727972 (pbk)

*QUINN, John
The Summer of Lily and Esme
Poolbeg, 1991
ISBN 1853 712086 (pbk)
(Winner of the Children's Book Trust
Bisto Book of the Year Award, 1991)

PATERSON, Katherine
Bridge to Terabithia
Gollancz, 1978
ISBN 0575 025506 (hb)
Puffin, 1980
ISBN 0140 312609 (pbk)

POPLE, Maureen
The Other Side of the Family
Orchard, 1989
ISBN 1852 13173X (hb)
Orchard, 1989
ISBN 1852 131446 (pbk)

SALWAY, Lance
Second to the Right
Limelight, 1989
ISBN 0333 516494 (pbk)

WERSBA, Barbara
The Dream Watcher
Bodley Head, 1988
ISBN 0370 311566 (pbk)

ROMANCE

BAER, Judy
Working at Love
Bantam, 1991
ISBN 0553 281925 (pbk)

BANKS, Lynne Reid
My Darling Villain
Bodley Head, 1986
ISBN 0370 307232 (pbk)

BLUME, Judy
Just as long as we're together
Heinemann, 1987
ISBN 0434 925934 (hb)
Piper, 1988
ISBN 0330 304747 (pbk)

BYARS, Betsy
Cybil War
Puffin, 1983
ISBN 0140 31458X (pbk)

CLEARY, Beverly
Fifteen
Puffin, 1977
ISBN 0140 309489 (pbk)

CONFORD, Ellen
If this is love I'll take spaghetti
Armada, 1984
ISBN 0006 724140 (pbk)

COONEY, Caroline B.
I'm not your other half
Methuen, 1987
ISBN 0416 062423 (pbk)

DANZIGER, Paula
There's a bat in bunk five
Heinemann, 1987
ISBN 0434 934135 (hb)
Pan, 1988
ISBN 0330 302345

*DOHERTY, Berlie
Granny was a Buffer Girl
Methuen, 1986
ISBN 0416 535909 (hb)
Lions, 1988
ISBN 0006 727921 (pbk)
(Winner of the Carnegie Medal, 1986)

FAIRWEATHER, Eileen
*French Letters: the Life and Loves of Miss
Maxine Harrison, Form 4A*
Women's Press, 1987
ISBN 0704 349035 (pbk)

SALWAY, Lance
Someone is Watching
Piccadilly, 1987
ISBN 0946 826986 (pbk)

SCOTT, Mike
Judith and the Traveller
Wolfhound, 1991
ISBN 0863 272991 (pbk)

Judith and Spider
Wolfhound, 1992
ISBN 0863 273475 (pbk)

STRACHAN, Ian
Wayne loves Custard
Methuen, 1990
ISBN 0416 150225 (hb)

TATE, Joan
Clee and Nibs
Puffin, 1990
ISBN 0140 341064 (pbk)

WILSON, Jacqueline
Waiting for the Sky to Fall
O.U.P., 1983
ISBN 0192 714856 (hb)
Lions, 1985
ISBN 0006 724388 (pbk)